APPROACHES

to Research in

SECOND LANGUAGE LEARNING

APPROACHES

to Research in

SECOND LANGUAGE LEARNING

Donna M. Johnson

University of Arizona

Longman

Approaches to Research in Second Language Learning

Longman, 10 Bank Street, White Plains, N.Y. 10606

Associated companies:
Longman Group Ltd., London
Longman Cheshire Pty., Melbourne
Longman Paul Pty., Auckland
Copp Clark Pitman, Toronto

Senior editor: Naomi Silverman
Production editor: Ann P. Kearns
Cover design: Patricia Lowy
Text art: Fine Line Inc.
Production supervisor: Anne P. Armeny

Library of Congress Cataloging-in-Publication Data

Johnson, Donna M.
    Approaches to research in second language learning / Donna M.
    Johnson.
            p.   cm.
    Includes bibliographical references and index.
    ISBN 0-8013-0604-3
    1. Second language acquisition—Research.   2. Language and
languages—Study and teaching—Research.   I. Title.
P118.2.J64   1991
401'.93—dc20   90-22292
                                                          CIP

4   5   6   7   8   9   10-MA-95

Copyright Acknowledgments

For Helen and Morgan

Contents

Acknowledgments

I would like to express my deep appreciation to the graduate students at the University of Arizona who read and responded to many chapters in this book. Their continual presence as a familiar, important audience provided a powerful source of motivation and their insightful questions and comments led to many improvements. I am especially grateful to Lihe Chen, Joy Egbert, Parvaneh Farzad, Margi Olsen, and Hongguang Ying.

Many other people and experiences have contributed in diverse ways to the writing of this book. First, I wish to express my gratitude to the scholars whose work I have cited. My professors at Stanford University in the 1970s, especially Robert Politzer, but also Elliot Eisner and Thomas Knapp, inspired my interest in a variety of approaches to research. At RMC Research Corporation, the collaboration among researcher colleagues from many disciplines was stimulating and enriching as were experiences at the University of Arizona in the culturally distinct worlds of the Departments of Educational Psychology and English.

I would like to express my gratitude to the many colleagues who provided support and encouragement, each from a unique perspective. Among them are: Doug Adamson, Pat Dunkel, Mary McGroarty, Shitala Mishra, Judy Nichols Mitchell, Gerald Monsman, Frank Pialorsi, Duane Roen, Muriel Saville-Troike, Helen Slaughter, Victoria Stein, and Rudolph Troike. The financial support of a Steinfeld Grant from the Faculty of Humanities at the University of Arizona was much appreciated. I am deeply grateful for that support, as well as for released time granted by the Department of English.

Special thanks go to the Longman staff, especially to Senior Editor Naomi Silverman for her competence and warm support, and to Ann P. Kearns and Karen Philippidis. To Longman's four anonymous reviewers I am most grateful. I found their careful reviews highly useful in revision and sincerely appreciate their contributions. Finally, I want to thank David.

PART I
Contexts for L2 Research

CHAPTER 1

Introduction to L2 Research

As long as you teach or work in second language (hereafter L2) programs, you will be reading and evaluating research and accepting or rejecting statements that researchers make about L2 learning and teaching. Whether or not you conduct research yourself, as a professional you will continue to seek information that will contribute to improving learning and teaching in second language, foreign language, and bilingual education programs. Research is one important source of information that can be used for this purpose. As we learn more, through research, about how people learn languages in different contexts, we become better able to adapt our methods and programs to better meet their needs. The purpose of this book is to provide an overview of the major approaches to research in second language use and learning. Its focus is on research conducted in formal contexts.

This chapter provides a general introduction to the book. It opens with four major goals for readers. The second section examines the importance of research for L2 teaching, addressing the relationship between teachers' expertise and the kinds of knowledge and insights they can obtain from research. The third section describes the background knowledge and resources that you should have to best benefit from the book. The fourth section contains a discussion of the orientations and organization of the book and defines some basic terms. The final section addresses contextual factors that influence L2 research.

GOALS FOR READERS

This book has several major goals for you as readers. After reading it you should be better able to: (1) understand research; (2) critically evaluate research questions, methods, findings, and conclusions; (3) benefit from research studies; and (4) contribute in some way to the research endeavor.

In addressing the first goal, understanding research, we will attempt to demystify research and, at the same time, show the challenges involved in conducting good research. While these two aims may seem contradictory, they are not. Any professional who has worked with L2 learners in a variety of settings is well aware that language acquisition is a complex phenomenon and that the challenges of teaching in varied settings are great. Armed with some knowledge about research, then, it is easy to be critical of researchers who fail to take into account important issues in formal learning environments. Yet I have found that when my graduate students have begun to carry out their own small pilot research projects, they realize that it is difficult to conduct research that they themselves would evaluate as both good and important. As a result, while they no longer view research as mysterious and incomprehensible by the end of the course, they do develop a respect for the research endeavor and the care with which researchers attempt to find answers to important questions.

An understanding of the major approaches that researchers use to find answers to questions will enable you to work toward the second goal, which is to increase your ability to critically evaluate research. Our approach will be to use a question-and-answer format to examine the key features of studies. These key features include, for example, research questions, characteristics of the subjects or participants, the definition and measurement of variables, findings, and implications.

The ability to critically evaluate studies, based on an understanding of research methods, will allow you to benefit from research. Teachers often reject a study because they do not understand parts of it, because it examines only a limited number of factors, because it does not provide clear-cut answers, or because it does not apply to their situation. A basic understanding of approaches to research, coupled with the attitude that L2 professionals can "apply" research in many ways, should allow you to benefit from research in new ways. You will be better prepared to construct meaningful personal conclusions from studies you read and to devise creative ways to use those insights to improve practice. Improving practice can include designing programs, creating courses and curricula, training teachers, and encouraging students.

In addition to helping you to understand, evaluate, and benefit from research, a fourth goal of this book is to prepare you to contribute to the research endeavor in L2 learning and teaching should you wish to do so. You can contribute in many ways. One way is through conducting your own informal, small-scale, or pilot research projects in the settings in which you work. Another way to contribute to the research effort is to collaborate with professional researchers. Such collaboration can benefit both researchers and teachers when they share their unique perspectives. Even more important, you can be active in helping to redirect the inappropriate application of research findings to practice. This can be done by using research findings and current theories with which you are familiar to support those practices that you believe are best for students. Each of these contributions can link research and practice in ways that benefit students.

APPLYING L2 RESEARCH:
REFLECTION AND ACTION

Let us further explore the topic of how teachers can benefit from research. What good is research to teachers? For what purposes should a teacher know about research methods and findings? These are legitimate questions that merit attention because, as we noted above, teachers do not always see immediate practical value in research. However, knowledge gained from research can open our eyes in many unexpected ways. It is crucial in providing us with a deeper understanding of what it takes to learn an additional language and function in a new culture.

Operating on Intuition?

At a recent professional conference I heard a teacher strongly proclaiming, "I don't base my teaching on any particular theory or research. It's all intuition, but it works." Several others near her exchanged knowing, approving glances. Yet these conference participants were attending a fascinating roundtable report of an ethnographic study of literate behaviors of Spanish-speaking children in their homes (Vasquez, 1988). While the teacher who spoke out felt strongly that she operated on intuition, she and the others were actively seeking out new information to inform their teaching. By pursuing knowledge about the literacy practices of young children in their own homes, these teachers were adding to the knowledge base that contributes to what they might view as "intuition."

The insights they were gaining from research contributed to their professional growth. The importance of research is not so much that it supplies definitive answers to questions such as "What is the best way to learn a language?" or "Which is the most effective method of L2 teaching?" It does not. Rather, research can help us gain a richer understanding of the many interrelated factors involved in learning. It can help us see how the ways we organize learning environments can promote or inhibit growth.

Experienced second and foreign language teachers may believe that they have a solid understanding of the art or craft of teaching, but may feel that research is either inaccessible, incomprehensible, or irrelevant to them. One highly experienced teacher stated to me, "When I came here [to graduate school to earn a second master's degree] I was afraid I would have to throw out everything I knew and start over." She quickly realized that recent advances in theory and research corroborated many of her own observations and beliefs about how students learn, increasing her confidence in what she was already doing. At the same time, however, the new knowledge she was gaining allowed her to build on that base and provided her with exciting new ways of viewing and supporting the learning process.

Applying Research as Re-seeing Learning

In addition to adding to a knowledge base, research findings can sometimes be applied to classroom practice in more direct ways. Notions of what it means to "apply" research vary widely, however. It is often assumed that research is conducted, teachers read research, and then teachers attempt to apply the findings of research. In this model teachers are viewed as "consumers" of research (Borg, 1981, p. 1), as indicated below.

Conduct research → Consume research → Apply research

Holders of this traditional consumer view of applying research tend to see teachers as passive recipients of information, not as readers who construct their own meanings from the events and texts with which they transact or interact. The consumer model is inadequate for several reasons. First, the direct application of research findings to practice is usually ill advised, even if it were possible. Studies are usually not conducted in situations that are similar in important ways to the environment in which the teacher practices. It is usually wrong to assume that phenomena that occur in one situation with one group of students (in a university English-as-a-foreign-language [EFL] class in Beijing, China, for example) will occur in the same way in another situation with another group of students (in a university English-as-a-second-language [ESL] class in the United States). Research findings cannot necessarily be generalized across settings (Politzer, 1981). While there are certain universal aspects of second language acquisition, other aspects of the process vary according to the individual and according to social and cultural circumstances (Ellis, 1985; McLaughlin, 1987).

Second, the consumer model of applying research is inadequate because readers of research may gain different insights from the same study. For example, from a study about L2 writing, one reader may be intrigued by what students can learn through talking about writing, while another reader's attention is captured by an approach to assessing writing development that is new to her. Each reader, then, constructs a unique meaning, gaining different insights from the same study, and will use those insights to revise personal views and practices in unique ways. The rather mechanical notion, then, that we should directly apply research findings to practice is not consistent with the ways that readers construct meaning as they read research reports. It is more productive to take the attitude that research provides an impetus that encourages us to reflect continually

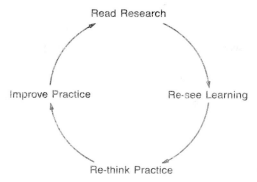

Figure 1.1. A View of Applying Research

on language use and learning processes, to rethink practice, and to take action to improve practice. This alternate model of applying research as re-seeing learning and teaching might be illustrated as in Figure 1.1.

Applying research, then, has both thought and action components; improving practice requires a continual process of reflection and action. The value of research for teachers is that it is one important source upon which they can draw to reflect and act. One purpose of this book is to encourage teachers and other readers to benefit from research in this way.

BACKGROUND KNOWLEDGE AND RESOURCES

The primary audience for this book is graduate students in the fields of second language acquisition and teaching, foreign language learning, and bilingual education. Most readers will have had some experience as a second or foreign language teacher or working with language-minority students. Teaching experience is not necessary, however, to benefit from the material. One or more courses in linguistics will provide the background to understand the nature of language—what it is students are trying to learn —as well as to understand the linguistic terminology and categories used for analysis in studies. A previous course in second or foreign language pedagogy will help you to understand the theoretical foundations and the approaches, methods, and techniques of second and foreign language teaching. It is not necessary, however, to have had prior courses in research design, language testing, or statistics to profit from this book; it provides an introduction to research. The book does not assume knowledge of statistics on the part of readers, nor does it attempt to teach statistics; many other resources are available for that purpose (see, for example, Brown, 1988; Hatch & Lazaraton, 1990; and reviews of books on quantitative research by Hamp-Lyons, 1989).

A large part of developing competence in academic subjects is a matter of mastering the specialized patterns of language use, the semantic patterns, and the genres of the subject (Lemke, 1988). Because this is just as true for studying L2 research as it is for any other subject, terms in this book will be defined as they are introduced. In addition, it would be useful to have some reference materials available. For example, even if you do have some background in linguistics, a dictionary of applied linguistics terminology (Richards, Platt, & Weber, 1985, for example) is a helpful resource.

ORGANIZATION AND ORIENTATION

Organization

This book consists of two parts. Two chapters make up Part I, the introductory section of the book. In the second section of this chapter we will consider contextual factors that affect topics of L2 research. These are second language acquisition theory, the contributing academic disciplines, sociopolitical conditions, and the institutional contexts in which research is conducted. Chapter 2 presents a discussion of developments that occurred in L2 research in formal contexts from the 1970s through the 1980s. I suggest that research during this period can be characterized by three major developments: (1) a more balanced focus on the social and personal nature of learning in formal settings, (2) changes in research methods, and (3) new roles for technology. This chapter provides a short historical backdrop against which readers can examine current and future research.

Part II of the book focuses on research method. Chapters 3 through 8 address the six prominent approaches to studies in second language learning. These are: (1) simple and complex correlational approaches, (2) case studies, (3) survey research, (4) ethnographic approaches, (5) experiments, and (6) multisite, multimethod, large-scale studies.[1] Each of these chapters follows a similar format. First, a brief description of the research approach is given along with findings of authentic studies employing that approach. Next, methodological issues are discussed. Finally, a sample study using that approach is described and analyzed using a question-and-answer format.

Chapter 9 discusses the developing teacher-researcher movement. In the final chapter, I offer some concluding remarks. The Appendix is a focused guide to the major scholarly reference works and journals for L2 researchers, graduate students, and teachers. The emphasis is on works available to audiences in the United States, although several key sources from other parts of the world are included as well.

Orientation

In this section we will consider the particular orientations of the book. We will discuss ways in which it is designed to provide a balanced view of research method and ways in which it emphasizes neglected areas of research.

Balance. We will attempt to give a balanced treatment to both quantitative and qualitative/interpretive approaches to research (sometimes referred to as positivist vs. naturalistic approaches; see Hammersley & Atkinson, 1983). The chapters on correlational, experimental, and survey research are primarily (although not totally) quantitative in orientation, while the chapters on case studies, ethnography, and multisite, multimethod studies are primarily (although not totally) qualitative in orientation. A key assumption is that each of these research approaches provides useful insights about language learning.

We will also attempt to give reasonably balanced attention to a variety of topics in L2 learning. These topics range from classroom learning strategies, to writing development, to cultural adjustment. Readers might select a topic of interest and examine that topic from the perspective of each of the major traditions of research. We will also give attention to learning through different modes. Although most L2 research in the early 1980s focused primarily on oral classroom language use (see Chaudron, 1988, and Allwright, 1988, for reviews), much recent work has been carried out in reading, writing, and various aspects of literacy development (Carrell, Devine, & Eskey, 1988; Hudelson, 1989; Johnson & Roen, 1989; Zamel, 1987). We will also examine studies of learners of a variety of ages, including children, adults, and the neglected adolescent.

In addition, because many L2 teachers and professionals work in a wide variety of countries and situations throughout their careers, we consider studies in various learning contexts. These situations even within the United States can range from teaching in prisons (Egbert, 1989) to designing English courses for the Green Angels, who assist tourists on Mexican roadways, to teaching languages for international business. Situations might also range from conducting tutoring programs for migrant children in cafeterias (Johnson, 1987), to organizing adult literacy programs with open enrollments and classes of 80 students held in cramped trailers to conducting small university courses in ESL composition for highly educated international graduate students. Because each setting has its own conditions and challenges that affect L2 learning, it is important to look at research in a variety of interesting and contrasting situations.

A Social Context Focus. Although we will aim for some balance in those areas, this book does have distinct orientations. One of those orientations is a focus on the role of social and contextual factors in L2 use and learning. Second languages are always used, learned, and taught in sociocultural contexts that affect learning opportunities and shape learning in significant ways. Therefore, each of the studies used to illustrate differing research approaches in Chapters 3 through 8 addresses in some way the influences of social or contextual factors in L2 learning.

Let us now briefly consider how we will view the terms "L2 learning," "L2 teaching," and "formal contexts," and consider the rationales for selecting studies conducted in school contexts.

Second Language Learning. We will use the term *second language learning* as an umbrella term for the learning, acquisition, or development of an additional language, whether a second language (L2), a third language (L3), or an n-th language (Ln). It also refers to the development of bilingualism or multilingualism and the learning of varieties of a language. This umbrella term encompasses learning in second language and foreign language (FL) settings as well as in situations in which a language is used as a lingua franca or language of wider communication. The term *second language use* is also an umbrella term used in the same way. Both terms include all modes of language use.

Language Teaching. Language teaching is defined broadly as creating situations that promote second language use and learning. The term "teaching" is thus not linked to any particular theoretical orientation to teaching, such as "direct teaching," nor to any particular language content, such as syntactic or rhetorical form. Rather, teaching involves organizing learning environments and language-use and/or language-learning tasks or activities that are intended to facilitate students' language development (Stern, 1983, p. 21).

Learning in Formal Contexts. Related to the focus on social context factors is an emphasis on research conducted in formal settings. The majority of the studies selected for discussion in this book are studies conducted in formal settings, which refer to the programs and courses that are sponsored by societal institutions. These institutions include universities, high schools, elementary schools, adult schools, language institutes, and businesses.

These institutional settings offer opportunities for many kinds of learning, including the learning resulting from instruction as well as learning that occurs in other ways, such as through informal social interaction, through work experiences, or through individual study. There are two reasons for a focus on research conducted in formal institutional contexts. One reason pertains to theoretical notions of what constitutes suitable settings for the study of language use and learning and the other pertains to audience concerns.

People learn additional languages in many different ways. Learning for some occurs outside of any formal institutional or school context. A prototypical example is a Turkish worker who immigrates to a West European country not knowing a single word of the local language but who manages on his own to learn to get along in the language (Klein, 1986, p. 16). For other learners, the classroom is the only context in which a new language is used. For still other students, learning occurs in both formal and informal contexts.

Opinions differ widely about the relative value of research examining spontaneous (naturalistic, untutored) second language learning versus instructed (guided or tutored) learning. Klein (1986) argues that spontaneous L2 acquisition should be granted priority in research and offers two rationales. One is a historical argument. Although language instruction is recent, he argues, L2 acquisition processes have occurred and evolved over millennia. This argument is not convincing because the evolution of these processes in humans is not the focus of most second language research.

The other argument that Klein proposes for granting first priority in research to spontaneous acquisition is a theoretical one. He suggests that the study of spontaneous learning can provide more knowledge of the underlying mechanisms or laws that govern language processing. When learners are instructed, he explains, these mechanisms or laws are modified and, therefore, more difficult to identify and study. He also proposes, however, that human language learning "resists" instruction to varying degrees, which implies that these processing mechanisms operate to some extent regardless of instruction. Klein suggests that we need to understand the processes of spontaneous learning so that they can be "taken into account by organizing language instruction in ways that would not run counter to the principles of language processing" (Klein, 1986, p. 54). His recommendation is that researchers should first study spontaneous acquisition, then study how acquisition can be "assisted and put under pressure" (p. 54).

Klein's assumption that naturalistic, untutored second language acquisition (SLA) is more important as an object of study than learning that occurs in classrooms is implicit in much of the SLA literature. However, the argument that spontaneous SLA in naturalistic, informal situations is simpler or purer than SLA in formal environments can be challenged on several grounds. First, if we consider that language learning occurs in many ways in many contexts, the selection of one type of context for study over another kind becomes a matter of choice, and contextual variation becomes a topic of research (see Tarone, 1988, for a theoretical treatment of variation in interlanguage).

Second, from the point of view of the individual learner, what is most basic or most natural is the particular experience of that learner, not the way other individuals learned an L2. For many learners of a foreign language, for example, naturalistic acquisition through interactions with native speakers of the language is simply not part of their experience. Vast numbers of English-as-a-foreign-language students, for example, use English only in a formal classroom. For these learners "naturalistic" or "pure" SLA is a phenomenon that does not exist.

Third, there is often no sharp distinction between tutored and untutored learning, even in classrooms; both kinds of learning occur in formal institutional settings in and out of classrooms. Indeed, much of what is taught in classrooms is not learned, while much that is learned was not explicitly taught. Classroom-centered research, in fact, often addresses "natural" language learning (Chaudron, 1988; Johnson, 1983). Similarly, methodologies have emphasized creating classroom activities that promote "natural" acquisition (Hawkins, 1988; Kaplan,

1988; Krashen & Terrell, 1982; Prabhu, 1987; Nunan, 1988). Thus, because naturalistic and tutored learning are not completely distinguishable, and because both kinds of learning occur inside and outside of classrooms and schools, there is little reason that L2 research conducted in informal environments should be valued as more basic and thus more important than L2 research conducted in formal situations.

Psycholinguist Kenji Hakuta, in *Mirror of Language* (1986), addresses this issue in a discussion of research on bilingualism. He claims that a prejudice exists against research conducted in bilingual education classrooms. Hakuta states, "There is a prevalent assumption that social science is like the physical sciences, and that phenomena should be studied in their 'purest' uncontaminated states before any additional complexities are figured in. Thus the inclination is to understand the process of first-language acquisition in monolingual children before trying to understand untutored second-language acquisition and to understand both of these before trying to understand second-language acquisition in bilingual education classrooms. . . . The point . . . is that 'pureness' of a phenomenon is a subjective term . . ." (p. 240).

The practical reason that we will emphasize research conducted in formal school contexts in this book is that such research is of great interest and importance to the audience of second language professionals, including language program administrators, teachers, and those who prepare teachers. Because the learning environments that teachers create and the contextual factors that affect learning in classrooms and societal institutions are crucial for many learners, they are of great practical interest. In conclusion, then, this book focuses on research in language use and learning in formal contexts because it is both theoretically important and of interest to teachers and other professionals who work in those settings.

CONTEXTS FOR L2 RESEARCH

We have seen that language learning occurs in a variety of informal and formal contexts. Similarly, research is conducted in a variety of situations that are related to the questions that are posed and the ways that studies are carried out. In this section we turn to the contexts in which research is conducted. We shall consider factors that influence the topics that researchers choose to study. In addition, in the appendix at the end of this chapter, we shall briefly examine the institutional contexts in which research is conducted and how these contexts shape research. (This chapter appendix will be of particular interest primarily to those who wish to engage in research as a profession.) An overview of how these theoretical, sociopolitical, and institutional context factors relate to the research endeavor should increase your ability to better understand and benefit from studies.

Contextual Influences on Topics of L2 Research

A wide variety of topics are addressed in L2 research. Where do these topics come from? What determines the important issues for research? Why is there no research on some of the questions that teachers most want answers to? There are three factors that exert a powerful influence on topics of L2 research. These are second language acquisition theory, the relevant academic disciplines, and sociopolitical and educational conditions within a nation or across nations.

Second Language Acquisition Theory in L2 Research. Theories of second language acquisition are the most important theoretical influence on topics that are selected for research. It is interesting to note that this was not the case as recently as the 1960s. Most research on L2 teaching and learning at that time was not grounded in a theory of second language acquisition (Politzer, 1981). As we shall see in Chapter 2, one of the major developments since then has been a growth in research in classroom learning and teaching based on second language acquisition theories.

It is not our purpose in this book to review second language acquisition theories. Thorough discussions are provided by Ellis (1985), Gardner (1986), Klein (1986), Krashen (1985), McLaughlin (1987), Spolsky (1989), and Tarone (1988). As we examine sample pieces of research, however, we will note the theoretical orientations of the researcher, because the explicit or implicit theories that motivate the research influence the questions that are addressed, the research methods, and the interpretations of the findings.

Theories of second language acquisition range from comprehensive theories that make claims about the relationships among a broad array of factors to those that attempt to account for very specific kinds of processes. Gardner's (1978, 1986) "socio-educational model," for example, addresses the relationships among wide-ranging factors with a particular emphasis on motivation. Similarly, Spolsky (1988, 1989) calls for a "general" theory of second language learning that can account for the multiple conditions that affect learning. Studies motivated by such views of language learning typically address many variables, focusing strongly on motivation and the relationships between social-psychological factors and classroom behaviors (Gardner, 1986) as well as on the social contexts that influence language learning (Spolsky, 1989; Wong Fillmore, 1989). Language proficiency is often assessed in a global manner.

Other L2 theorists have developed claims that address more specific aspects of learning. Krashen's widely debated input theory (Krashen, 1985; White, 1987) stressed the nature and importance of linguistic input to learners in developing sentence-level grammar. Researchers interested in this theory have studied questions such as how modifications of linguistic input affect comprehension (Enright, 1986; Pica, Young, & Doughty, 1987). McLaughlin's (1987) "cognitive theory" centers on types of cognitive processing. Other cognitive approaches involve, for example, examining the relevance of connectionist models of cognition to SLA (Gasser, 1990). The role of linguistic universals, as well, is an important topic of research for scholars interested in whether and in what ways the constraints of a universal grammar (UG) are still in force for the learning of languages beyond a first language (Rutherford, 1987, p. 131; Schachter, 1988). Discourse and interaction theories emphasize the contributions of conversational interaction to learning (Gass & Madden, 1985; Ellis, 1985). Sociolinguistically oriented researchers are interested in language variation and its relation to L2 use and interlanguage development (Adamson, 1988; Ellis & Roberts, 1987; Gass, Madden, Preston, & Selinker, 1989; Tarone, 1988). Many recent studies conducted in formal contexts are either motivated by a theory of L2 acquisition or appeal to a theory in interpreting findings.

Disciplinary Links. Although L2 acquisition theories exert important influence on topics of research, the related disciplinary interests of researchers also influence the topics they address. Academic disciplines such as linguistics, anthropology, sociology, psychology, and education provide rich research traditions and an ever-developing variety of issues and questions that relate to L2 use, learning, and teaching (see Stern, 1983, for an overview and historical account of the influence of these disciplines, and Beebe, 1987, for another multidisciplinary view).

Linguistics has been the major contributing discipline to L2 scholarship and research, while psychology has traditionally been the second most influential discipline. In the last two decades, however, researchers have given increasing attention to the roles of social and cultural factors in language learning. The so-called hybrid disciplines of sociolinguistics, psycholinguistics, and social psychology, as well as cognitive psychology, have been particularly influential in contributing insights into L2 and FL learning. In this section we will examine a few of the issues that L2 researchers with various disciplinary interests have addressed.

Second language research still draws most heavily on linguistic issues and insights. Linguistics defines the nature of language, providing an understanding of the language system that students are attempting to learn. However, L2 research tends to concentrate on those areas that are important areas of study within linguistics and to neglect other areas. For example, studies of the acquisition of syntax and morphology have been the main focus of interlanguage studies ever since the beginning of the Chomsky era of transformational grammar, yet vocabulary development has received less attention. Scholars working in other schools of linguistics have different emphases. Those working in the Hallidayan tradition, for example, are interested in the functions of language and the linguistic realizations of those functions (Halliday & Hasan, 1985).

Linguistics has contributed a great deal to L2 research in formal settings by providing ways to examine classroom communication and the texts that students read and produce. Discourse analysts (Cazden, 1988; Varonis & Gass, 1985), conversational analysts working from an interactional sociolinguistic perspective (Gumperz, 1986), and text analysts (Halliday & Hasan, 1985) use linguistic categories and insights to describe learning and teaching as linguistic processes. Michaels (1986), for example, has used discourse analysis in an ethnographic study to examine oral narrative accounts of first graders in a multiethnic classroom. She shows that African American children's narrative style did not match the teacher's schema for appropriate narrative style, resulting in misunderstandings and, therefore, less effective teaching and learning.

Researchers with a sociological orientation are interested in descriptions of social life and the effects of social forces on the individual. How educational institutions contribute to maintaining the social order in society has been one topic of study. Auerbach (1986), for example, claims that competency-based adult education ESL programs tend to socialize immigrant adults for existing, menial jobs in society rather than preparing them for the language demands of higher-level jobs. She supports her claim through an analysis of course content and the language functions that students are expected to learn.

Sociolinguistic studies examine L2 use in relation to its social context. Milk (1980), for example, found that when young L2 learners in bilingual classrooms worked in small groups with peers, they talked more and used a wider range of speech acts, particularly controlling and informing acts, than when they participated in teacher-directed instruction. Long and Porter (1985) have summarized similar findings for the interlanguage talk of adult L2 learners. In Wolfson's presentation of sociolinguistics written for an L2 audience (1989) she discusses a broad range of studies in areas such as sociolinguistic and pragmatic transfer, language and gender, language variation, and English as a world language.

Studies with an anthropological orientation focus on the relationships between language use and culture. Au's (1980) work in Hawaii, for instance, shows how reading lessons can be offered in a culturally appropriate way for minority children. By hearing lessons that resemble "talk story" and storytelling, which are major speech events in Hawaiian culture, children were better able to fully engage their cognitive and linguistic resources in learning to read.

Psychological studies have focused on topics such as cognitive processing (Faerch & Kasper, 1987; McLaughlin, 1987), test construction and validation (Bachman & Palmer, 1981; Bergan, Johnson, & Smith, 1984; Henning, 1987; Oller, 1979), L2 learning strategies among high school and college students (O'Malley et al., 1985; Politzer & McGroarty, 1985), and the roles of cognitive structures such as scripts and schemata in L2 reading comprehension (Carrell, Devine, & Eskey, 1988). Some researchers draw upon a particular theory of cognitive development, such as Vygotskian theory, to describe and analyze the kinds of environments that can promote second language and literacy development as well as intellectual development (Cazden, 1988; Hawkins, 1988; Moll, 1989).

Social psychologists have focused a great deal of attention on the roles of motivation—including global, situational, and task motivation—in L2 learning

(Brown, 1987; Gardner, 1986). Social psychologists are also interested in intergroup relations, relationships between individuals and groups, and the ways that language attitudes relate to learning (Beebe, 1987; Genesee, 1987).

In addition to the influences of the disciplines of linguistics, sociolinguistics, sociology, anthropology, psychology, and social psychology, the field of educational research has also had a strong impact on studies of L2 use and learning in formal settings. This field offers a vast literature and several research traditions, particularly in the study of teaching (Wittrock, 1986). The major research paradigms in the study of teaching, according to Shulman (1986), have been: (1) the process-product studies of the past three decades that examine relationships between teacher behaviors and student outcomes; (2) studies of academic learning time (ALT) in the 1970s that examined student engagement and outcome behaviors; (3) the social and cognitive mediation of teaching by students; (4) teacher cognition; and (5) sociolinguistic and ethnographic studies of classroom ecology.

Second language educational researchers operating in the first of these paradigms, the process-product paradigm, studied relationships between teaching processes and language-learning outcomes (Ramirez & Stromquist, 1979; Spada, 1987). The academic-learning-time paradigm was applied in a study of the key features of effective bilingual programs (Tikunoff, 1983). More recently, L2 researchers interested in social and cognitive mediation have used think-aloud protocols and retrospective accounts to examine L2 students' thought processes as they write and converse (see Faerch & Kasper, 1987, for a comprehensive discussion; Fiksdal, 1988). Unfortunately, little L2 work has been done in the teacher cognition paradigm (Gonzales, 1990). Shulman's (1986) fifth paradigm, namely, studies of classroom ecology, has been a very important one in L2 research, as indicated above, drawing on insights and methods from sociolinguistics and anthropology.

In addition to the paradigms used in research on teaching, L2 educational research studies have focused on documenting the diffusion and implementation of new or exemplary programs. Some studies in this line of research draw on communication theory to examine how innovations are disseminated and implemented. Researchers have studied these processes for bilingual programs (Horst et al., 1980), ESL programs (Nunan, 1988; Prabhu, 1987), computer use (Chen & Paisley, 1985; COMSIS, 1984), and whole language programs (Clark, 1987). An important emphasis in such studies is on the contextual factors that constrain or facilitate the implementation of a program in a new school site.

Each discipline, then, contributes its own research traditions and topics of interest. It is important to realize that no single view or set of questions from a single discipline can account for the complex and interacting social, cultural, cognitive, and linguistic processes involved in L2 use and learning. The field of second language learning is, and should be, multidisciplinary (Hatch, 1989).

The Sociopolitical Contexts for L2 Research. Although SLA theory and the other disciplinary interests of L2 researchers influence research topics, sociopolitical conditions within a nation or across national boundaries also affect topics of L2 research. These conditions are many, but might include changing notions of nationalism, war, economic hardship, migration, economic competitiveness, and laws related to these conditions.

In Uganda, in India, and in other formerly colonized countries, the roles of English, particularly the status and functions of varieties of English in society, are topics of hot debate, scholarly discussion, and research (see the journals *World Englishes* and *English Today* and B. Kachru, 1986, 1988). Similarly, attitudes toward language varieties in these settings become important topics of research.

As economic hardship or war forces people to leave their homeland and immigrate to other countries, the host society must respond in many ways to the needs of immigrants. The cultural adjustment and language learning of specific populations of immigrants then becomes an important research topic. In Europe, for example, the influx of large numbers of foreign workers (guest workers) intensified interest in examining naturalistic adult second language acquisition in the host countries (see Klein, 1986, 1989; Purdue, 1984). Similarly, after the Vietnam War, when streams of Southeast Asian immigrants arrived in the United States, one response of the federal government was to fund programs to facilitate refugees' "resettlement," their equal treatment under the law, and their successful "integration" into society. The integration process, of course, included L2 classes. These refugee programs included funds to study the effects of such classes on language learning. Tollefson (1985, 1986) has reported on the issues involved in adequately evaluating these programs.

In the United States, concerns about this nation's economic competitiveness in the world has, in part, motivated a renewed interest in foreign language teaching. Reports such as that of the President's Commission on Foreign Languages also gave an impetus to foreign language research, just as it was supported by the National Defense Education Act after the Sputnik crisis in 1957.

Second language research often emerges in response to specific legal requirements. In the United States, federal legislation often mandates that particular kinds of research be carried out. Many federally funded research projects are undertaken to comply with these legal mandates. For example, several of the larger bilingual education studies have been conducted in response to the 1975 and 1983 provisions of the Bilingual Education Act. Education laws usually require research into the effectiveness of programs funded under the law. The stated purpose of such research is usually to obtain evidence to promote or demote the program, or to revise the regulations that govern the programs. Nevertheless, program continuation often depends as much or more on political considerations as it does on research results. Federal research monies have been available for bilingual education, for bilingual special education, for Chapter I and Migrant programs, for structured immersion programs, and more recently, in the late 1980s, for foreign language programs and literacy programs. Second language research, then, is conducted to comply with laws requiring research on the operation and effectiveness of programs. The programs themselves are often created to respond to the educational and social needs of populations of L2 learners.

CONCLUSION

In the first section of this chapter we presented the major goals for readers of this book: to understand and be able to critically evaluate research, to benefit from research, and to contribute to the research endeavor. We examined the importance of research for L2 teaching, addressing the relationship between what teachers may view as their intuitive expertise and the kinds of knowledge and insights they can obtain from research. We argued against a mechanistic consumer model of applying research in favor of viewing research as a source of information that can encourage us to reflect on language use and learning processes and to take action to improve practice.

In the final section we explained the contexts for L2 research. First, we argued that three contextual factors influence L2 research topics: second language acquisition theory, the related academic disciplines, and sociopolitical conditions. The nature and relative weight of influence of these factors is also related, however, to the institutional contexts in which L2 research is conducted (see the appendix at end of this chapter). That is, the institutional context, whether a university, a private research firm, or an industry, can influence the topics, purposes, and audiences for research. This chapter has provided only a brief introduction to contextual issues in research. Yet some understanding of these factors and how they shape the conduct of research should help address the goals set forth in the first section of the chapter. In the following chapter we will examine some of the ways that L2 research is changing.

NOTE

1. A note on the rationale for the sequencing of Chapters 3 through 8: Traditionally, in scholarly works on both L2 research methods and educational research methods, quantitative (especially experimental) approaches have been viewed as most important and given top priority. This priority has been shown by devoting both a prominent position and more space to these approaches. Qualitative methodologies have traditionally been less valued in these two overlapping fields and their subordinate position has been indicated by devoting less space to them and by placing them at the

end of books (J. D. Brown, 1988; Smith & Glass, 1987, for example). Thus, a traditional order of presentation of methods for this book might be: descriptive, survey, experimental, qualitative. The organization of Chapters 3 through 8 departs from the standard approach and reflects my view that a variety of methodological approaches are useful for gaining insights into L2 learning and that the method used should fit the question addressed. Therefore, both quantitative and qualitative approaches are given significant attention with neither relegated to a subordinate position. Graduate-student readers of the book can carry on the "quantitative-qualitative debate" throughout these chapters as they compare contrasting methodologies. For example, the placement of case studies in Chapter 4 not only reflects their importance in L2 research but allows readers to see the strong contrasts between case-study methods and the correlational methods presented in Chapter 3. Case studies are also placed early in the book for a pedagogical purpose. That is, for many graduate students, they are both a feasible and an appealing approach for initiating pilot research projects. While these six chapters can be read in almost any order, I have found that this order of presentation is effective.

REFERENCES

Adamson, H. D. (1988). *Variation theory and second language acquisition.* Washington, DC: Georgetown University Press.

Allwright, R. (1988). *Observation in the language classroom.* London: Longman Group U.K.

Au, K. H. (1980). Participation structures in a reading lesson with Hawaiian children: Analysis of a culturally appropriate instructional event. *Anthropology & Education Quarterly, 11,* 91–115.

Auerbach, E. (1986). Competency-based ESL: One step forward or two steps back? *TESOL Quarterly, 20*(3), 411–429.

Bachman, L., & Palmer, A. S. (1981). A multitrait-multimethod investigation into the construct validity of six tests of speaking and reading. In A. Palmer, P. Groot, & G. Trosper (Eds.), *The construct validation of tests of communicative competence.* Washington, DC: Teachers of English to Speakers of Other Languages.

Beebe, L. M. (1987). *Issues in second language acquisition: Multiple perspectives.* New York: Harper & Row/Newbury House.

Bergan, J., Johnson, D. M., & Smith, A. N. (1984). *Executive summary of the Head Start Measures Project: Path-referenced assessment for Head Start children.* Tucson: University of Arizona, Center for Educational Evaluation and Measurement.

Borg, W. R. (1981). *Applying educational research: A practical guide for teachers.* White Plains, NY: Longman.

Brown, H. D. (1987). *Principles of language learning and teaching* (2nd ed.). Englewood Cliffs, NJ: Prentice Hall.

Brown, J. D. (1988). *Understanding research in second language learning.* Cambridge: Cambridge University Press.

Carrell, P., Devine, J., & Eskey, D. (1988). *Interactive approaches to second language reading.* Cambridge: Cambridge University Press.

Cazden, C. (1988). *Classroom discourse: The language of teaching and learning.* Portsmouth, NH: Heinemann.

Chaudron, C. (1988). *Second language classrooms: Research on teaching and learning.* Cambridge: Cambridge University Press.

Chen, M., & Paisley, W. (Eds.). (1985). *Children and microcomputers.* Beverly Hills, CA: Sage.

Clark, M. (1987). Don't blame the system: Constraints on "Whole- Language" reform. *Language Arts, 64,* 384–396.

COMSIS Corporation. (1984, November). *Review of the state of the art of educational technologies implemented in programs serving LEP students funded by the Department of Education: Final report.* Rosslyn, VA: National Clearinghouse for Bilingual Education.

Egbert, J. L. (1989). Prison ESL: Building a foundation for teaching English in unconventional settings. *English for Specific Purposes, 8,* 51–64.

Ellis, R. (1985). *Understanding second language acquisition.* Oxford: Oxford University Press.

Ellis, R., & Roberts, C. (1987). Two approaches for investigating second language acquisition. In R. Ellis (Ed.), *Second language acquisition in context.* Reading, MA: Addison-Wesley.

Enright, D. S. (1986). "Use everything you have to teach English": Providing useful input to young language learners. In P. Rigg & D. S. Enright (Eds.), *Children and ESL: Integrating perspectives* (pp. 115–162). Washington, DC: Teachers of English to Speakers of Other Languages.

Faerch, C., & Kasper, G. (1987). *Introspection in second language research.* Clevedon, England: Multilingual Matters.

Fiksdal, S. (1988). Verbal and nonverbal strategies of rapport in cross-cultural interviews. *Linguistics and Education, 1,* 3–17.

Gardner, R. C. (1978). *Social psychological aspects of second language acquisition* (Research Bulletin 445). London, Canada: University of Western Ontario, Department of Psychology.

Gardner, R. C. (1986). *Social psychological aspects of second language learning.* London: Edward Arnold.

Gass, S. M., & Madden, C. G. (1985). *Input in second language acquisition.* Rowley, MA: Newbury House.

Gass, S., Madden, C., Preston, D., & Selinker, L. (1989). *Variation in second language acquisition: Psycholinguistic issues.* Clevedon, England: Multilingual Matters.

Gasser, M. (1990). Connectionism and universals of second language acquisition. *Studies in Second Language Acquisition, 12,* 179–199.

Genesee, F. (1987). *Learning through two languages: Studies of immersion and bilingual education.* New York: Harper & Row/Newbury House.

Gonzales, L. (1990, April). *How bilingual student teachers acquire the cognition for teaching.* Paper presented at the annual meeting of the American Educational Research Association, Boston.

Gumperz, J. J. (1986). Interactional sociolinguistics in the study of schooling. In J. Cook-Gumperz (Ed.), *The social construction of literacy* (pp. 45–68). Cambridge: Cambridge University Press.

Hakuta, K. (1986). *Mirror of language.* New York: Basic Books.

Halliday, M. A. K., & Hasan, R. (1985). *Language, context, and text: Aspects of language in a social-semiotic perspective*. Victoria, Australia: Deakin University.

Hammersley, M., & Atkinson, P. (1983). *Ethnography: Principles and practice*. London: Tavistock Publications.

Hamp-Lyons, L. (1989). Recent publications on statistics, language testing, and quantitative research methods: I. *TESOL Quarterly, 23,* 127–132.

Hatch, E. (1989, February). *Multidisciplinary perspectives in SLA*. Plenary address presented at the Second Language Research Forum, Los Angeles.

Hatch, E., & Lazaraton, A. (1990). *The research manual: Design and statistics for applied linguistics*. New York: HarperCollins/Newbury House.

Hawkins, B. A. (1988). *Scaffolded classroom interaction and its relation to second language acquisition for language minority children*. Unpublished doctoral dissertation, University of California, Los Angeles.

Henning, G. (1987). *A guide to language testing: Development, evaluation, research*. New York: Harper & Row/Newbury House.

Horst, D. P., Douglas, D. E., Friendly, L. D., Johnson, D. M., Luber, L. M., McKay, M., Nava, H. G., Peistrup, A. M., Roberts, A. O. H., & Valdez, A. (1980). *An evaluation of project information packages as used for the diffusion of bilingual projects* (Vol.2) (Report No. VR-460). Mountain View, CA: RMC Research Corporation. (ERIC Document Reproduction Service No. ED 193 954)

Hudelson, S. (1989). Writing in a second language. In R. B. Kaplan (Ed.), *Annual Review of Applied Linguistics* (Vol. 9, pp. 210–222). Cambridge: Cambridge University Press.

Johnson, D. M. (1983). Natural language learning by design: A classroom experiment in social interaction and second language acquisition. *TESOL Quarterly, 17,* 55–68.

Johnson, D. M. (1987). The organization of instruction in migrant education: Assistance for children and youth at risk. *TESOL Quarterly, 21*(3), 437–459.

Johnson, D. M., & Roen, D. H. (1989). *Richness in writing: Empowering ESL students*. White Plains, NY: Longman.

Kachru, B. B. (1986). *The alchemy of English*. Oxford: Pergamon Press.

Kachru, B. B. (1988). The sacred cows of English. *English Today, 4*(4), 3–8.

Kaplan, R. B. (Ed.). (1988). *Annual Review of Applied Linguistics* (Vol. 8). Cambridge: Cambridge University Press.

Klein, W. (1986). *Second language acquisition*. Cambridge: Cambridge University Press.

Klein, W. (1989, February). *Utterance structure*. Plenary address at the Second Language Research Forum, Los Angeles.

Krashen, S. (1985). The input hypothesis. White Plains, NY: Longman.

Krashen, S., & Terrell, T. (1982). *The natural approach: Language acquisition in the classroom*. Oxford: Pergamon Press.

Lemke, J. (1988). Genres, semantics, and classroom education. *Linguistics and Education, 1,* 81–99.

Long, M., & Porter, P. (1985). Group work, interlanguage talk, and second language acquisition. *TESOL Quarterly, 19,* 207–228.

McLaughlin, B. (1987). *Theories of second language learning*. London: Edward Arnold.

Michaels, S. (1986). Narrative presentations: An oral preparation for literacy with first graders. In J. Cook-Gumperz (Ed.), *The social construction of literacy* (pp. 94–116). Cambridge: Cambridge University Press.

Milk, R. (1980). *Variation in language use patterns across different group settings in two bilingual second grade classrooms*. Unpublished doctoral dissertation, Stanford University.

Moll, L. (1989). Teaching second language students: A Vygotskian perspective. In D. M. Johnson & D. H. Roen (Eds.), *Richness in writing: Empowering ESL students* (pp. 55–69). White Plains, NY: Longman.

Nunan, D. (1988). *The learner centred curriculum*. Cambridge: Cambridge University Press.

Oller, J. W., Jr. (1979). *Language tests at school: A pragmatic approach*. London: Longman.

Office of Technology Assessment. (1987, March). *Trends and status of computers in school: Use in Chapter 1 programs and use with limited English proficient students*. Washington, DC: Science, Education and Transportation Program, OTA, U. S. Congress.

O'Malley, J. M., Chamot, A. U., Stewer-Manzanares, G., Russo, R., & Kupper, L. (1985). Learning strategy applications with students of English as a second language. *TESOL Quarterly, 19*(3), 557–584.

Pica, T., Young, R., & Doughty, C. (1987). The impact of interaction on comprehension. *TESOL Quarterly, 21*, 737–758.

Politzer, R. L. (1981). Effective language teaching: Insights from research. In J. E. Alatis, H. B. Altman, & P. M. Alatis (Eds.), *The second language classroom: Directions for the 1980's* (pp. 23–35). New York: Oxford University Press.

Politzer, R. L., & McGroarty, M. (1985). An exploratory study of learning behaviors and their relationship to gains in linguistic and communicative competence. *TESOL Quarterly, 19*, 103–123.

Prabhu, N. S. (1987). *Second language pedagogy*. Oxford: Oxford University Press.

Purdue, C. (Ed.). (1984). *Second language acquisition by adult immigrants: A field manual*. Rowley, MA: Newbury.

Ramirez, A., & Stromquist, N. (1979). ESL methodology and student learning in bilingual elementary schools. *TESOL Quarterly, 13*, 145–160.

Richards, J., Platt, J., & Weber, H. (1985). *Dictionary of applied linguistics*. London: Longman Group U.K.

Rutherford, W. E. (1987). *Second language grammar: Learning and teaching*. London: Longman Group U.K.

Schachter, J. (1988). Second language acquisition and its relationship to Universal Grammar. *Applied Linguistics, 9*, 219–235.

Shulman, L. (1986). Paradigms and research programs in the study of teaching. In M. C. Wittrock (Ed.), *Handbook of research on teaching* (3rd ed.) (pp. 3–36). New York: Macmillan (American Educational Research Association).

Slavin, R. E. (1989). PET and the pendulum: Faddism in education and how to stop it. *Phi Delta Kappan, 70*, 752–758.

Smith, M. L., & Glass, G. V. (1987). *Research and evaluation in education and the social sciences*. Englewood Cliffs, NJ: Prentice Hall.

Spada, N. M. (1987). Relationships between instructional differences and learning outcomes: A process-product study of communicative language teaching. *Applied Linguistics, 8*, 137–161.

Spolsky, B. (1988). Bridging the gap: A general theory of second language learning. *TESOL Quarterly, 22*, 377–396.

Spolsky, B. (1989). *Conditions for second language learning*. Oxford: Oxford University Press.

Stern, H. H. (1983). *Fundamental concepts of language teaching*. Oxford: Oxford University Press.

Tarone E. (1988). *Variation in interlanguage*. London: Edward Arnold.

Tikunoff, W. (1983). *Significant bilingual instructional features study*. San Francisco: Far West Laboratory.

Tollefson, J. W. (1985). Functional competencies in the U.S. Refugee Program: Theoretical and practical problems. *TESOL Quarterly, 20*, 649–664.

Tollefson, J. W. (1986). Research on refugee resettlement: Implications for instructional programs. *TESOL Quarterly, 19*, 753–764.

Varonis, E., & Gass, S. M. (1985). Non-native/non-native conversation: A model for negotiation of meaning. *Applied Linguistics, 6*, 71–90.

Vasquez, O. A. (1988, November). *Ethnographic perspectives on literacy in a minority setting*. Paper presented at the meeting of the National Council of Teachers of English, St. Louis, MO.

White, L. (1987). Against comprehensible input: The Input Hypothesis and the development of second-language competence. *Applied Linguistics, 8*, 95–110.

Wittrock, M. C. (Ed.). (1986). *Handbook of research on teaching* (3rd ed.). New York: Macmillan (American Educational Research Association).

Wolfson, N. (1989). *Perspectives: Sociolinguistics and TESOL*. New York: Harper & Row/Newbury House.

Wong Fillmore, L. (1989). Teachability and second language acquisition. In M. L. Rice & R. L. Schiefelbusch (Eds.), *The teachability of language* (pp. 311–332). Baltimore: Paul H. Brookes.

Zamel, V. (1987). Recent research on writing pedagogy. *TESOL Quarterly, 21*, 697–715.

APPENDIX: INSTITUTIONAL CONTEXTS
FOR CONDUCTING L2 RESEARCH

Additional understanding of the nature of L2 research can be gained by considering the institutional settings in which research is conducted. Studies conducted in different settings have distinctly different characteristics. Factors such as who initiates and funds the research, for what purpose, who conducts the research, on what topic, and for what audience vary widely according to the research setting. How results are disseminated and used to affect policy, practice, or theory also vary widely. Figure 1.2 lists these factors and can serve as a guide for the discussion to follow.

Research is carried out in a variety of institutional contexts ranging from universities to government agencies to industry. The most commonly known setting is the university, where professors and academic professionals, often in collaboration with graduate students, conduct research. University-based research may be funded by public agencies, private foundations, or internal university

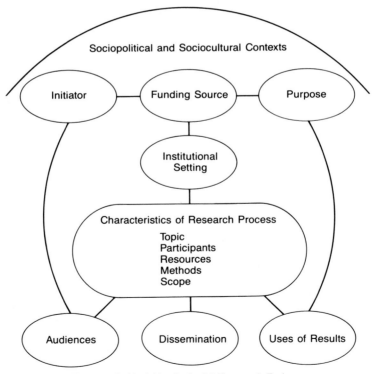

Figure 1.2. Variables in the L2 Research Endeavor

sources, or it may be unfunded. The major purpose of such research is usually to add to the body of knowledge in the field and to contribute to theory development. Topics are generally initiated by professors; therefore, topics are shaped more by L2 theory and theoretical concerns in related disciplines than they are by sociopolitical concerns. Many studies are small in scope because professors have teaching and service responsibilities, and often have limited resources and facilities. In addition, university-based studies often focus on the L2 use or learning of university students because these students are readily accessible as subjects or participants. Reports of the studies are presented at conferences and usually appear in scholarly journals and books because the major audience for this research is the academic community.

Significant L2 research is also carried out in centers, labs, and private research firms. In the United States, the Center for Applied Linguistics (CAL) in Washington, D.C., is an example of an influential center. By obtaining funding from sources such as government agencies and private foundations, it has conducted research on a wide variety of L2 issues. Researchers are professionals with MA's or PhD's in second language acquisition, linguistics, education, and related areas.

Private research firms operate in a similar manner. Researchers are often full-time, professional researchers with MA's and PhD's, who compete for contracts from the federal government and other agencies. Some examples of U.S. firms and sample research topics are RMC Research Corporation (studies of bilingual education evaluation and teacher preparation), SRA Technologies and Aguirre Associates (structured immersion), American Institutes for Research (bilingual program evaluation), SRI International (Chapter I), and Educational Testing Service (test development).

Studies carried out in labs, centers, and private firms are often large in scale (i.e., funded at $500,000 or more) and carried out over one, two, or three years. In contrast to university-based research, the topics are determined by the sponsor and are, therefore, often more motivated by policy concerns, which reflect the sociopolitical context, than by questions about L2 theory. The reports and products of these studies are delivered to the client who sponsored the research and disseminated through clearinghouses and networks such as ERIC, as well as through presentations at professional conferences. Many researchers later publish articles and chapters in scholarly journals or books.

Government agencies not only sponsor but also conduct research that relates to L2 learning. For example, the Office of Technology Assessment (OTA) of the U.S. Congress conducted a study of the roles of computers and other technologies in schools. The purpose of that study was to help make decisions about reauthorization legislation for Chapter I programs that serve low achieving as well as L2 students (Office of Technology Assessment, 1987). The U.S. military also funds research in areas such as uses of technology in language testing and cognitive factors in language learning (O'Malley et al., 1985).

Occasionally private industries conduct L2 studies. International Business Machines (IBM), for example, evaluated its Writing to Read computer program with ESL students. This research was aimed at determining the effectiveness of a commercial program so that the results could be used to market and sell a product to audiences of potential buyers. Because of its commercial motivation, results of research of this type are not necessarily published in scholarly journals and are sometimes sharply criticized by academicians. Slavin (1989), for example, has criticized studies of the Writing to Read program on the grounds that comparison groups were not comparable in important ways to experimental groups.

Departments of education in the larger states, such as California, New York, and Texas, often conduct research. The purpose of the research is usually to gain information that will help establish, support, or revise policy. For instance, the validity of the cut-off scores for categorizing students as "limited English proficient" (LEP) or proficient in English was a crucial issue when state-mandated tests were first used to place large numbers of students in programs. Such research may be conducted in-house or contracted out to a university, research firm, or district.

Large school districts have evaluation and research units that conduct research, including, most commonly, mandated evaluations of federally funded programs such as migrant education, bilingual education, or Chapter I programs. Results are reported to the funding agency, but are sometimes also published in journals. Cross-institutional collaboration among districts, universities, centers, and private firms is very common.

While researchers working in these various settings may collaborate and present their work at the same professional conferences, conflicts arise about the value of studies conducted in each setting. Some contract researchers view university-based researchers as overly theoretical, not interested in producing studies that will affect policy or practice, and overly concerned with conducting research to advance their own theories. On the other hand, some university researchers criticize contract research for lacking adequate theoretical frameworks, for producing multiple-authored work, or for bowing to the wishes of a sponsor by not addressing certain questions or addressing them in limited ways. An understanding of these contexts and the conflicting demands they make on researchers is essential because it adds to our ability to critically evaluate and interpret L2 research.

CHAPTER 2

Some Developments in L2 Research

Our major focus in this book is on L2 research in formal contexts and methods for carrying it out. To understand current L2 research, it is useful to examine developments that have occurred in research in recent years. Research is cumulative in the sense that researchers attempt to build on and improve upon previous work. It is not the purpose of this chapter to provide a history of L2 research (useful discussions can be found in Allwright, 1988; Chaudron, 1988; Krashen, 1982; Stern, 1983, and other sources). Rather, its purpose is to highlight a few key developments to provide some diachronic context within which to examine current and future research. We will focus on three general developments that characterize the ways in which L2 research has evolved. The developments are of three types, the first conceptual, the second methodological, and the third technological. They are: (1) a more balanced focus on both the social and personal nature of L2 use and learning; (2) expanded quantitative and qualitative methodological approaches; and (3) new roles for technology. We will examine changes in each of these areas using illustrative studies.

A MORE BALANCED VIEW OF THE SOCIAL AND PERSONAL NATURE OF LEARNING

Research in the decades of the 1970s and 1980s moved toward a more balanced view of the social and personal nature of learning. Language learning always occurs in a social context that affects individuals in different ways (Goodman,

This chapter is a much revised and expanded version of a chapter in M. McGroarty, & C. Faltis, (Eds.) (in press). *Languages in school and society: Policy and pedagogy*. Berlin: Mouton de Gruyter.

1988; Politzer, 1981; Wong Fillmore, 1983). Recent research has led to new insights about individuals' learning processes, strategies, attitudes, and cultural background, as well as to new insights about the ways that these factors interact with classroom and social contexts to shape language learning.

We will briefly discuss two studies that provide examples of insights into the personal and social nature of learning. A naturalistic study of the private speech of young language learners by Saville-Troike (1988) illustrates how children use language in the service of intrapersonal goals, while Goldstein's (1987) correlational study of language preferences of high school learners adds to our knowledge about interpersonal relationships and the social-psychological nature of language learning among adolescents.

Personal Strategies in the Silent Period

Saville-Troike's (1988) study provides one of the best illustrations of the personal side of second language development in childhood. She set out to determine the nature of L2 learners' private speech and to analyze ways that private speech can reveal the use of learning strategies that contribute to children's acquisition of English. The children she observed were speakers of Chinese, Korean, and Japanese. Working in both nursery school and elementary school settings, she and her colleagues used wireless microphones to tape-record the naturally occurring private speech of nine children ranging in age from 3;3 (3 years, 3 months) to 8;3. They audiotaped and videotaped the children over a period of several months.

Saville-Troike found that three of the children were "other-directed" in their early social orientation and did not go through a silent period. The other six—the majority of the children—were "inner-directed," reflective children who went through silent periods ranging from 5 to 23 weeks. One child, in fact, remained silent and learned no English. During the silent period the five who did learn English used virtually no overt English speech with others but did continue to interact nonverbally with English speakers and with their first-language (L1) peers using their first language. For five of these six children, the nature of their private speech indicated that they were actively engaged in using the L2 for intrapersonal cognitive purposes in ways that contributed to learning. For example, they used strategies such as repeating others' utterances, chanting phrases (revealing attention to and awareness of morphological patterns), creating new words with English phonological structure, recalling meaningful portions of scripts for events, and rehearsing utterances for later social performance for the teacher.

As Saville-Troike (1988) states, these findings illustrate the children's metalinguistic awareness of sound, form, and meaning. They suggest that some children exercise self-regulatory control of L2 learning strategies at a younger age than expected for other domains of knowledge (p. 587). The results have implications for interaction theories of second language acquisition. That is, they show that the kinds of interactions that can contribute to L2 acquisition go beyond two-way verbal interactions.

This study contributes to knowledge about important aspects of the intrapersonal side of child L2 learning about which we previously had little, if any, information. Implications for teaching are several. First, teachers should expect that many, though not all, learners will go through a silent period. Second, teachers should understand that most children going through a silent period are engaged in attending to sound, form, and meaning with the intent to learn to communicate with English speakers in order to participate more fully in school and social life. They should, therefore, provide opportunities for meaningful L1 verbal interaction as well as meaningful L2 nonverbal interaction, without demands to speak. This study shows, as has other research, that children go about the language-learning task in their own way and at their own pace (Hudelson, 1989; Wong Fillmore, 1983).

Talking the Right English

While this naturalistic work in children's private speech has helped to illuminate the personal strategies of learners, other research has also shed light on the social factors involved in L2 learning. Goldstein's (1987) quantitative sociolinguistic study of target language varieties illustrates the importance of social-psychological and affective factors in the L2 acquisition of adolescents. She provided some evidence that high school L2 learners are well aware of variation in the target language (English) and have preferences for the varieties they want to speak and learn. When asked about his language goals, one teenager stated "to the right people you talk the right English" (p. 429). For the adolescent learners in her study, Standard English was not necessarily the target language or the only target language. Some of them preferred African American English over Standard English as a target language and some preferred to know and use both varieties.

Goldstein investigated the relationship between two variables, extent of contact and feelings of identification with African Americans, and the frequency with which subjects used two features of African American English: negative concord (e.g., They won't tell nobody else) and distributive *be* (indicating intermittent rather than permanent qualities; e.g., You sometimes be scared). Her subjects were 28 Spanish-speaking male high school students, 15 to 19 years of age. They were advanced users of ESL who had lived in New York for at least two years and had not studied English before their arrival. Goldstein found no relationship between her measure of identification with African Americans and the use of the two features of African American English. She did, however, find statistically significant relationships between a measure of contact with African American friends/acquaintances and frequency of use of these features in an informal interview in which they discussed friends and the fear of death. The adolescents with extensive or medium contact did not use negative concord categorically, however, but variably.

The importance of this study for teachers is that some deviations from Standard English in a learners' language may not be errors at all. Rather, they may be features of the target language variety that they choose to employ. We will examine this study in more depth in the chapter on correlational research.

Interactions between Social Contexts and Personal Factors

Each of these studies shows, although in very different ways, that L2 learning takes place in social contexts that affect different learners in different ways. For many of the learners in Saville-Troike's study, their L2 use went "underground," but their private speech reflected what occurred in the social context. That is, it reflected what occurred through L1 interactions and through L2 interactions that the learners observed or in which they participated nonverbally. Goldstein's study illustrates the importance of peer relations in shaping adolescents' target language use and their goals for learning. As these and other studies have shown, both child and adolescent learners have personal goals and reactions to language use situations, and they engage in personal strategies to use and acquire an L2 in the classroom and in the broader social environment. These studies represent a clear departure from the 1970s tradition of morpheme acquisition studies, which neither addressed language variation nor linked language use and development to its social context. One of the major advances in research in the last two decades has been the attempt to illuminate and explain the complex interactions between the social contexts for L2 learning and the strategies, processes, attitudes, and developing communicative competence of learners. These are only two examples of such research. We will see others throughout the book.

DIVERSITY IN RESEARCH METHOD

Attempts to describe and explain the complex and interacting factors involved in the social and personal sides of language use and learning have paralleled important changes in research methodology that allow researchers to examine these complexities more adequately. The overall change is that the field embraces a wider repertoire of quantitative and qualitative methods (Chaudron, 1988). In the 1960s, 1970s, and much of the 1980s quantitative experimental methods were favored in research in L2 learning and teaching. The experiment was valued as the best approach to research because it could establish cause-and-effect relationships. Improving research was seen as improving measurement and statistical techniques and conducting more tightly controlled experiments. While those goals certainly remain, and are important, the options for research method have expanded dramatically. The proliferation and wider acceptance of qualitative and ethnographic approaches have had a powerful impact on the field. In this section, we will review several developments in qualitative and quantitative approaches, and in approaches that combine methods, and we will illustrate these with sample studies. But before we do this, we will draw a distinction between two paradigms of research.

Contrasting Paradigms

The basic beliefs and assumptions that underlie studies in the experimental/ quasi-experimental/correlational paradigm (studies that are primarily quantitative in orientation) are fundamentally different from those that guide studies called interpretive, ethnographic, or constructivist (which are primarily qualitative in orientation). There is much debate about the value of quantitative and qualitative approaches to research. The issues are complex and a great deal has been written on these topics. It is not within the scope of this book to provide an extended discussion of the ongoing debates. Many excellent sources are available for that purpose.[1] Rather, in our initial discussion we will briefly outline the positivist/ constructivist dichotomy proposed by Guba and Lincoln (1989), with the caveat that there is always danger in any dichotomy. Dichotomies are useful only for taking an initial look and making initial contrasts.[2]

Guba and Lincoln dichotomize inquiry into conventional and constructivist approaches. They contrast the conventional paradigm (also called positivist or scientific) with the constructivist (also called hermeneutic or interpretive). Each paradigm reflects an underlying belief system that affects the nature of inquiry. They compare the paradigms on three dimensions: ontology, epistemology, and methodology. Each of these dimensions is interrelated. For example, methodology derives from ontology and epistemology. Our discussion here is organized around their three-part framework.

Ontology deals with philosophical issues about the nature of reality. Holders of a realist ontological view assert that there is an objective reality, or at least an objective reality that can be discovered within a particular perspective or discipline. The goals of inquiry are to discover the nature of that reality and to uncover causal laws. These assumptions are basic to the conventional paradigm. On the other hand, the relativist view that characterizes the constructivist paradigm, according to Guba and Lincoln, asserts that realities are mental constructions of phenomena, that there are multiple socially constructed realities, and that "truth" is problematic. Rather than searching for truth, the goal of inquiry is to arrive at an informed and sophisticated construction on which there is consensus among competent people. They also suggest that such a construction is always open to change and to reconstruction.

Epistemology deals with the relationship of the knower to the known. An objectivist epistemology holds that inquiry can be objective and free of values. A state of subject-object dualism is assumed in which the observer remains detached and distant from the object of study. An assumption of the conventionalist paradigm is that if research is properly carried out, it can be free of bias, free of subjectivity, and free of values. In contrast, holders of a monistic, subjectivist epistemology assert that it is not possible to separate the inquirer from the object of inquiry, nor should such a separation be a goal. Rather, according to Guba and Lincoln (1989), it is the interaction between the two that creates the data and shapes the findings (p. 88). Human beings cannot set their subjectivity aside. Rather, they bring their values into their research through the theories they employ as guiding frameworks, through choices about what to study and what to exclude from study, and through the methodologies they use.

Guba and Lincoln point out that methodology derives from epistemology and ontology. They dichotomize methodology as either interventionist or hermeneutic. A goal of conventional, scientific, interventionist methodology is to discover cause-and-effect relationships. This is accomplished by manipulating the natural environment, setting up a situation for study, and controlling variables. Contextual factors are controlled as well so that their effects can either be eliminated or isolated for study. Cook and Campbell (1979) stated it this way: "causal forces are usually confounded in nature and most can be clearly unconfounded when putative causes are varied 'at will' " (p. 31). Interventionist methodology requires that the researcher intervene, manipulating the situation to determine causes of certain effects. This methodology, according to Guba and Lincoln, follows from a realist ontology and an objectivist epistemology.

A hermeneutic methodology, in contrast, follows from a relativist ontology and a subjectivist epistemology. Guba and Lincoln define this methodology as involving a continuing dialectic of iteration, analysis, critique, reiteration, and reanalysis. These processes lead to a joint construction of a case as all inquirers and respondents participate in the continuing dialectic. The goals of inquiry are not to discover cause-and-effect relationships, but to make sense of a case, to understand a situation. The dialectic of inquiry is aimed at a new social construction.

The present discussion has provided only the briefest overview of two contrasting paradigms as interpreted by two scholars who strongly favor naturalistic and constructivist approaches. Other qualitative researchers (Howe & Eisenhart, 1990) point out that setting up positivism as the polar opposite of qualitative research is pointless because positivism is no longer a tenable epistemological position in the philosophy of science. The point for now is that basic philosophical assumptions about the nature of reality and the relationship of the knower to the known guide inquiry of all types. No research is unbiased or objective. Informed readers of research and participants in collaborative research need an awareness of the range of views on these very basic issues. As we go through the six major approaches to research in Chapters 3 through 8, the ways that these differences are played out in real studies will become more apparent. Let us now turn to some specific developments within the broad areas of qualitative and quantitative L2 research.

Qualitative Research

Qualitative approaches to research have gained a strong foothold in L2 research. While the case study had always had a secure place in studies of naturalistic child language acquisition, it had not until more recently been viewed as a major, rigorous approach to research in formal L2 classroom settings (Brown, 1988). And although ethnography has played important roles in educational research and sociolinguistic research (Spindler, 1974; Gumperz & Hymes, 1972), its use in L2 research in formal settings has not been widespread. Case studies, ethnography, and a range of other primarily qualitative approaches now play an increasingly important role in L2 research in formal settings (see Chapters 4, 6, and 8).

Not only are qualitative approaches in general more accepted as legitimate methods but there is also an increasingly wide range of methods under intense discussion. These have diverse labels including ethnographic, microethnographic, critical ethnographic, naturalistic, interpretive, constructivist, artistic, symbolic interactionist, interpretive interactionist, democratic, neo-Marxist, and feminist (Erickson, 1986; see Atkinson, Delamont, & Hammersley, 1988, for a discussion contrasting U.S. and British qualitative research). This diversity is a positive development because it expands the options for ways of looking and ways of understanding phenomena. Moreover, it suggests differing views about what phenomena are worth studying.

For a field in which cultural issues play a crucial role in everyday practice, this diversity can only enrich inquiry. Ethnographic work, with its attention to contextual and cultural interpretation, has added to our knowledge of how students approach L2 learning, how culture interacts with language learning, and how teachers and institutions can be culturally sensitive (Au, 1980; Cazden, 1987; Erickson, 1986; Heath, 1983; Mehan, Moll, & Reil, 1985).

Ethnographic approaches have been most widely used with children. Unfortunately, for learners in middle schools, high schools, universities, and various adult settings, ethnographic studies are still all too scarce. An increase in such studies with learners of all types and in a variety of institutional settings should do much to enrich L2 research (van Lier, 1988; Watson-Gegeo, 1988).

Quantitative Approaches

Important changes have taken place in quantitative approaches as well. These approaches, which are discussed in Chapters 3, 5, and 7, include experimentation or quasi-experimentation, correlational studies, and survey research. Quantitative methods differ from qualitative methods in that they emphasize the systematic measurement and quantification of variables, statistical analysis of the quantitative data, and the use of mathematical models and causal inferencing (Linn, 1986, p. 92). A key problem in applying experimentation to studies of learning in actual classrooms is that true, tightly controlled experiments of any length or magnitude are not feasible or even ethical or legal in many formal settings. The first important development, then, is more variety in acceptable quasi-experimental designs for studying planned changes in teaching-learning environments.

Second, for those conducting correlational research, there now exist more sophisticated statistical procedures that allow researchers to take larger numbers of interacting factors into account within a study. Quantitative research is often criticized for its reductionist nature. That is, it focuses on too few factors, it reduces these factors to numbers, and simply does not attend to much potentially important and interesting contextual information. Researchers using correlational methods have attempted to achieve greater validity by accounting for more factors within a single study. Rather than studying only a few variables, many now attempt to account for complex clusters of factors (Kamil, Langer, & Shanahan, 1985, p. 107). For example, rather than studying the relationship between two variables, such as anxiety and achievement, Gardner's (1985) social-psychological research on the learning of French as a foreign language has involved examining relationships among large numbers of variables including various types of attitudes, motivations, and achievement using powerful computer programs.[3] This helps bring the study a bit closer to the complexities of real life and helps counter the criticism that too many factors are ignored. It is important to emphasize that the quantitative versus qualitative distinction, like any dichotomy, does not adequately characterize research. That is, while any particular piece of research may be primarily oriented toward the quantitative or interventionist paradigm (to use Guba and Lincoln's terminology), it may also involve some qualitative analysis and description. Conversely, a primarily qualitative and interpretive ethnographic study may include numerical data.

Multisite, Multimethod, Large-Scale Research

Changes have occurred in the nature of large-scale studies.[4] In this type of research investigators have examined the effectiveness of language programs or teaching methods in terms of learning outcomes. In the 1960s, researchers conducted large-scale studies of major methods of language teaching, such as traditional grammar-translation and audiolingual methods in an attempt to determine which was most effective (see discussions of these studies in Krashen, 1982; Politzer, 1981; Stern, 1983). These studies employed experimental designs with little emphasis on adequately describing what was occurring in the classrooms.

Not surprisingly, the findings of such studies were not very conclusive. Politzer (1981) wrote that two of the main messages of these studies were that "they caused or perhaps rather confirmed a healthy skepticism in the pure habit formation type of audiolingualism which had dominated language teaching in the 1950's and early 1960's" and "raised some doubts about the possibility of obtaining conclusive results from large-scale research in comparing methods of foreign language teaching" (p. 24).

In the 1970s, L2 research in general turned away from such studies of teaching behaviors toward a stronger focus on the learner.[5] Those large-scale studies that were conducted in the late 1970s and the early 1980s were funded to examine not methods of language teaching but the effectiveness of bilingual education as an approach to promoting the acquisition of English by language minority students in the early grades. Bilingual education programs were compared to "regular" programs or to "ESL-only" programs. However, just as the large-scale studies comparing L2 teaching methods were not very conclusive, these studies comparing bilingual education programs to nonbilingual education programs produced mixed and inconclusive results for three reasons. First, some researchers attempted to compare groups of bilingual-program students to comparison groups who were simply not comparable in important characteristics such as English language proficiency (Douglas & Johnson, 1981). It became clear that traditional experimental designs were not feasible. Second, programs were not studied longitudinally even though program goals were stated as long-term and much research indicates that L2 learning is a long-term endeavor (Collier, 1989; Cummins, 1984). Third, adequate descriptions of classroom instruction were rarely included in studies (Horst et al., 1980).

More recent large-scale studies are different in a number of ways. First, most researchers have abandoned the naive search for the one best program. It is recognized that the "best" learning environment for any group of students depends on many factors. Recent research, then, addresses more varied questions about how and why certain teaching/learning approaches work in particular situations for learners of different types (cf. Tikunoff, 1983; Noggle et al., 1982, 1983). Second, rather than relying on experimental designs with little description of classroom processes, researchers employ a variety of both quantitative and qualitative data-collection and analysis techniques. These multiple methods allow them to better attend both to classroom processes and to the contextual conditions that shape learning environments. Program evaluators, for example, conducted both formative and summative evaluations. Third, there have been efforts to examine bilingual education programs longitudinally rather than on a short-term basis (Ramirez, Yuen, Ramey, & Merino, 1986). Finally, a current emphasis in program evaluation is the active involvement of program participants and evaluators in more collaborative, democratic approaches to studying programs (Guba & Lincoln, 1989). Each of these developments in multisite research has worked toward providing greater insights into the factors that contribute to successful L2 learning.

We will now review three sample studies, one ethnographic; one complex quantitative; and one multisite, multimethod, large-scale. Each represents the types of developments discussed. The ethnography is a study of cultural factors in L2 acquisition. The quantitative study addresses multiple factors related to participation in the language classroom. The multisite study is an evaluation of an educational program in which both qualitative and quantitative approaches were used to attend to contexts and processes as well as outcomes.

Acculturation and Second Language Acquisition

Willett (1987) conducted an important ethnographic study of two young children, one Korean girl, and one Brazilian girl, who were acquiring English in a preschool setting. Through five months of observations and through interviews with parents and teachers, she studied how their interaction patterns might be culturally shaped. Willett found that the two girls approached social participation, L2 use, and learning in ways that reflected their respective cultural values. Jeni, the Korean, began speaking English soon. She sought out interaction with adults, generally not joining in with her peers. Her pronunciation was poor and she made little use of formulaic phrases, compared to the Brazilian girl. On the other hand, Jeni made rapid progress in semantic and syntactic development. Alisia, the Brazilian girl, did not speak English for about three months, but joined in many peer activities nonverbally. When she did begin to use English, her pronunciation and intonation were native-like and she used formulaic chunks appropriately.

Willett suggests that the girls' interaction styles reflected the values of their sociocultural environments at home. One contrast she drew was between an emphasis on peer sociability in the Brazilian family and on Confucian values and one-on-one learning interactions with adults in the Korean family. Willett concluded that Jeni's superior syntactic development may have resulted from her adult interactions, while Alisia's appropriate use of formulaic routines may have resulted from peer interaction. This study is important because it illustrates how culturally shaped language socialization patterns from home can affect both interaction patterns and L2 learning.

Language-Class Anxiety and Participation

Ely's (1986) study of student participation in first-year university Spanish courses provides a good example of a classroom study employing complex quantitative methods to examine relationships among a number of social and affective factors in the foreign language (FL) classroom. Ely studied the relationships among students' affective characteristics, their oral participation in the language classroom, and learning outcomes. As Ely notes, it is commonly assumed that extraversion is an affective characteristic that promotes L2 proficiency, but research results on the issue have been mixed. Therefore, Ely chose to measure risktaking, sociability, and discomfort in the specific context of classroom interaction, rather than as general personality traits. He predicted that these measures would be positively associated with measures of voluntary oral participation. He obtained measures of risktaking, sociability, and discomfort on his 75 subjects through the use of a questionnaire. He also obtained measures of a number of other variables including motivation, class attitude, concern for grade, and foreign language aptitude. Direct observations were conducted of classroom participation, which was defined for this study as self-initiated oral contributions. Several language proficiency measures were also administered.

Ely found that self-reported language class risktaking positively predicted classroom participation. Classroom participation, in turn, positively predicted oral correctness. However, language class discomfort was a significant negative predictor of language class risktaking and language class sociability. Ely suggests that some students must be made to feel more psychologically comfortable in class before they will take linguistic risks, and that teachers should devise and test the effectiveness of strategies for lessening language class discomfort (Ely, 1986, p. 23). This study illustrates how quantitative research attempts to address relationships among many factors within one study. It will be discussed in more detail in Chapter 3.

Evaluation of the Migrant Program

A study of the Migrant Education Program (Johnson, 1987) offers an example of multisite, multimethod, large-scale research that focused on process as well as product and on the contexts for learning. The Migrant Education Program provides supplementary services to elementary and secondary students whose schooling has been interrupted because of moves. Migrant students' families generally move because the parents are involved in seasonal agricultural and fishing industries. Many migrant students, therefore, need assistance in keeping up with their content subjects, in learning English, and in coping with health and other problems. As part of a two-year statewide evaluation of the total program, our research team conducted a study of the organization of migrant supplementary instruction. We were particularly interested in the interactions among teachers and aides responsible for educating migrant students and whether their joint efforts contributed to providing educational continuity for the students.

Using a range of qualitative and quantitative data-collection techniques, we examined programs in a sample of 11 school districts in California. These techniques included 86 classroom observations; interviews with migrant and "regular" teachers, aides, administrators, and parents; and the collection of questionnaire, achievement, proficiency, and grade advancement data.

We found that migrant supplementary instruction, focusing mainly on so-called basic skills, was provided almost entirely by teacher aides with much dedication but little training. Migrant aides worked in the regular classroom in 68% of the instructional sessions we observed and in a pullout setting in 32% of the sessions. We examined the relationship between the pullout sessions and regular classroom activities through observations and interviews, and found a lack of continuity between the two instructional settings. That is, when migrant elementary students were pulled out of the regular classroom for instruction, their regular teachers showed very low levels of awareness of the students' activities or progress with their migrant program aides. Supplemental instruction at the secondary level, however, was often more integrated with regular classroom work.

At the program level, we found a general lack of planning among the various programs serving migrant students, including Chapter I, bilingual education, and migrant education. Because collaborative planning and strong administrative support for such planning were critical features of the high-quality supplemental programs, many of our recommendations focused on reducing the disjointedness in migrant students' education.

In summary, we have seen a refocusing in both quantitative and qualitative L2 research, as well as the use of a combination of these methods in large-scale studies. In the qualitative arena, both researchers and teachers benefit from the rich cultural and contextual descriptions provided in ethnographic and interpretive research. This is a positive development. Interestingly, ethnographic research has not yet achieved the role some had predicted it would play in L2 research. At the end of the decade of the 1970s Politzer noted: "Ethnographic research leading to understanding of the cultural processes of second language teaching and learning and a resulting increase of second language teaching efficiency should be among the attainable goals of the 1980s" (Politzer, 1981, p. 30). A solid place for ethnographic research as an attainable goal of the 1980s, however, was not fully realized even though significant progress was made. The future should bring increased numbers of ethnographic and other qualitative studies of L2 learners of all age groups.

In quantitative studies such as those of Ely, Gardner, and many others, the attempt to account systematically for a wider array of interacting variables has served to improve the ecological validity of the studies and to make them more meaningful to teacher readers. This, too, is a positive development.

Multisite, multimethod, large-scale studies of L2 programs, because they use a variety of methods, can build on the advantages of both qualitative and quantitative approaches to provide a broad and rich picture of a program or issue across many sites. The goals of these studies have progressed from attempting to determine whether program A is more effective than program B through the use of basic experimental methods focusing on outcomes, to goals such as describing effective practices and providing a more adequate accounting of the contextual and process factors that shape L2 learning and instruction.

COMPUTERS IN LANGUAGE-LEARNING ENVIRONMENTS

A third development that has affected L2 research in a number of ways is technological in nature. Computer technology is an important topic of L2 research as well as a tool for researchers. The phenomenal increase in the use of computers and other technologies in society has influenced L2 learning from preschools to universities. In a study of technology conducted for the U.S. Congress, the Office of Technology Assessment (OTA) determined that, nationally, 40% of all Chapter I teachers who taught ESL used computers (Office of Technology Assessment, 1987). A large proportion of the students in Chapter I programs are acquiring English as an additional language. To what extent will future language learning and teaching be influenced by computers? Predictions differ widely. Some educators remind us that in many settings there are no computers, nor are there likely to be any for some time to come. Others have projected that students in elementary and secondary schools in the United States will spend a very substantial proportion of the school day interacting with computers, either alone or in small groups. Despite the conflicting predictions, there is little doubt that computer technology will play increasingly important roles in L2 learning, teaching, and testing, and, as a result, in research as well. The appropriate role of computer technology in language learning has become an important topic of L2 research (Dunkel, 1991; Peyton & Mackinson-Smyth, 1989).

Computers are also widely used as tools for research and for communication about research. Not only are sophisticated programs available for the analysis of quantitative data,[6] but programs are also available for qualitative data analysis and for text analysis (Biber & Finegan, 1989; Grabe, 1987). Computer-mediated communication has speeded the exchange of information among researchers, creating new communication cultures, new forms of social interaction, and changing the ways that journals and publishers function (Silverman, in press). Computer-mediated communication has also created new patterns of discourse, blurring the traditional dichotomy between informal conversation and academic writing, for example (Murray, 1988).

A Survey of CALL

We will briefly discuss one study of the roles of computer technology in L2 learning. Under contract to the Carnegie Corporation of New York, I conducted a survey of the state of the art in computer-assisted language learning (CALL) in the public schools, grades K–12 (Johnson, 1985). Among the goals of the work of the Carnegie Corporation is the "prevention of damage to children." Therefore, one objective of the study was to determine how computers were being used to promote L2 acquisition and whether these approaches were beneficial to students.

Over a period of several months, I gathered information by (1) reviewing the L1 and L2 computer-learning literature, (2) interviewing key researchers and practitioners in CALL, and (3) visiting several school programs that were considered exemplary. My report addressed a wide range of issues including equal access and opportunity, software development and dissemination systems, computers in composition, typical practices, model programs, and research. I will address only two findings and a recommendation here. One of the findings had to do with equal access and equal opportunities for language-minority students. I found that:

> Language minority students who are limited in English proficiency have fewer opportunities to use and interact with computers than . . . the general population of students. They often experience a double barrier, the first resulting from their being in low SES, primarily minority schools, and the second resulting from their lack of English proficiency. In addition, the opportunities that they do have to interact with and use computers are often qualitatively inferior to those of other students. (Johnson, 1985, p. II-2)

I also found that even in some programs considered exemplary, the software that young ESL students were asked to use was poor in quality and primarily focused on grammatical forms, many of which were not particularly important. I recommended a model for the creation of functional L2 learning environments (p. III-10). The model specified employing computers as tools for authentic communication and for accomplishing intellectually challenging, nonremedial tasks in the context of culturally appropriate whole activities. The basis for the model was a blending of current second-language-acquisition theories with notions of culturally appropriate forms of communication, and Vygotskian theories of cognitive development.[7]

Another finding, relevant to our purposes here, had to do with the types of research being conducted. Based on a review of the current research literature, I categorized studies into four types: (1) CAI/CALL feasibility and effectiveness studies, (2) studies of learning and transfer, (3) research in learner characteristics, and (4) studies of social interaction and status. In studies of the first type, researchers examined the feasibility of implementing computer-based L2 learning programs by documenting the implementation process (Chen & Paisley, 1985; COMSIS, 1984). Other studies in this category attempted to establish the effectiveness of the program by comparing it to some other "traditional" L2 program, often with less than conclusive results (Ramos, 1984, for example). In the second category, there were few studies of transfer of learning, although one implicit assumption behind the use of many computer-assisted instruction (CAI) "drill and practice" programs is that the learning of discrete items transfers to other language-use contexts. Researchers investigating learner characteristics, the third topic, have suggested that because learners vary in their attitudes and approaches to using CALL lessons, software should be not only "intelligent," but "sensitive" to such differences (Chapelle & Jamieson, 1986). Studies in the fourth category addressed relationships between computer work and social factors such as verbal interaction, cooperation, and student status. Findings of some studies illustrated how, rather than isolating students, computer work promoted new forms of social interaction and increased the status of students who became valued "computer experts."

One area of clear progress in CALL research in the last decade lies in the broader range of questions that researchers are addressing. In addition to asking how a computer-based program was implemented, or whether the program was more effective than other forms of L2 instruction, researchers are addressing a range of additional questions that reflect the many ways that computers are used. These questions take account of the active role of the learner and the interactive nature of computer work in its social context. For example, in research on the social effects of computer work, research questions have evolved from seeking the average effects of the medium on the social life of classrooms, to an accounting of the richness of interactions among the computer, the teachers, the learners, the task, and its functional goals (Johnson, 1991). Because computers will become more prevalent in L2 learning environments, their appropriate roles in enhancing learning should continue to be important topics of study in L2 research. There is no question that their roles as tools in conducting and communicating about research will expand in exciting ways.

CONCLUSION

In this chapter we have examined three general developments in L2 research. First, a more balanced focus on both the social and personal nature of learning can be seen in a number of studies. Work in individual differences in the learning strategies of children in varying social contexts has made a contribution, as has work in the social-psychological orientations of teenagers toward the varieties of English that they hear, use, and learn. The second trend is methodological. Expanded quantitative and qualitative/interpretive research approaches have enriched our options for conducting more meaningful L2 research, for more adequately examining teacher and student interactions, and for improving the validity of studies. Improved validity makes the research more useful to teachers as they reflect on its meaning for them and modify their own views of learning and effective teaching. Third, the growing use of computer technology in formal L2 learning environments is introducing far-reaching changes into the conduct and communication of L2 research.

NOTES

1. A particularly interesting source is Eisner and Peshkin, 1990. Also see van Lier (1988, pp. 53–65) for a view of the value of ethnographic approaches to L2 classroom research.

2. In Chapters 3 through 8 the specific ways that many of these differences are played out are illustrated in the context of a particular methodology (e.g., correlational vs. case-study research, case-study vs. survey research, survey vs. ethnographic research, etc.). Thus, readers can carry on the quantitative-qualitative debate throughout these chapters, not only in the context of a particular method, but in the context of authentic real-life studies. Guba and Lincoln's evaluational model is discussed in Chapter 8.

3. Other important technological developments in the area of measurement, such as item response theory (IRT), have had a major impact on testing. Applications of IRT can be found in Henning (1986). Applications of the two-parameter model applied to bilingual test development are reported in Bergan, Johnson, and Smith (1984). For a review article on L2 testing see Bachman (1990). See Stansfield (1986) for a collection of papers on technology and language testing based on a research colloquium held at Educational Testing Service, Princeton, NJ, in 1985. See Lazaraton, Riggenbach, and Ediger (1987) for an interesting report of a survey addressing applied linguists' literacy in research methodology and statistics.

4. The term "multisite, multimethod, large-scale research" comes from Miles and Huberman (1984), *Qualitative Data Analysis*. They describe a very systematic (perhaps too mechanical) set of methods for qualitative data collection and analysis. We will use the term, however, to refer to any large-scale study that involves a number of institutions (sites), and in which researchers employ a variety of both quantitative and qualitative data-collection and analysis techniques.

5. This shift was documented by Politzer (1981) in an article surveying the state of the art in research on language teaching. He conducted a content analysis of journals to determine the numbers of articles focusing on learning versus teaching. The journals he analyzed were the four major U.S. journals that published research in FL/L2 teaching: the *TESOL Quarterly, Language Learning, Foreign Language Annals,* and *The Modern Language Journal*. He determined the frequency of data-based articles addressing FL learning processes (including, for example, pupil errors, aptitudes, learning styles, and others) and FL teaching (including an independent teaching variable).

6. See note 3.

7. Mehan, Moll, and Reil (1985) and Cole and Griffin (1983) discuss the Vygotskian theory underlying functional computer projects for elementary children. De Avila, Cohen, and Intili (1981) demonstrated that functional math and science learning environments for bilingual students produced gains in both achievement and English. Hakes (1981) reports on a National Institutes of Education (NIE)-funded study of a math and science computer project on the Acoma reservation in New Mexico that employed culturally appropriate storytelling techniques to teach about concepts such as energy.

REFERENCES

Allwright, R. (1988). *Observation in the language classroom*. London: Longman Group U.K., Ltd.

Atkinson, P., Delamont, S., & Hammersley, M. (1988). Qualitative research traditions: A British response to Jacob. *Review of Educational Research, 58,* 231–250.

Au, K. H. (1980). Participation structures in a reading lesson with Hawaiian children: Analysis of a culturally appropriate instructional event. *Anthropology & Education Quarterly, 11,* 91–115.

Bachman, L. F. (1990). Assessment and evaluation. In R. B. Kaplan (Ed.), *Annual Review of Applied Linguistics* (Vol. 10) (pp. 210–226). New York: Cambridge University Press.

Bergan, J., Johnson, D. M., & Smith, A. (1984). *Executive summary of the Head Start Measures Project.* Tucson: University of Arizona, Center for Educational Evaluation and Measurement.

Biber, D., & Finegan, E. (1989). Drift and evolution of English style: A history of three genres. *Language, 65,* 487–517.

Brown, J. D. (1988). *Understanding research in second language learning: A teacher's guide to statistics and research design.* Cambridge: Cambridge University Press.

Cazden, C. B. (1987). *Classroom discourse: The language of teaching and learning.* Portsmouth, NH: Heinemann.

Chapelle, C., & Jamieson, J. (1986). Computer-assisted language learning as a predictor of success in acquiring English as a second language. *TESOL Quarterly, 20,* 27–46.

Chaudron, C. (1988). *Second language classrooms: Research on teaching and learning.* Cambridge: Cambridge University Press.

Chen, M., & Paisley, W. (1985). *Children and microcomputers: Research on the newest medium.* Beverly Hills, CA: Sage.

Cole, M., & Griffin, P. (1983). A socio-historical approach to remediation. *The Quarterly Newsletter of the Laboratory of Comparative Human Cognition, 5,* 69–74.

Collier, V. P. (1989). How long? A synthesis of research on academic achievement in a second language. *TESOL Quarterly, 23,* 509–531.

COMSIS Corporation. (1984, November). *Review of the state of the art of educational technologies implemented in programs serving LEP students funded by the Department of Education: Final report.* Rosslyn, VA: National Clearinghouse for Bilingual Education.

Cook, T. D., & Campbell, D. T. (1979). *Quasi-experimentation: Design & analysis issues for field settings.* Chicago: Rand McNally.

Cummins, J. (1984). *Bilingualism and special education: Issues in assessment and pedagogy.* Clevedon, England: Multilingual Matters. Co-published in the United States by College-Hill Press, San Diego.

De Avila, E., Cohen, E., & Intili, J. (1981, August). *Final report: Multicultural improvement of cognitive abilities.* Stanford, CA: Stanford University.

Douglas, D., & Johnson, D. M. (1981, April). *An evaluation of Title VII evaluations: Results from a national study.* Paper presented at the Annual Meeting of the National Association for Bilingual Education, Boston.

Dunkel, P. (Ed.). (1991). *Computer-assisted language learning and testing: Research issues and practice.* New York: HarperCollins/Newbury House.

Eisner, E., & Peshkin, A. (1990). *Qualitative inquiry in education: The continuing debate.* New York: Teachers College Press.

Ely, C. (1986). An analysis of discomfort, risktaking, sociability, and motivation in the L2 classroom. *Language Learning, 36,* 1–25.

Erickson, F. (1986). Qualitative methods in research on teaching. In M. C. Wittrock (Ed.), *Handbook of research on teaching* (3rd ed.) (pp. 119–161). New York: Macmillan (American Educational Research Association).

Gardner, R. (1985). *Social psychology and second language learning*. London: Edward Arnold.

Goldstein, L. M. (1987). Standard English: The only target for nonnative speakers of English? *TESOL Quarterly, 21,* 417–436.

Goodman, K. (1988, July). *Language and learning: Toward a social-personal view*. Paper presented at the Brisbane Conference on Language and Learning, Brisbane, Australia.

Grabe, W. (1987). Contrastive rhetoric and text-type research. In U. Connor & R. Kaplan (Eds.), *Writing across languages: Analysis of L2 text* (pp. 115–137). Reading, MA: Addison-Wesley.

Guba, E. G., & Lincoln, Y. S. (1989). *Fourth generation evaluation*. Newbury Park, CA: Sage.

Gumperz, J. J., & Hymes, D. (1972). *Directions in sociolinguistics: The ethnography of communication*. New York: Holt, Rinehart & Winston.

Hakes, J. (1981). *Final report: Computer storytelling mathematics for Pueblo Indian upper elementary level students*. Albuquerque, NM: All Indian Pueblo Council.

Heath, S. B. (1983). *Ways with words*. Cambridge: Cambridge University Press.

Henning, G. (1986). Quantitative methods in second language acquisition research. *TESOL Quarterly, 20,* 701–708.

Horst, D. P., Johnson, D. M., Nava, H. G., Douglas, D. E., Friendly, L. D., & Roberts, A. O. H. (1980, May). *A prototype guide to measuring achievement level and program impact on achievement in bilingual projects*. Mountain View, CA: RMC Research Corporation (VR-460). (ERIC Document Reproduction Service No. ED 193 955)

Howe, K., & Eisenhart, M. (1990). Standards for qualitative (and quantitative) research: A prolegomenon. *Educational Researcher, 19*(4), 2–9.

Hudelson, S. (1989). A tale of two children: Individual differences in ESL children's writing. In D. M. Johnson & D. H. Roen (Eds.), *Richness in writing: Empowering ESL students* (pp. 84–99). White Plains, NY: Longman.

Johnson, D. M. (1985, November). *Using computers to promote the development of English as a second language: A report to the Carnegie Corporation*. Tucson: University of Arizona. (ERIC Document Reproduction Service No. ED 278 211)

Johnson, D. M. (1987). The organization of instruction in Migrant Education: Assistance for children and youth at risk. *TESOL Quarterly, 21,* 437–459.

Johnson, D. M. (1991). Second language and content learning with computers: Research in the role of social factors. In P. Dunkel (Ed.), *Computer-assisted language learning and testing: Research issues and practice* (pp. 61–83). New York: HarperCollins/ Newbury House.

Kamil, M. L., Langer, J. A., & Shanahan, T. (1985). *Understanding research in reading and writing*. Boston: Allyn & Bacon.

Krashen, S. (1982). *Principles and practice in second language acquisition*. Oxford: Pergamon Press.

Lazaraton, A., Riggenbach, H., & Ediger, A. (1987). Forming a discipline: Applied linguists' literacy in research methodology and statistics. *TESOL Quarterly, 21,* 263–277.

Linn, R. L. (1986). Quantitative methods in research on teaching. In M. C. Wittrock (Ed.), *Handbook of research on teaching* (3rd ed.) (pp. 92–118). New York: Macmillan.

Mehan, H., Moll, L., & Reil, M. (1985, June). *Computers in classrooms: A quasi-experiment in guided change.* Final report to the National Institute of Education. La Jolla: University of California, San Diego.

Miles, M. B., & Huberman, A. M. (1984). *Qualitative data analysis.* Beverly Hills, CA: Sage.

Murray, D. (1988). The context of oral and written language: A framework for mode and medium switching. *Language in Society, 17,* 351–373.

Noggle, N. L, Garza, H. A., Weiner, F. S., Abrica-Carrasco, R., & Johnson, D. M. (1982). *The education of California's migrant students: An evaluation of the migrant education program—Technical addendum* (RMC Report No. UR-495). Mountain View, CA: RMC Research Corporation.

Noggle, N. L, Garza, H. A., Weiner, F. S., Abrica-Carrasco, R., & Johnson, D. M. (1983). *The education of California's migrant students: An evaluation of the migrant education program—Final Report* (RMC Report No. UR-495). Mountain View, CA: RMC Research Corporation.

Office of Technology Assessment. (1987, March). *Trends and status of computers in school: Use in Chapter 1 programs and use with limited English proficient students.* Washington, DC: Science, Education, and Transportation Program, OTA, U. S. Congress.

Peyton, J. K., & Mackinson-Smyth, J. (1989). Writing and talking about writing: Computer networking with elementary students. In D. M. Johnson, & D. H. Roen (Eds.), *Richness in writing: Empowering ESL students* (pp. 100–119). White Plains, NY: Longman.

Politzer, R. (1981). Effective language teaching: Insights from research. In J. E. Alatis, H. B. Altman, & P. M. Alatis (Eds.), *The second language classroom: Directions for the 1980's* (pp. 23–35). New York: Oxford University Press.

Ramos, N. J. (1984). *The utilization of computer technology in a bilingual classroom.* Unpublished doctoral dissertation, Texas A & I University, Kingsville, TX.

Ramirez, J. D., Yuen, S. D., Ramey, D. R., & Merino, B. (1986). *First year report: Longitudinal study of immersion programs for language minority children.* Arlington, VA: SRA Technologies.

Saville-Troike, M. (1988). Private speech: Evidence for second language learning strategies during the "silent" period. *Journal of Child Language, 15,* 567–590.

Silverman, N. (in press). From the ivory tower to the bottom line: An editor's perspective on college textbook publishing. In P. Altbach, G. Kelly, H. Petrie, & L. Weis (Eds.), *Perspectives on textbooks and society.* Albany, NY: SUNY Press.

Spindler, G. D. (1974). *Education and cultural process: Toward an anthropology of education.* New York: Holt, Rinehart & Winston.

Stansfield, C. W. (1986). *Technology and language testing.* Washington, DC: Teachers of English to Speakers of Other Languages.

Stern, H. H. (1983). *Fundamental concepts of language teaching.* Oxford: Oxford University Press.

Tikunoff, W. J. (1983). Five significant bilingual instructional features. In W. J. Tikunoff (Ed.), *Compatibility of the SBIF features with other research on instruction for LEP students* (pp. 5–18). San Francisco: Far West Laboratory. (SBIF-83–R.9/10)

van Lier, L. (1988). *The classroom and the language learner: Ethnography and second language classroom research.* London: Longman Group U.K.

Watson-Gegeo, K. A. (1988). Ethnography in ESL: Defining the essentials. *TESOL Quarterly, 22,* 575–592.

Willett, J. (1987). Contrasting acculturation patterns of two non–English-speaking preschoolers. In H. T. Trueba (Ed.), *Success or failure? Learning and the language minority students* (pp. 69–84). New York: Harper & Row/Newbury House.

Wong Fillmore, L. (1983). The language learner as an individual: Implications of research on individual differences for the ESL teacher. In M. Clarke, & J. Handscombe (Eds.), *On TESOL '82: Pacific perspectives on language learning and teaching* (pp. 157–174). Washington, DC: Teachers of English to Speakers of Other Languages.

PART II
Approaches to Research

CHAPTER 3

Correlational Approaches

Are students who are highly anxious about composing in a second language (L2) overly concerned with correct form? Is it true that the more you interact with native speakers of a target language the more you will learn? Is membership in a certain cultural group associated with the use of particular learning strategies? These are examples of questions that researchers using correlational approaches have asked.

Correlational research has long been one of the major approaches to L2 research. It is widely used not only by L2 researchers, but by psychologists, sociologists, sociolinguists, and educational researchers. The term *correlational* refers not to how one collects data, but to the kinds of research questions that are addressed, how data are represented, and the kinds of analyses that are undertaken to answer the questions posed.

In the first part of this chapter we will look at the use of simple correlations between two variables to explore why correlation is used in L2 research. Then a set of criteria for assessing correlational studies is suggested and we will use these criteria to examine a sample study. The sample study employs simple correlational techniques to assess the language-use goals of high-school students. In the second part of the chapter we will examine more complex correlational approaches in which researchers attempt to explore the relationships among sets of variables.

WHAT IS CORRELATIONAL RESEARCH?

The purpose of correlational studies is to understand relationships among characteristics of people or other entities. Examples of research questions in correlational research include: "What is the relationship between cultural background and the use of specific communication strategies?" "What is the relationship between syntactic competence and sociopragmatic competence?" "What is the relationship between anxiety and L2 writing quality?" Each of these questions addresses the relationship between two characteristics or variables.

A *variable* is "a defined characteristic that varies; it has at least two values and usually more" (Smith & Glass, 1987, p. 12). Let us consider an example. Anxiety about writing in a second language is a variable because it varies across students; that is, some students are more anxious than others when trying to compose a paper in a second language. To assign a value to the degree of anxiety that students feel, they are given a test (a measure) of writing anxiety. Their score on the measure might range, for example, from 1 to 10. These scores on the variable of writing anxiety are simply indicators that are intended to represent the actual *construct* or *trait* of anxiety. A construct or trait is an abstract concept or idea about some quality of an individual (Smith & Glass, 1987, p. 4; Borg, 1987, p. 120). A hypothetical construct cannot be observed or measured directly; rather, the researcher operationally defines the construct as something that can be measured, such as students' answers to the series of questions on the writing apprehension measure. In reading correlational studies, it is always important to consider how adequately the measure represents the construct.

Other variables that are important in L2 research are language proficiency, motivation, cultural and linguistic background, and a host of other student characteristics. Variables may also be characteristics of teachers, such as experience or language ability. Variables may be characteristics of classes, such as ethnic composition or class size, or characteristics of other entities, such as universities, schools, or programs. Most L2 studies involve the study of linguistic variables, such as the use of particular types of discourse features, speech acts, or grammatical structures. Through the use of correlational techniques, researchers attempt to learn how the variables they have measured are related to one another.

Correlational studies are most often defined in opposition to causal studies such as experiments. In experiments, researchers attempt to determine that one variable causes another, while in most correlational studies they do not intend to make causal claims. In correlational studies, researchers ask questions in the form "What is the relationship between extraversion and L2 oral proficiency?" rather than "Does extraversion cause higher levels of L2 oral proficiency?" Or a researcher might ask "What is the relationship between explicit knowledge of rhetorical form and L2 reading comprehension?" rather than the experimental question "Does knowledge of rhetorical form cause better comprehension?"

How would you conduct a correlational study? Let us consider a hypothetical example. You might want to know if it is the case that the more content-focused feedback L2 teachers give to their students in teacher-student interactive journals, the more the students' L2 proficiency will improve. To examine this question you would obtain a measure of the amount of feedback each learner received and some measure of the growth each student made in L2 proficiency. You would then determine the degree of association between feedback and improvement by calculating a correlation coefficient. A correlation coefficient is a number, a quantitative measure, that represents the degree of relationship between the two variables. The number indicates the direction (positive or negative) and degree of relationship between feedback and improvement. Because the research question is posed in terms of a relationship, the answer is stated as a relationship. That relationship is ~correlation.

An example of an actual study related to Krashen's input theory (1985) helps to illustrate how correlational techniques are sometimes used. Polak and Krashen (1988) were interested in whether a relationship existed between English spelling competence and voluntary English reading for Polak's intermediate-level community college ESL students. Through correlation they examined the relationship between two variables: (1) spelling accuracy (which they assessed through dictation) and (2) current voluntary reading (which they assessed through a short questionnaire). They found positive correlations indicating that, for the three different groups of students they studied, those who reported that they did more free reading made fewer spelling errors regardless of their first language. After cautioning readers that causality cannot be implied, they concluded: "Our results suggest that voluntary reading will help spelling and lead to what is at worst a harmless implication: Students should be encouraged to do pleasure reading on their own. Besides spelling, there is good evidence that voluntary reading leads to improvement in many areas of language, including reading ability, vocabulary, grammar, and writing style" (Polak & Krashen, 1988, p. 145). In fact, this study does not show that voluntary reading causes ("helps") spelling accuracy; rather, it merely illustrates that an association exists between the two variables as measured. It may be that other factors caused or contributed to spelling accuracy. This example illustrates one way that researchers use correlational methods to examine the relationship between two variables for groups of students.

USES OF CORRELATION IN L2 RESEARCH

Correlational studies are traditionally classified as relationship studies or prediction studies. In *relationship studies,* researchers study the relationship between measures of different variables obtained at approximately the same time. In the Polak and Krashen example cited above, measures of the two variables were taken at about the same time. Second language researchers have made wide use of correlational techniques to explore a variety of relationships. Listed below are examples of relationships that either have been or could be investigated through correlational techniques.

Relationship Studies

Variable 1	*Variable 2*
Verbal interactions	Oral proficiency
Integrative cultural attitudes	Global proficiency
Syntactic competence	Sociolinguistic competence
Control of anaphoric devices	Composition quality
Use of learning strategies	Achievement gains
Spelling accuracy in L2	Voluntary reading in L2
Attention to form	Composing anxiety
Discourse input modifications	Listening comprehension

For each pair of variables you can ask, "What is the relationship between [variable 1] and [variable 2]?" The results of relationship studies are often used to make claims about theoretical issues in L2 learning. One use of relationship studies, for example, has been to study the factors that make up complex phenomena such as communicative competence or motivation for language learning.

In *prediction studies,* researchers are concerned with measuring variables that can be used to predict performance on another variable, either at some future time or at the same time. Some topics of this type are listed below.

Prediction Studies

Variable 1	*Variable 2*
Discussing concepts in L1	Academic achievement in L2
Composition placement scores	Composition course grades
TOEFL exam scores	Success in university studies
Scores on SPEAK test	Student ratings of teaching
Oral language proficiency scores	Reading achievement

are used to predict future success in written work in university classes. The basic assumption is that those who score below a certain level on the TWE will not have sufficient overall proficiency to do well in a U.S. university, while those who score above that level will be likely to succeed. Questions in prediction studies take the form "How well do TWE scores predict the grades that international students receive on their written university work?" or "How well does the SPEAK test predict a foreign graduate student's ability to teach successfully in a U.S. university?" In the U.S. military context, decisions about admitting individuals to a language training program might be made on the basis of measures of aptitude and other predictors of success in foreign language learning.

An important and complicated prediction question for students in grades K–12 that has affected policy has been "How well do scores on state-mandated language proficiency assessment procedures predict (correlate with) the academic success of L2 learners in elementary and secondary schools?" Because scores on any single test do not correlate very well with future performance, educators use multiple measures and observe student performance in a variety of contexts. The results of prediction studies, then, are used as one source of information to make decisions about admissions to and placement in language and educational programs.

A word of caution is needed: Correlational studies provide information about *groups* of students or other entities. It is important to understand that they do not tell us much about individuals. It would be inappropriate to assume that group trends necessarily apply to any one individual.

VALIDITY AND RELIABILITY IN MEASUREMENT

What kinds of data are collected for correlational studies? Among the most common means of collecting data are various measures of language proficiency (listening, speaking, reading, writing), tests of academic performance, quantitative observations of language use, questionnaires, and attitude scales.

Correlational research is by nature *quantitative*. That is, constructs are measured using techniques that yield numerical results. These numbers, which are assumed to represent the construct, are then analyzed. Valid and reliable measurement, then, is crucial for good correlational research. Let us consider basic definitions of reliability and validity.

Validity

Simply stated, a measure is *valid* if it measures what it is intended to measure. Let us say, for example, that a researcher wishes to measure L2 oral proficiency for the purpose of correlating it with academic progress in high school. To measure L2 proficiency the researcher tape-records interviews with students and scores them on phonological criteria. As you can imagine, a student could be highly proficient in L2 vocabulary, syntax, and written discourse, but less proficient in pronunciation. The interview, then, which amounts to nothing more than a pronunciation test, is not a valid measure of proficiency for such a study. It has little meaning because it does not assess the important aspects of proficiency. We cannot infer that the score on that indicator adequately represents the construct the researcher intends to assess. Validity is not an absolute notion, however. Rather, a high level of validity is a goal to strive for. You must always ask how valid a measure is for a particular purpose and for particular persons in a particular context.

Reliability

The reliability of a measure refers to the accuracy or consistency of measurement. There are many sources of error that can reduce the accuracy of measurement. In evaluating a bilingual program, I once observed second-grade students taking a paper-and-pencil "self-concept" test. The test was being administered by a teacher to a group of about 20 children. Several of these students were busily engaged in circling answers on the wrong page. This kind of problem is just one of many sources of error that can render scores useless.

Much L2 research involves observations of verbal behavior or ratings of students' writing. In such cases it is important to provide evidence that the observations or ratings are reliable. This is accomplished by determining *interrater reliability,* sometimes called or *interobserver reliability* or *interjudge reliability*. To do this, two or more persons rate the same phenomenon. Their ratings are then compared to see how well they agree with one another. The researcher may determine the percentage of agreement, may correlate the ratings of the two raters, or may use a variety of more sophisticated techniques to determine the degree of consistency across judges.

In reading and assessing correlational studies, it is crucial to assess the adequacy of the measures. How can this be done? First, researchers should report evidence that the measures they have used in a correlational study are valid and reliable. This evidence may come from previous research. In addition, however, evidence for the validity and reliability of the measures should be provided for the study being reported. This is important because a measure that was adequate for one group of students in one situation may be inadequate in another situation. Regardless of the evidence reported, you should assess the adequacy of the measures for yourself.

CRITERIA FOR ANALYZING CORRELATIONAL STUDIES

In reading and evaluating research that employs correlational techniques, you should attempt to answer the questions below. Considering the answers to these questions will help you decide how to interpret the study, how much confidence to place in the results, and what can be learned from the various aspects of the research.

1. What is the research question?
2. In what context was the research conducted?
3. What are the theoretical orientations of the researcher(s)?
4. Who were the subjects/participants in the study? How many were there and how were they selected? What are their relevant characteristics?

5. What variables were assessed? How were they defined and measured? How adequate (valid and reliable) were the measures?
6. What correlational analyses were performed and with what results?
7. What conclusions are drawn? Are generalizations about the results appropriate?
8. What is the contribution of the study to our knowledge of social or contextual factors in L2 learning?
9. What are the stated implications for L2 learning in formal contexts?

SAMPLE CORRELATIONAL STUDY: VARIATION IN TARGET LANGUAGE GOALS

A study by Goldstein (1987) provides an interesting example of research employing correlational techniques. I selected this study because it addresses an important social-psychological issue in L2 learning in a multicultural high school setting: What are students' goals in language learning and why? Goldstein found that African American English, rather than Standard English, served as a target language for some of the Hispanic teenage students with whom she worked. She further provided evidence that those students who had extensive contact with African American peers used features of African American English more often than did those who had less contact with African American peers.[1] (It is useful to read the full report of the study in addition to the analysis that follows.)

1. What is the research question?

The researcher had two purposes in this study. The first was to document that teenage nonnative speakers (NNSs) of English have language-use goals other than Standard English. The second purpose was to determine what factors were related to learners' choice of a target language model. Goldstein (1987) explained that

> one goal of the study . . . was to demonstrate that nonnative speakers do have target language models other than standard English. We also need to delineate the sociolinguistic factors which might influence whether or not a particular variety will serve as a target. The second goal of the study, therefore, was to explore the relative effects of two factors—extent of contact and feelings of identification with black Americans—on nonnative speakers' frequency of use of selected features of black English. (p. 419)

2. In what context was the research conducted?

This was a doctoral dissertation study conducted in three high schools in metropolitan New York.

3. What are the theoretical orientations of the researcher?

The researcher draws on theoretical notions from sociolinguistics and social-psychology. She grounds her work in the sociolinguistic principle that speech communities are heterogeneous, not homogeneous, and that diverse varieties of English are spoken by teenagers. She claims, building on work by Beebe (1985) and others, that teenage L2 learners are aware of this linguistic diversity in their environment and make active choices about the variety or varieties of a language they wish to use.

Goldstein introduces her report by quoting Carlos, one of the students in the study, who explains what he knows about sociolinguistic variation:

> "White people, they talk different from black, and the teachers, they talk different, you know." (Carlos, a nonnative speaker of English). (Goldstein, 1987, p. 417)

The author then asks readers to:

> Listen to the voices of Carlos [and others] . . . They . . . understand that their speech community is not homogeneous, that they are exposed to many varieties of English, and that learners of English as a second language can make choices among these varieties. (p. 418)

Social psychologists in general are interested in how the thoughts, feelings, attitudes, and behaviors of individuals are related to other people in their social environment. The social-psychological basis of the study lies in its examination of the relationships between learners and their peers. Specifically, the author chose to assess these teenagers' feelings of identification with their African American peers.

4. Who were the subjects/participants in the study? How many were there and how were they selected? What are their relevant characteristics?

The researcher studied 28 high school students, all males, and all native speakers of Spanish. They ranged from 15 to 19 years in age. The participants had lived in New York City or Jersey City for at least two years and had not studied English before their arrival to the metropolitan area. All had become proficient speakers of English in the local area and were enrolled in or had completed an advanced ESL course.

5. What variables were assessed? How were they defined and measured? How adequate (valid and reliable) were the measures?

The researcher examined two independent variables. The first of these constructs was contact with African American peers and the second was identification with African American peers. She defined and assessed these variables as follows:

The contact measurement asked subjects to complete a chart on which they named their friends (up to 10) and indicated their ages, ethnicity, race, the language spoken with each, the amount of time spent with each and the extent of their relationship. (Goldstein, 1987, p. 421)

Contact, then, was quantified as a score representing the number of African American friends and acquaintances named.

The second construct, identification with African American peers, was operationalized as follows:

For the identification measurement, feelings of identification with black Americans were operationally defined as subjects' choosing black Americans as their reference group. . . . A subject rated how well each of 30 descriptors fit his ideal self, black Americans, and white Americans on a 5–point scale ranging from *very well* to *not at all.* (pp. 421–422)

These descriptors, including items such as *busy, helpful, cool, fashionable, generous,* and *considerate,* were listed in both Spanish and English. To quantify this measure, "similarity scores" were calculated. (The method of calculating the similarity scores is not explained in the published report.) Five teenagers indicated African American peers as a reference group and 23 indicated white peers as a reference group.

Goldstein studied two dependent variables, distributive *be* and negative concord within the clause:

distributive *be* [is] a form characteristic only of black English in which uninflected *be* is used to indicate qualities which are intermittent rather than permanent. (p. 418)

Goldstein provides this example: "When I watch a movie, a scary movie, right, I be you know, I sometimes be thinking of it, you know, how you sometimes be scared . . ." (p. 418). She defines negative concord:

negative concord within the clause [is] a rule which incorporates a copy of the *not* in the main verb phrase (VP) or in a preverbal noun phrase onto all indefinites after the main VP. (p. 418)

An example of negative concord she provides is, "If I tell them a secret, they won't tell nobody else." (p. 418)

To elicit these two forms, the researcher paired students who were friends and interviewed them for 40 to 50 minutes about friendship, including in her interview discussions about death and about fighting. She selected these topics to elicit less formal speech from the students. She also had them enact role-plays during the sessions, which were taped and later transcribed.

6. What correlational analyses were performed and with what results?

There are many kinds of correlation coefficients and these are explained in detail in books on statistics. The choice of a coefficient depends on the nature of the data. The correlational analyses that were performed are described as follows:

> Pearson product-moment correlations were carried out to determine if a relationship existed between extent of contact with black Americans and the frequency with which subjects used negative concord and distributive *be*. The correlations were significant for both. (p. 425)

To state that the correlations were significant means they were (not only positive in this case but) high enough that it is unlikely the relationships were simply due to chance. This result means that those students who reported the most contact with African American peers were those who most often used these features of African American English.

The author also calculated another kind of correlation coefficient (called a point biserial correlation coefficient) to determine the degree of relationship between the students' choice of African Americans as a reference group and the frequency with which they used negative concord and distributive *be*. These correlation coefficients were not statistically significant. This is interpreted to mean that Goldstein found no evidence that having African Americans as a reference group was associated with the use of the two linguistic features. She suggests, however, that one possible explanation for this finding is that the measure used to assess reference group may not have been valid. That is, the measure may not have assessed what it was intended to assess. Goldstein bases the conclusions below on additional analyses of individual students.

7. What conclusions are drawn? Are generalizations about the results appropriate?

The author draws the following conclusions:

> the evidence is very strong that contact is a necessary condition for grammatical assimilation (p. 428). . . . Extensive or medium contact with black Americans was a necessary, but not sufficient, condition for subjects to use negative concord categorically (that is, like speakers of black English) and for subjects to use distributive *be* (p. 427). . . . other factors, in addition to extent of contact, are related to the assimilation of grammatical variants. (p. 428)

This study did not provide evidence about the process of assimilation because it did not involve examining change in the adolescent males' English over time. Rather, it involved the study of the relationship between self-reported contact and the use of particular features of language at one point in time. Rather than concluding that "contact does play a role in grammatical assimilation" (p. 426), one can only conclude, based on evidence provided from this study, that contact and certain grammatical features in the students' language use are associated, and that contact may play a role in grammatical assimilation.

8. What is the contribution of the study to our knowledge of social or contextual factors in L2 learning?

This study illustrates the importance of examining the social context in which adolescents are using and learning the L2 and the nature of the interaction of adolescents with that social context. The author correctly stresses that many studies of SLA contain the incorrect assumption that a learner is functioning in a homogeneous target language environment and that the learner's only target language is the standard variety. As a result of this incorrect assumption, researchers often compare the learner's language only to the standard. They assume that forms that deviate from Standard English, for example, are interlanguage forms when they may, in fact, be forms of another variety that the individual student intends to use and acquire. This study effectively shows that teenagers who are advanced users of English as an additional language are aware of the sociolinguistic diversity in their high school social environments, and many have as a goal the use of more than one variety of the L2. That is, their goal is a heterogeneous competence.

This study of adolescents adds to similar findings from other studies of children. For example, Milon (1975) illustrated how a Japanese child in Hawaii acquired and preferred to use the variety of English used by his peers, rather than the variety used by teachers. First he used the Hawaiian Creole of his peers over the Standard English of his teachers. But when he moved to a new neighborhood, he used the Standard English of his peer reference group.

Beebe (1985) proposes that language learners are not simply passive recipients of input, but that they adopt a language variety or varieties by consciously or unconsciously choosing to attend to some target language models over others. There is a great deal of sociolinguistic and L2 research evidence that the following input preferences for language learning hold: peers over teachers, peers over parents, own social group over other social group, friends over nonfriends, high-contact over low-contact group, higher-prestige group over lower-prestige group (Beebe, 1985; Dulay, Burt, & Krashen, 1982). Beebe has suggested that these preferences are related to the solidarity function of language, the attempt to establish and maintain social solidarity through language.

She points out that there are, however, exceptions to these patterns of solidarity preferences. For example, a learner might have a status-oriented preference, choosing to use the higher-status variety of the language over the variety spoken by peers. Beebe (1985) concludes, "I would like to hypothesize that preference for higher-prestige models and teacher models is most likely status-oriented, whereas preference for peer models, friends, and own ethnic group models is solidarity-oriented. Whether status or solidarity takes priority is a function of personal values which are, in turn, highly affected by social and situational context" (p. 413). Preston (1989), in a discussion of interactional factors in sociolinguistic L2 research, also suggests that solidarity among learners is an important variable contributing to second language acquisition and calls for more studies that correlate performance features in learners' developing interlanguage with solidarity variables. The Goldstein study makes a contribution to this general body of research by establishing a relationship between contact and language features for high school students.

9. What are the stated implications for L2 learning in formal contexts?

Teachers need to understand that students, particularly those beyond the beginning levels, will determine their own language-use goals for English and these may not necessarily include Standard English. Teachers should know what those goals might be and be aware of linguistic features of those varieties. This is important because what may appear to be an error in the student's language may be the appropriate use of another variety of English. Attempts to eradicate these features may be fruitless. Rather, Goldstein (1987) suggests that teachers should "help their students determine whether or not standard English is necessary to their public lives and to discuss with their students the situations in which they would need to use standard English" (p. 433).

Most teachers and students feel that knowledge of and control over the prestige variety of a language, in addition to a respect for and an understanding of other varieties, will empower students in their public lives (see Sledd, 1972, for another view). Therefore, teachers need to give students information about the relevant varieties of English in their environment and some of the key distinguishing features of those varieties. Students are aware of variation in the languages they know well, and teachers can build on that knowledge. Students need to know in what situations it is appropriate to use different varieties to accomplish their own purposes.

Similarly, in contexts in which English is used as a language of wider communication, such as in parts of Asia and Africa, norms for appropriate and creative uses of English are different from those in the United States, the United Kingdom, or Australia, for example. Smith (1987) and Kachru (1987) remind us that there are more nonnative users than there are native users of English in the world and that norms for nativized varieties are in the making. As with wider social groups, teenagers participate in the social construction of their own norms within their own social groups.

A COMPLEX CORRELATIONAL APPROACH

In reading and thinking about simple correlational studies that address the relationship between two variables, questions inevitably arise about the role of other variables that were not studied. Because L2 use and learning are such complex phenomena, simple correlational studies that examine only two variables inevitably fail to account for other important factors. As a result, much correlational research, rather than being *bivariate,* assessing the relationship between two variables, is *multivariate.* In multivariate correlational studies, researchers attempt to account for relationships among a number of variables within the same study.

In these studies researchers determine the nature and magnitude of relationships among multiple variables by performing a variety of complex statistical analyses. Although a discussion of such procedures is far beyond the scope of this book (a topic for advanced statistics courses), we will devote time and space to this approach to research for two important reasons.

First, studies that examine complex clusters of variables have a clear advantage over bivariate correlational studies in that they have the potential for greater validity (Kamil, Langer, & Shanahan, 1985). Because they account for more variables, they are more adequate than bivariate studies in representing the complexities of real language-learning situations. Teachers, perhaps more than anyone, are well aware of the complexities of classroom learning, and they draw on this background knowledge in interpreting reports of complex studies.

Second, a top-down approach to exploring research may be a better, although nontraditional, way to start for most readers. Some might argue, from a quantitative or bottom-up perspective, that a brief look at this type of study is superficial if one does not first learn the statistics involved. But I believe that view is not necessarily correct. By examining the types of questions that are addressed in complex correlational studies and the overall conceptual approach used, readers can then decide if they wish to pursue the courses in statistics that will allow them to fully understand the mathematical modeling used in such research. Just as language learners tolerate incomplete knowledge of the target language, so too will you need to tolerate an incomplete knowledge of the mathematical models involved in complex quantitative studies.

In this section we will examine one complex correlational study to illustrate how such research is conducted. As a result, you should be able to read complex correlational studies with at least some degree of understanding of the conceptual issues even though you may not be familiar with the statistical procedures used.

SAMPLE COMPLEX CORRELATIONAL STUDY: AFFECT, RISKTAKING, AND L2 PROFICIENCY

The sample study we will review was conducted by Ely (1986) with university foreign language (FL) students who were studying Spanish. Ely used a complex correlational approach, called "causal modeling," to study the relationships among students' oral participation in the FL classroom, their affective characteristics, and learning outcomes. In this type of research, although correlational techniques are used, researchers attempt to establish cause-and-effect relationships among variables. They use verbs such as "influence" and "affect" in stating their hypotheses and in drawing conclusions. Cause-and-effect relationships are usually studied through experimental approaches, but in this case the basis for making causal claims is the theory upon which the hypotheses are based (Smith & Glass, 1987, pp. 188–191). It is important to realize, however, that any study based on correlational information cannot establish causality. We will use the same questions we used for simpler correlational studies to examine this study.

1. What is the research question?

The researcher's broad questions were: What affective factors are associated with oral participation in the classroom? Is voluntary oral participation in the classroom associated with greater proficiency? Because this study involves a large number of variables and hypotheses, the best way to become familiar with them is to examine Figure 3.1 at this point. The lines with arrows indicate which variables were expected to be related to one another. Each of these is called a "causal path." Overall, Ely (1986) posited that:

> (1) affective variables influence a student's voluntary classroom participation and (2) voluntary classroom participation (through various cognitive processes) in turn affects second language proficiency. (p. 4)

He proposed additional hypotheses about how affective variables are related to one another. He hypothesized that language class discomfort decreases risktaking and sociability in Spanish. As he explains:

> It was felt that the presence of such discomfort discourages a student from taking risks with the language and also inhibits the student's interaction with others in Spanish. (p. 5)

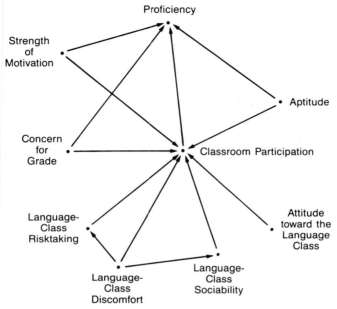

Figure 3.1. Theoretical Model for Investigation (*Source:* From "An Analysis of Discomfort, Risktaking, Sociability, and Motivation in the L2 Classroom" by C. Ely, 1986, *Language Learning, 36,* pp. 1–25. Copyright 1986. Reprinted by permission.)

In addition to proposing that discomfort decreases risktaking and sociability, Ely hypothesized that (1) discomfort decreases participation, and (2) risktaking and sociability increase classroom participation. Participation was expected to be a positive predictor of proficiency. The other relationships he proposed can be seen in Figure 3.1. The hypotheses about relationships among variables that are represented in this figure constitute the "theoretical model" that was investigated. The model was constructed based on current theory and on previous research.

2. In what context was the research conducted?

This was a dissertation study conducted in Spanish foreign language classrooms in a U.S. university.

3. What were the theoretical and other orientations of the researcher?

This study is social-psychological in orientation. The author's theoretical objectives were to determine how affective variables were related to L2 classroom interaction and achievement. He drew on previous theoretical and empirical work on "good language learners" (Naiman, Frohlich, Stern, & Todesco, 1978; Heyde Parsons, 1983) and on social-psychological studies of language learners that have investigated relationships between classroom anxiety, participation, and achievement (for an overview, see Gardner, 1985).

4. Who were the subjects/participants in the study? How many were there and how were they selected? What were their relevant characteristics?

Six teachers and 75 students participated in the study. The author describes the subjects:

> The subjects were students enrolled in first year Spanish courses at a university in northern California. The study involved six classes: three classes of students in their first quarter of Spanish study (Level 1) and three classes of second quarter students (Level 2). (Ely, 1986, p. 7)

The students gave written consent to participate in the study but were not aware of the specific questions being investigated. Ely does not explain his rationale or criteria for selecting these particular classes. He does, however, provide additional information about the characteristics of the students through the measures that he administered. For example, some of the students had studied Spanish in high school and some used Spanish in their homes. The report does not provide information about ethnicity.

5. What constructs were assessed? How were they defined and measured? How adequate (valid and reliable) were the measures?

Ely (1986) points out that, although it is commonly assumed that extraversion, a general personality trait, promotes L2 proficiency, the results of research on this topic have been mixed. Therefore, rather than measuring global personality traits such as extraversion, he chose to investigate risktaking, sociability, and discomfort in the specific context of the foreign language class. His study centered on three "situation-specific" constructs:

- *Risktaking* was defined as "an individual's tendency to assume risks in using the L2 in the second language class" (p. 3).
- *Sociability* was defined as "a desire to interact with others in the second language class by means of the L2" (p. 3).
- *Discomfort* was defined as "anxiety, self-consciousness, or embarrassment felt when speaking the L2 in the classroom" (p. 3).

Ely developed questionnaire items to assess these constructs. Six items were developed to assess risktaking, five for sociability, and five for discomfort (see the appendix at the end of this chapter for sample items). Questionnaire items were also developed to assess other constructs represented in Figure 3.1, including attitude toward the language class (four items), concern for grade (one item), and strength of motivation (seven items). Strength of motivation was defined as the degree to which an individual desires to learn the foreign language (p. 3). The item development process also involved pilot-testing the items, conducting item analyses to investigate their adequacy, and eliminating inappropriate items. Careful item development is important, because correlational research of this type is very dependent upon valid and accurate measurement of variables.

Reliability assessments of the scales used in the study yielded coefficients ranging from .65 (which is low) to .86 (an adequate level). The value of using self-report questionnaire data in providing valid information about affective characteristics is always open to question, as the author notes (p. 22). While we also might criticize the study for employing a small number of items, this consideration must be balanced against the response burden placed on students who are asked to fill out questionnaires.

Foreign language aptitude was assessed with the Modern Language Aptitude Test, a well-established measure of language aptitude. The author reports split-half reliability coefficients of .93 for college males and females that were reported by Carroll and Sapon (1959). While this is sufficient to establish reliability, it would be preferable to also report reliabilities obtained with this group of students.

The students' self-initiated classroom participation was directly observed and audio-recorded by two native Spanish-speaking observers. Ely (1986) explains how the variable of classroom participation was defined:

> Classroom participation was operationalized as the number of times a student asked or answered a question or provided information in Spanish without being individually nominated to do so. (p. 13)

A total of 200 minutes of observations were coded from tape recordings. To reduce biases of the observers, they were not informed of the questions being investigated. To assess the reliability (consistency) of these observations, several measures of interrater agreement were calculated. In all cases the two coders agreed with one another over 90% of the time. These levels of agreement are sufficiently high to indicate that the observations were acceptably reliable.

Spanish language proficiency was assessed only once during the quarter using two methods. First, it was measured through a story-retelling task accompanied by pictures. The story was constructed using vocabulary and structures from the course and the retelling was scored on both fluency and on the accuracy of those items taught in the course. Second, written correctness was assessed through a final exam. Reliabilities were assessed by calculating interscorer and test reliabilities. On all measures these were over 90%, levels considered high.

6. What correlational analyses were performed and with what results?

This was a complex study with a number of complex analyses. (For example, Ely used path analysis, with an ordinary least-squares multiple regression procedure to examine the validity of the causal model depicted in Figure 3.1.) An explanation of these analyses is not our purpose here. The point is that the researcher used correlational procedures to determine the nature and magnitude of the relationships among the variables.

As expected, results indicated that language-class discomfort was a significant negative predictor of language-class risktaking and language-class sociability. Also, as expected, language-class risktaking was a significant positive predictor of classroom participation. Discomfort, sociability, and motivation were not found to be predictors of participation, however.

Classroom participation was a significant positive predictor of oral correctness, but only for the first-quarter students. It did not predict oral fluency or written correctness for either group of students.

7. What conclusions are drawn? Are generalizations about results appropriate?

The author states his conclusions in terms of predictions. As we discussed above, the broad purpose of correlational research is to understand patterns of relationships among variables. One goal of such research is to allow us to predict one variable from another or from several others. If two variables correlate with one another, then knowing a person's status on one variable allows us to predict what that person's status on the related variable or variables might be. Thus, to conclude that language-class discomfort was a significant negative predictor of language-class risktaking (for these 75 students) means, for example, that many of the individuals who reported that they were not comfortable in the class were those who also reported that they were not risktakers. We can "predict" status on one variable based on status on the other variable. These predictions are based on group data. They do not necessarily hold for any individual.

Ely is careful not to imply that a correlational study can unequivocally establish cause-and-effect relationships. As he appropriately points out,

> a cross-sectional, correlationally-based study is not capable of definitively proving causality. For this it would be necessary to conduct research following an experimental paradigm or using repeated measurements obtained over time. (Ely, 1986, p. 22)

The author is also careful not to generalize the findings to other age groups and to other groups of learners in different situations. He indicates, for example, that results might be very different for U.S. secondary school foreign language students because of the nature of peer relationships among adolescents. He also points out that the results are not necessarily generalizable to ESL, EFL, and bilingual situations.

His conclusions are appropriate, although it is also important to realize that the results cannot be generalized to different cultural groups, a point that Ely does not discuss directly. The cultural context of this study was a U.S. university classroom composed primarily, we assume, of Anglo-American students and some Hispanic students. In some cultures excessive handraising, "callouts," and volunteering to speak up in the classroom are not appropriate behaviors. Because students bring with them their own culturally shaped scripts for appropriate classroom behavior, we can expect relationships among affective factors, voluntary participation, and achievement to be quite different in different cultural contexts.

Indeed, McGroarty (1989) has found cultural differences in both attitudes and learning strategies among adult ESL learners who had been in the United States for just over one year. She found, for example, that Spanish-speaking adults tended to favor interactive approaches to classroom language study, while Chinese and Japanese speakers favored the use of strategies based on memory and on conscious attention to grammatical form. Cultural background is one source of systematic variation in the factors involved in second language acquisition. Thus the Ely study provides interesting information about the relationships among affective and social interactional factors in one cultural setting, but we do not know how these relationships might have varied according to the students' background, nor can the findings be generalized to other classroom, institutional, or cultural settings.

8. What is the contribution of the study to our knowledge of social and contextual factors in L2 learning?

As is true of many other complex correlational studies, one of the valuable features of this study is that, by addressing a number of variables, it takes into account the fact that language learning involves a complex host of interacting factors. Similarly, by using three different measures of language proficiency, an attempt was made to define proficiency in a broad, rather than a narrow, sense.

Although Ely found that voluntary oral participation was associated with oral correctness for Level 1 students, this relationship did not hold for the Level 2 students. Participation was not associated with either oral fluency or written correctness for either level. While some studies have shown voluntary verbal participation to be related to achievement (Naiman et al., 1978; Seliger, 1977), others have found a lack of relationship (Day, 1984). These findings remind us that the two commonsense notions that practice makes perfect, and that the more students engage in oral classroom practice the more they will learn, do not necessarily hold. Many other factors and other types of interactions and transactions with texts contribute to overall proficiency.

One important contribution of this study, however, is that it defines affective factors that are important for voluntary verbal interaction in a context-specific manner. That is, affective factors were defined, not as general personality traits, but for a specific situation. Thus the study takes account of social context by recognizing that students' perceptions of their sociability, willingness to take risks, and feelings of discomfort vary from one setting to another. Obviously, affective factors can also be studied for different tasks.

An interesting finding of the study was that discomfort was a negative predictor of risktaking in the typical classroom context. This finding, that students who are uncomfortable are less likely to take risks, is important for teachers because optimal levels of risktaking in using the L2 are believed to enhance learning (Beebe, 1983; Ellis, 1985). The Ely (1986) study can lead us to consider other important questions regarding discomfort and risktaking and how they relate to growth. We need to know how these factors operate in varying task and activity contexts for students of different cultural backgrounds and with different personalities. For example, how does risktaking in interactive journal writing compare to risktaking in teacher-led, small-group oral interaction and what are the effects on language use and learning? Research by Shimizu-Iventosch (1988) indicates, for example, that beginning Japanese foreign language students take risks with both content and form in journals. Another question we might ask is, How does discomfort vary according to the nature of the task? Evidence from correlational and case study research in L2 writing anxiety indicates, for example, that excessive concern with correctness of form is one factor related to L2 writing anxiety for university students in some tasks (Gungle & Taylor, 1989; Rose, 1984; Taylor & Johnson, 1989). The situational, cultural, and task factors affecting discomfort, risktaking, and active participation are important areas for continued research.

9. What are the stated implications for L2 learning in formal contexts?

Ely (1986) suggests how his research might guide teachers:

> Teachers may find in these results an indication of the importance of language class risktaking and classroom participation in various language learning situations. However . . . simply exhorting students to take more risks and participate more may not be effective. Apparently, before some students can be expected to take linguistic risks, they must be made to feel more psychologically comfortable and safe in their learning environment. To this end, classroom teachers may wish to devise and test the relative effectiveness of various strategies for lessening language class discomfort. (p. 23)

Although Ely does not suggest strategies, this discussion of implications guides us to think about the effects of discomfort and challenges us to develop learning environments and language-learning tasks that are optimally effective both in the affective and in the cognitive realm.

CONCLUSION

The major advantage of correlational research is that it can alert us to associations among variables that are important in the learning process. Multivariate studies that examine relationships among a number of variables are usually more interesting than bivariate studies because they better represent the real complexities of phenomena.

The key disadvantage of correlational studies is their essentially reductionist nature. Constructs such as language proficiency must be reduced to a number or a set of numbers. For this reason, the value of a correlational study depends heavily on how well the theoretical constructs (such as attitudes, proficiency, communicative competence, etc.) are defined and how they are measured. A very narrow definition of a construct, or a measure of a construct with questionable validity and reliability, renders a study less meaningful.

From the traditional experimental point of view, the inability of a correlational study to determine cause-effect relationships is a drawback. We do not know, for example, whether reading for pleasure causes higher levels of proficiency (as Polak and Krashen, 1988, and Huang and Van Naerssen, 1987, proposed) or whether higher levels of proficiency promote reading. Similarly, in correlational studies of the relationship between attitudes and proficiency, we do not know whether attitudes influence proficiency or whether proficiency affects attitudes (as Strong, 1984, suggested). Gardner (1989) points out that it is highly likely that causality operates simultaneously in both (or many) directions, because language learning is a complex and dynamic process. These issues of causality cannot be resolved using correlational methods. In fact, the positivist assumption that cause-effect relations exist and can be objectively determined at all is hotly debated by philosophers and researchers. These challenges to positivism undermine the experimentalist's criticism of correlational research. The criticism of reductionism remains the most serious.

Another limitation of correlational research is that, because it requires studying groups, the larger the better, it does not provide us with rich insights about individual language learners. Researchers who wish to explore in more depth the processes and strategies that individuals use in learning and communicating, or a learner's language and literacy development over time, may turn to more qualitative approaches. Case studies, for example, can better provide these kinds of insights, as we will see in the next chapter.

NOTE

1. Consistent with current convention, the term African American is used, rather than
black.

REFERENCES

Beebe, L. (1983). Risk-taking and the language learner. In H. W. Seliger & M. H. Long
(Eds.), *Classroom oriented research in second language acquisition* (pp. 39–65).
Rowley, MA: Newbury House.

Beebe, L. M. (1985). Input: Choosing the right stuff. In S. M. Gass & C. G. Madden
(Eds.), *Input in second language acquisition* (pp. 404–414). Rowley, MA: Newbury
House.

Borg, W. (1987). *Applying educational research* (2nd ed.). White Plains, NY: Longman.

Carroll, J. B., & Sapon, S. M. (1959). *Modern language aptitude test (MLAT) manual.*
New York: The Psychological Corporation.

Day, R. (1984). Student participation in the ESL classroom or some imperfections in
practice. *Language Learning, 34,* 69–102.

Dulay, H., Burt, M., & Krashen, S. (1982). *Language two.* New York: Oxford
University Press.

Ellis, R. (1985). *Understanding second language acquisition.* Oxford: Oxford University
Press.

Ely, C. (1986). An analysis of discomfort, risktaking, sociability, and motivation in the
L2 classroom. *Language Learning, 36,* 1–25.

Gardner, R. C. (1985). *Social psychology and second language learning: The role of
attitudes and motivation.* London: Edward Arnold.

Gardner, R. C. (1989). Attitudes and motivation. In R. Kaplan (Ed.), *Annual Review of
Applied Linguistics (1988), 9,* 135–148.

Goldstein, L. M. (1987). Standard English: The only target for nonnative speakers of
English? *TESOL Quarterly, 21,* 417–436.

Gungle, B. W., & Taylor, V. (1989). Writing apprehension and ESL writers. In D. M.
Johnson & D. H. Roen (Eds.), *Richness in writing: Empowering ESL students* (pp.
235–248). White Plains, NY: Longman.

Heyde Parsons, A. (1983). Self-esteem and the acquisition of French. In K. M. Bailey,
M. H. Long, & S. Peck (Eds.), *Second language acquisition studies* (pp. 175–187).
Rowley, MA: Newbury House.

Huang, X., & Van Naerssen, M. (1987). Learning strategies for oral communication.
Applied Linguistics, 8, 287–307.

Kachru, B. B. (1987). Discourse and stylistic strategies in contact literatures. In L. E.
Smith (Ed.), *Discourse across cultures: Strategies in world Englishes* (pp. 125–140).
Englewood Cliffs, NJ: Prentice Hall.

Kamil, M. L., Langer, J. A., & Shanahan, T. (1985). *Understanding research in reading
and writing.* Boston: Allyn & Bacon.

Krashen, S. (1985). *The input hypothesis.* White Plains, NY: Longman.

McGroarty, M. (1989, February). *Cultural styles in adult language learning.* Paper
presented at the Second Language Research Forum, Los Angeles.

Milon, J. P. (1975). Dialect in the TESOL program: If you never you better. In M. Burt & H. Dulay (Eds.), *On TESOL '75* (pp. 159–170). Washington, DC: Teachers of English to Speakers of Other Languages.

Naiman, N., Frohlich, M., Stern, H. H., & Todesco, A. (1978). *The good language learner*. Research in Education Series No. 7. Toronto: The Ontario Institute for Studies in Education.

Polak, J., & Krashen, S. (1988). Do we need to teach spelling? The relationship between spelling and voluntary reading among community college ESL students. *TESOL Quarterly, 22,* 141–146.

Preston, D. (1989). *Sociolinguistics and second language acquisition.* Oxford: Basil Blackwell.

Rose, M. (1984). *Writer's block: The cognitive dimension.* Carbondale and Edwardsville: Southern Illinois Press.

Seliger, H. (1977). Does practice make perfect? A study of interaction patterns and L2 competence. *Language Learning, 27,* 263–278.

Shimizu-Iventosch, M. S. (1988). *Dialogue journals: Students' risk-taking on content and form.* Unpublished master's thesis, University of Arizona.

Sledd, J. (1972). Bi-dialectalism: The linguistics of white supremacy. In D. L. Shores (Ed.), *Contemporary English: Change and variation* (pp. 319–330). Philadelphia: J. B. Lippincott.

Smith, L. E. (Ed.). (1987). *Discourse across cultures: Strategies in world Englishes.* Englewood Cliffs, NJ: Prentice Hall.

Smith, M. L., & Glass, G. V. (1987). *Research and evaluation in education and the social sciences.* Englewood Cliffs, NJ: Simon & Schuster/Prentice Hall.

Strong, M. (1984). Integrative motivation: Cause or result of successful second language acquisition? *Language Learning, 34,* 1–14.

Taylor, V., & Johnson, D. M. (1989). Apprehension in foreign language writing. Manuscript submitted for publication.

APPENDIX: SAMPLE QUESTIONNAIRE ITEMS
FROM COMPLEX CORRELATIONAL STUDY

These are the questionnaire items used by Ely (1986) in the study described above. They are listed by scale here, although they were not separated by scale when administered to subjects.

Try taking the questionnaire yourself. If you are currently a first or second quarter/semester student in an L2/FL class, answer truthfully. If not, try to remember how you felt when you were in such a language class. Substitute the language you studied for "Spanish" in the items below.

1 = strongly disagree, 2 = moderately disagree, 3 = slightly disagree, 4 = slightly agree, 5 = moderately agree, 6 = strongly agree.

Language-Class Risktaking Scale

1. I like to wait until I know exactly how to use a Spanish word before using it.   1   2   3   4   5   6
2. I don't like trying out a difficult sentence in class.   1   2   3   4   5   6
3. At this point, I don't like trying to express complicated ideas in Spanish in class.   1   2   3   4   5   6
4. I prefer to say what I want in Spanish without worrying about the small details of grammar.   1   2   3   4   5   6
5. I prefer to follow basic sentence models rather than risk using the language.   1   2   3   4   5   6

Language-Class Sociability Scale

1. I'd like more class activities where the students use Spanish to get to know each other better.   1   2   3   4   5   6
2. I think learning Spanish in a group is more fun than if I had my own tutor.   1   2   3   4   5   6
3. I enjoy talking with the teacher and other students in Spanish.   1   2   3   4   5   6

4. I don't really enjoy interacting with the other students in the Spanish class. 1 2 3 4 5 6

5. I think it's important to have a strong group spirit in the language classroom. 1 2 3 4 5 6

Language-Class Discomfort Scale

1. I don't feel very relaxed when I speak Spanish in class. 1 2 3 4 5 6

2. Based on my class experience so far, I think that one barrier to my future use of Spanish is my discomfort when speaking. 1 2 3 4 5 6

3. At times, I feel somewhat embarrassed in class when I'm trying to speak. 1 2 3 4 5 6

4. I think I'm less self-conscious about actively participating in Spanish class than most of the other students. 1 2 3 4 5 6

5. I sometimes feel awkward speaking Spanish. 1 2 3 4 5 6

Strength of Motivation Scale

1. Outside of class, I almost never think about what I'm learning in class. 1 2 3 4 5 6

2. If possible, I would like to take a second-year Spanish course. 1 2 3 4 5 6

3. Speaking realistically, I would say that I don't try very hard to learn Spanish. 1 2 3 4 5 6

4. I want to be able to use Spanish in a wide variety of situations. 1 2 3 4 5 6

5. I don't really have a great desire to learn a lot of Spanish. 1 2 3 4 5 6

6. Learning Spanish well is not really a high priority for me at this point. 1 2 3 4 5 6

7. I don't really feel that learning Spanish is valuable to me. 1 2 3 4 5 6

Attitude toward Language-Class Scale

1. I find Spanish class to be very boring.	1	2	3	4	5	6
2. I would say that I'm usually very interested in what we do in Spanish class.	1	2	3	4	5	6
3. I don't really like the Spanish class.	1	2	3	4	5	6
4. In general, I enjoy the Spanish class.	1	2	3	4	5	6

Concern for Grade Scale

1. It is very important to me to get a good grade in Spanish this quarter.	1	2	3	4	5	6

CHAPTER 4

Case-Study Approaches

How does scaffolded interaction promote second language and literacy development? What strategies do high school students use in reading L2 texts? How do individual learners differ in their approach to learning a new language and culture? These are examples of the kinds of questions a researcher can explore through a case-study approach.

In the previous chapter we analyzed correlational studies in which researchers quantify variables and establish the nature and degree of relationship among them. You may have found yourself thinking about how individual students respond, feel, perform, or comprehend. Or perhaps you found yourself thinking about how such phenomena differed in contexts in which you have participated. You may also have wished that the data were not all numbers! In this chapter we will examine a very different approach to research—the case study.

We will first define the essential characteristics of a case study. We will then explore the types of issues that can be addressed using case-study methods. Next, we will discuss methods of conducting case studies. Finally, criteria are presented for analyzing a case study and we will apply these criteria to a sample study.

WHAT IS A CASE STUDY?

A case study is defined in terms of the unit of analysis. That is, a case study is a study of one case. A case-study researcher focuses attention on a single entity, usually as it exists in its naturally occurring environment.

A close study of one case allows researchers to find answers to different types of questions from those for which correlational techniques are appropriate. While correlational studies tell us about relationships among variables for groups of students, case studies can provide rich information about an individual learner. They can inform us about the processes and strategies that individual L2 learners use to communicate and learn, how their own personalities, attitudes, and goals interact with the learning environment, and about the precise nature of their linguistic growth.

As in monolingual child-language research, in research in second language acquisition and bilingual/multilingual language acquisition, the case is most often a person who is learning an additional language. Well-known examples are studies by Hakuta (1976, 1986) of a Japanese child learning English; by Schumann (1978) of a Spanish-speaking adult's language learning and acculturation; and by Wong Fillmore (1976) of five children's cognitive and social strategies in learning English.

The unit of analysis (i.e., the case) might also be a teacher, a classroom, a school, an agency, an institution, or a community. In research in interactional sociolinguistics, the case may be a communicative interaction in a particular situation (Gumperz, 1986). The researcher may examine only one case or may choose to study several cases and compare them. The number of cases is always small, however, because the essence of the case-study approach is a careful and holistic look at particular cases.

The purpose of a case study is to describe the case in its context. Guided by a research question, a researcher studies the case and those aspects of the environment that pertain to that case and that shed light on the research question. Stake (1988) offers this definition of a case study: "The case study is a study of a 'bounded system,' emphasizing the unity and wholeness of that system, but confining the attention to those aspects that are relevant to the research problem at the time" (p. 258). This definition requires that case studies be generally *naturalistic*. That is, the individual or other entity is studied in its naturally occurring state and environment. As we will see, however, a variety of methods, naturalistic or otherwise, can be used to address the research question.

A case study may stand alone as a single substantive study or it may constitute one portion of a larger study employing additional approaches. For example, case studies of programs, and comparisons across these case studies, often form part of a program evaluation. Similarly, a long-term ethnographic study may include briefer, individual case studies (see Michaels, 1986, for example).

USES OF CASE STUDIES

In this section we will review several case studies to illustrate the types of questions that researchers have investigated, the contexts in which they have studied phenomena, their methods of collecting data, and their findings.[1] The studies represent a range of topics for learners at different levels. They also include studies of cases other than learners.

Learning Portuguese

Schmidt and Frota (1986) conducted a case study of Schmidt's learning of Portuguese during a five-month period in Rio de Janeiro. They were interested in charting his linguistic development as a beginning learner, his growth in conversational competence, and the relative contributions of classroom instruction and informal interaction to his learning.

Schmidt kept a daily journal and recorded in a "semisystematic" manner salient aspects of his own learning experiences in and out of class, such as specific conversational exchanges, communication and learning strategies, and hypothesis formation and confirmation. The researchers complemented his subjective diary account with a second, more objective, source of data. At one-month intervals they taped 30- to 60-minute unstructured conversations in Portuguese. These were transcribed and then analyzed for interaction patterns and for aspects of the Portuguese noun and verb phrase.

The report provides an extensive analysis of data and discussions of Schmidt's language development in relation to SLA theory. We will mention only a few of the many findings. Schmidt had particular difficulties with Portuguese articles. The authors hypothesized that his persistent omission of the indefinite article, for example, could have been due, in part, to transfer from Arabic, a language he knew well and which has no indefinite article (Schmidt & Frota, 1986, p. 255).

Discourse analysis of his taped conversations with Frota revealed that he had problems with affirmative answers to questions. In Portuguese an appropriate affirmative response to the question "Did you live in Egypt?" *(Voce morou no Egito?)* would not be "Yes" *(sim),* but "I lived" *(Morei).* He failed to master this structural pattern even though it was explicitly taught in class. The analysis also revealed that he used repetition as a strategy in conversation to hold the floor, to gain time to plan, and to say a phrase again more completely or smoothly. Regarding the contributions of class work, Schmidt and Frota concluded that Schmidt's class provided resources that he could put to immediate use outside of class and helped him to interpret what he had heard but not understood in interaction.

The findings of a case study cannot necessarily be generalized to other learners. Learners who are less linguistically sophisticated than Schmidt, for example, might use very different strategies and exhibit somewhat different learning outcomes (see Schmidt, 1983). Rather, it is useful to compare the findings of case studies and search for useful general principles.

Coping with Academic Content in a Second Language

An important goal of ESL instruction in high schools and universities is to prepare students for academic success. In a number of case studies, researchers have examined the demands of listening, speaking, reading, and writing tasks in content courses and how advanced ESL students cope with these tasks.

What are the academic listening experiences of ESL students in university courses? Benson (1989) explored this question by studying an Arabic-speaking ESL student in one university course in his master's program. To gather information Benson conducted interviews with his subject and with one of his subject's professors, observed classes, audio- and video-recorded some of the classes, collected the subject's papers and class notes, and collected the professor's lecture notes.

The findings focus on how listening to learn in this student's content course differed from merely listening to comprehend in his former ESL courses. He focused heavily on the information he thought would be on tests. He took notes on main points, omitting subsidiary points, omitting statements with which he did not agree, and omitting information arising through class discussion. He never participated verbally by asking or answering questions in class, nor did he view listening as the most important way to learn. Benson concluded that if the purpose of advanced listening courses for L2 students is to prepare them adequately for the academic setting, the courses should stress actual content learning, should relate content to past and anticipated experiences, and should require the use of various modalities (listening, speaking, reading, and writing), including notetaking. He proposed that such courses should promote the kinds of active student participation that are valued in academic settings.

Adamson (in press) has also studied ESL students in academic content courses and illustrated how success in such courses is highly dependent not only on academic study strategies but also on how well teachers are able to provide effective ways for students to engage their own background knowledge in class activities and in testing practices. He and his graduate students conducted 34 case studies of intermediate, high school, and university students to determine what problems they were having and how they coped. These teacher-researchers each tutored a student in a content course for 10 hours or more over 6 to 10 weeks. They audio-taped the sessions and took field notes. In addition, they observed the content classes, interviewed the teachers, and gathered relevant documents.

A few findings from one of the case studies will illustrate the nature of the challenges the students faced. A high school history teacher (E. S. Shepps) studied one of her own high school students, a Thai speaker who planned to become an electrical engineer. Focusing on his notetaking and test-taking practices, she found that he depended most upon material written on the board. He concentrated on this information because he assumed it was most important for tests and because he felt he could not concentrate on listening and taking notes on the teacher's lecture at the same time. This strategy resulted in his missing material that was mentioned only orally but appeared on tests. She discovered that her student did best when he had knowledge of a topic; otherwise his learning was somewhat superficial, consisting of memorizing names and events. He did poorly on multiple-choice tests because he often did not know the vocabulary in the item. On the other hand, when assessment involved essays and conversations rather than discrete tests, he experienced much more success because he could express himself on his own terms, drawing on language and content that he knew. Shepps's overriding conclusion was that the discrete tests she was using did not tap the student's knowledge of history. It is not difficult to see some parallels between patterns exhibited by this high school student and the university student studied by Benson.

Scaffolding, Problem Solving, and Second Language Learning

Case-study methodology is also an effective means of illuminating the ways that L2 learning and content learning interact for younger students. Hawkins (1988), drawing on notions of scaffolding and on Vygotsky's notion of the zone of proximal development, studied how fourth-grade ESL students cope with academic content and language demands. She studied seven children to search for (1) evidence of scaffolding in the interaction of the teachers and students and (2) concrete signs of language learning or independent problem solving that resulted from the scaffolded interaction. She was also interested in finding out (3) what type of classroom activity motivated scaffolded interaction.

She videotaped the seven children every day for two months in each of their classes (math, science, social studies, ESL reading, ESL grammar, and computer writing). These classes were taught by several teachers. Therefore, the children were motivated to clarify issues when, for example, they had to explain what they had learned in social studies to the ESL teacher and then write about it for her.

Hawkins (1988) used several types of discourse analysis to address her research questions. She did find evidence of scaffolding and some concrete signs of language learning resulting from instances of scaffolded interaction. She also found evidence of independent problem solving. In fact, the students achieved cognitive accomplishments that they are not normally thought capable of attaining because of their level of proficiency in the L2.

The answer to Hawkins's third research question was that scaffolding was more likely to be present in situations and activities that were both interactively and cognitively demanding—that is, in activities in which students were actively involved in the interaction and the emphasis was on interpretive and critical comprehension (p. 28). The importance of this study is that it clearly illustrates not only how scaffolded interaction can promote second language and literacy development, but also how some continuity in content across settings (from the individual student's point of view) contributes to these goals (p. 127).

Second Language Writing

The case-study approach has been widely used to examine writing processes in L1 research (Lauer & Asher, 1988) and L2 research as well. Urzua (1987), through a case-study approach, examined the oral and written interactions and texts of four Southeast Asian children who participated in writing activities such as dialogue journals and peer response groups. One of her conclusions was that allowing students some control over topics gave them the freedom to build on their own knowledge and to share that knowledge with others. This finding is consistent with the Adamson and Shepps case discussed above. Urzua also concluded that when children chose their own topics, their voices came through more strongly and they were more effective writers. In addition, she documented that they could successfully revise their papers based on group peer-review sessions.

Peyton and Seyoum (1989) used a modified case-study approach to examine written journal interactions between a teacher and her students. The teacher (L. Reed) was highly experienced and successful in using dialogue journals with her students. The study focused on how this exemplary teacher's strategies promoted student participation in written dialogue. A commonsense assumption is that asking students written questions to which they are expected to respond will elicit not only more writing but more complex writing from the students. They found that this was not true for this teacher and her students.

The researchers studied the interactions of 12 limited-English-proficient students in Reed's sixth-grade class. Six of the students were Asians and 6 were Hispanics from El Salvador and Mexico. Peyton and Seyoum analyzed a sample of 15 consecutive written interactions for each student to determine to what extent the teacher either initiated or responded to topics and to what extent she either requested replies or made personal contributions that did not solicit a response.

They found that the teacher did not initiate topics in more than about one-fourth of her journal entries. Rather, she tended to respond to the students' ongoing topics. She used this pattern for students at low and mid, as well as high English proficiency levels. Moreover, she did not rely heavily on the common-sense strategy of asking questions to solicit a reply. Rather, she made personal contributions in the majority of the entries, offering her own opinions and adding information about a topic. When she did ask questions, she often posed them in the context of her personal contribution.

The analyses of the students' writing revealed that while teacher questions were successful in eliciting replies, students tended to write more when they were responding to a teacher entry that contained a question along with a personal contribution. The researchers concluded that "the success of the dialogue journal interaction lies precisely in the teacher's participation as an active partner in a meaningful, *shared* communication" (Peyton & Seyoum, 1989, p. 330).

Working with university students, Jones (1985) used a case-study approach to investigate factors that inhibit drafting for writers composing in English as a foreign language. He used video recordings and interviews to examine the composing processes of two students. Drawing on notions of monitoring, Jones described one student as an "overuser" of the monitor and the other as an "underuser" of the monitor. His study revealed that the overuser, who was more proficient in grammar and vocabulary than the underuser, monitored in ways that inhibited her composing process. Because the student's compositions did not reflect her full competence, Jones concluded that overmonitoring during drafting can have an inhibiting effect on written communication. Other researchers, however, working with L2 writers in different situations, have obtained different findings in their case studies (Raimes, 1985).

Reading Strategies

Case-study methods are useful for investigating processes in reading as well as composing. Hosenfeld (1984) conducted an exploratory case study of Ricky, a ninth-grader who was determined to learn Spanish as a second/foreign language, but who was having trouble reading passages in his class textbook. She worked with him, using a "think-aloud" technique, to discover what strategies he was using to understand a text and to teach him to use more effective strategies. Hosenfeld explained that "a thinking aloud approach consists of asking students to perform tasks and to verbalize their thought processes; an introspective/ retrospective approach consists of asking students to reflect upon their operations as they perform a task or after they have completed it" (pp. 231–232).

In her first session with her subject at his school, Hosenfeld taught him to think aloud in English while he read the Spanish text aloud. He learned to do this quickly. She found that he read word-by-word, continually turning to the glossary to find the meaning of words. It appeared that these strategies were based on advice from a previous teacher, as well as his desire to achieve "perfect" comprehension in order to do the exercises in the textbook.

During four subsequent half-hour sessions with Ricky, Hosenfeld taught him some of the strategies that successful readers had reported using in her previous research. She successfully led him to guess the meanings of many words from cognates and from morphological information. She also led him to use contextual information from the sentence, the text as a whole, illustrations, and his own background knowledge to derive meaning successfully.

It appears that Ricky's strategies were closely tied to what he perceived as the important purposes for reading. It would be interesting to address how his strategies might have differed if he were reading an authentic text for a real purpose.

Adult Literacy

The case study is a useful approach for inquiry into literacy development. Rigg (1985) describes a case study of a middle-aged Mexican migrant woman as she was tutored in reading and writing in Spanish and English. Rigg took notes as another adult (Rigg's student) tutored Petra using a variety of techniques such as examining environmental print on food cans (labels for salt, tomatoes), using a language-experience approach to produce and read recipes, and sustained silent reading of magazines and *fotonovelas*. Rigg provides a vivid narrative account of what she and her student learned about how sociocultural and economic contexts affect views of literacy, access to literacy, and goals for learning. They discovered, for example, that their own theory of reading differed widely from Petra's view of literacy and her goals for using print. Petra's goals for writing were drawing clear letters and writing her name on her possessions. Rigg also describes Petra's economic circumstances as a migrant worker and how her family situation may have inhibited her goals for literacy. She concluded that she and her colleague should have entered into a Freirian dialogue with Petra.[2]

Modifying Input Strategies:
The Conversion of a Teacher

Teachers in their classroom interactions may also be the focus of a case study. As classrooms become more linguistically and culturally diverse, more teachers find that promoting second language acquisition is a new part of their professional role (Rigg & Allen, 1989). Enright (1986) documented how an elementary teacher, Molly, adapted her teaching when she switched from teaching in an all-English environment to teaching in a classroom that included both native English-speaking students and ESL students of a wide variety of proficiency levels. In his case study Enright (1986) describes "the way it is in one ESL classroom" (p. 119). Data were collected through a variety of techniques, including naturalistic observations, interviews, and the gathering of teachers' plans and journals as well as students' work. Enright examined the range of interactive events that Molly organized for her new class. His analysis focused on specifying patterns of instructional adaptations.

He found and describes a variety of general adaptations, such as new grouping strategies and input strategies. For example, discourse strategies that Molly used included repeating, recycling, and rephrasing. In his report, Enright provides a description of each strategy with examples that clearly illustrate how classroom language use was meaningful and focused on activities in which the teacher and students were engaged. Enright (1986) reports that Molly's way of dealing with the diversity in her classroom was to "contextualize and re-contextualize her input and her students' own language use both within and across her classroom events" (p. 148). First, she established predictable classroom events, allowing children to take on increasingly linguistically demanding roles within the events. Second, she created new contexts within predictable events. Third, she used similar language across classroom events, each providing a different context, meaningful, but with differing degrees of abstraction. This notion of "contextual contrast" is both theoretically important in view of recent semantic theory (Lemke, in press; Lakoff, 1987) and practical for promoting learning. More qualitative studies of this nature will add rich insights to our knowledge of teachers' changing thought processes and the contextual conditions that promote L2 learning.

   These studies provide only a sampling of the kinds of issues that researchers have investigated using case studies. Questions that address an individual's linguistic development, composing processes, reading strategies, communicative interactions, and attitudes about literacy are all well suited to a case-study research approach.

ISSUES IN CASE-STUDY METHODOLOGY

There are fewer widely agreed upon, strict methodological criteria for case studies than there are for studies in the hypothetico-deductive paradigm such as experiments, correlational studies, and quantitative surveys. Rather, case-study methodology is flexible and is formulated to suit the purpose of the study. It can vary along a number of dimensions. Case studies are most often primarily *qualitative,* although they often involve the quantification of some information. They are usually primarily *naturalistic,* relying on the collection of naturally occurring data. In addition, however, various procedures may be used to elicit data. Case studies are usually *descriptive* in that they describe phenomena, or they may go beyond description to contextual or cultural interpretation. Case studies may be *longitudinal,* conducted over a lengthy period of time, as are many important studies of second language acquisition, but many are of short duration.

   What, then, are the important methodological issues in case-study research? In this section we will discuss five key issues: (1) initial problem formulation; (2) defining the unit of study and its boundaries; (3) data-collection techniques and researcher roles; (4) analysis—the search for patterns; and (5) communicating the experience in a report.

The Initial Research Question

Case studies begin with a research question as do correlational studies. Where do these questions come from? They may come directly from experience or from theory. These two sources of research questions are not mutually exclusive. Some claim that naturalistic case studies are seldom related to theory (Smith &

Glass, 1987, p. 257). This is clearly not the case for much L2 research, particularly research that has focused on language use and language and literacy development. Case study research has been very important in advancing second language acquisition theory (see McLaughlin, 1987, for one review). The questions that motivate case studies often arise out of knowledge gaps or discontent with currently accepted explanations for phenomena. The attitude "I have to see for myself" drives researchers to see how it works for a particular case. Researchers often illustrate how the experiences of one learner are either consistent with or diverge from theoretical claims. They may simply describe what they learn or they may propose new explanations for phenomena, contributing to theory development. Case study research questions, then, may lead to description or to better theory.

A key difference between a case study and a correlational study is that in many case studies the researcher starts with research questions, but also develops and refines them as the study progresses. An example from a study of a larger case will help illustrate this point. The example comes from a descriptive, qualitative case study of the roles of bilingual education offices in state departments of education (Nava et al., 1984). As a consultant for this study, I conducted two of the nine case studies. We were interested in describing the activities of these offices in serving the bilingual education needs of their respective states. An issue that emerged as important during our site visits and interviews was the relative attention given to Spanish-speaking versus Native American groups within the states we were studying. We, therefore, looked further into the issue than originally planned and found that states differed widely in areas such as materials development, language-assessment guidelines, and allocation of personnel and material resources for Native Americans. As we learned about each case, then we modified and reoriented our study questions to gain understanding of issues.

The Unit of Study: Determining the Boundaries of the Case

The essence of a case study is that it focuses holistically on an entity, whether a student, teacher, or program. The purpose is to understand the complexity and dynamic nature of the particular entity, and to discover systematic connections among experiences, behaviors, and relevant features of the context. "A case study tells a story about a bounded system" (Stake, 1988, p. 256). One goal of the researcher, then, is to define the bounded system, to determine the boundaries of the unit of study. These boundaries depend on the goals of the study.

Let us consider two examples. In the Benson (1989) study of university academic listening, the bounded system included not only the listening and notetaking activities of the student but also the professor's lectures, lecture notes, and her expectations for student performance. A better example is the Hudelson (1989) case study of two elementary students' writing reviewed below. The focus of study was the two children and their writing, drawing, and conversation as they worked with Hudelson. In addition, however, the bounded system included the nature of Spanish-language instruction, English-for-speakers-of-other-languages (ESOL) sessions, and the English language arts curriculum. These experiences all contributed to shaping both the children's views of writing and the writing they produced.

In these examples, individual students were the focus of study. When the unit of study is a class, a district, a language institute, a community, a political unit that sets language-education policy, or a national program, researchers must determine different types of boundaries. What is the nature of a bounded system at one of these levels? Let us consider a different example. I conducted case studies of two school districts' Migrant Education Programs in collaboration with a team of researchers (Johnson, 1987). While our major focus was on the Migrant Program, to adequately describe and evaluate the program in each district it was important to examine related programs such as ESL and bilingual programs, the so-called regular program, and the interactions among these programs from the point of view of administration, teachers, aides, and students. We also interviewed parents to discover how they perceived the program. Thus the boundaries that we set for our study encompassed the important programs and contextual factors that contributed to shaping students' educational experiences.

A Working Research Design. Discovering what aspects of the case and its natural environment are relevant to the goals of the study requires that the research design be flexible. A *research design* is a plan, a set of guidelines for the researcher's activities. The design lays out, step by step, what needs to be accomplished to carry out the study. Unlike a correlational or experimental research plan, which is fully specified in advance and carefully adhered to, a case-study design is further developed as the study progresses. The researcher develops a *working design* that sets out the questions to be addressed, the unit selected for study with its tentative boundaries, the entities or situations or people to be studied, the various data-collection procedures, guidelines for analysis, and how much time will be involved. As information is gathered and the researcher gains an understanding of the phenomena being studied, new issues will come to light that need exploration and the boundaries of the study may need to be shifted. Refocusing, deciding what is important to look at and what areas are not fruitful, is an important process in the ongoing case-study design.

Data-Collection Techniques

A wide range of techniques can be used to collect information for case studies. As you can see from the sample studies discussed above, data collection can be entirely *naturalistic,* in which researchers collect information from the natural setting as unobtrusively as possible, or it may involve *eliciting* language or other information. Very often both naturalistic data and elicited information are gathered to provide different perspectives on the same issue. Researchers may also gather existing information. We will briefly discuss data collection techniques that are most used in L2 case studies. These techniques are naturalistic observations, elicitation methods including interviews and verbal reports, and the collection of written materials.

Naturalistic Observations. Observing natural communication in a school setting, particularly oral or written interactions among students and between students and teachers, is one of the most common and important data-collection techniques in case studies. How can the information be recorded? Notetaking, audio-recording, and video-recording are the major methods used to record data on verbal interactions. The major problem with notetaking is that there is not time to record everything, so decisions must be made about what to record and what to exclude. Using a tape recorder helps solve this dilemma, but introduces other problems. While the obvious advantage of audio-recording is that all interaction that is audible is recorded and can be analyzed later in a number of ways, the presence of the tape recorder can inhibit students or teachers, especially at first. Because machines may fail or humans may forget to turn them on, a backup is a good idea. In addition, students may move out of range, and even in range, much speech turns out to be inaudible. To pick up speech that might otherwise be inaudible, microphones can be attached to key students (Saville-Troike, 1988).

Video technology allows researchers to capture the nature of the physical setting, the identity of participants in interactions, and many aspects of nonverbal communication such as gestures, bows, and eye contact. Grouping patterns can be captured as well, particularly if the person recording is an informed member of the research team. Video-recording, like audio-recording, however, tends to make some people uncomfortable. But if adults understand the purpose of the recordings, and recordings are made regularly over an extended period of time, the inhibiting and other effects of the intruding machines are likely to lessen. Videotapes, like audiotapes, can be analyzed repeatedly in a variety of ways while live observations, of course, cannot.

Computers can be useful tools in gathering certain kinds of live observational data. For example, a lap-top computer can be faster than a pen in recording live observations of classroom events. Similarly, many kinds of software can record certain aspects of a student's interaction with the computer such as questions attempted, answers, texts produced, and so on.

Another naturalistic technique involves taking notes about one's own language-learning experiences in a diary or journal, as Schmidt did (Schmidt & Frota, 1986). This technique involves retrospective, rather than live observation.

Case studies relying on this technique are often referred to as *diary studies* (see Bailey, 1983, 1985 for discussions).

Written production resulting from everyday classroom activities might be considered naturalistic if it was not elicited by an outside researcher. Because most student writing is elicited in some way by the instructor, however, we could conclude that the only truly naturalistic writing is that which is spontaneously produced by students, such as notes and letters to one another. Dyson (1987) refers to this kind of writing as the "underground writing curriculum." For our purposes, however, let us define naturalistic classroom writing broadly, to include any writing not elicited by the researcher that is either part of normal class activities or "underground" writing. Classroom writing samples can come from papers and notes from content courses, assignments written for L2 classes such as interactive or dialogue journal interactions, written computer discussions, peer reviews of papers, collaboratively composed stories or compositions, and content or literature response papers.

Elicitation Techniques. Elicitation implies that it is the researcher who elicits information. The most crucial question to consider in reading research using elicitation procedures is how the information the researcher obtained (e.g., language production or comprehension, strategies, processes, attitudes, opinions, or practices) might have varied according to the nature of the task and the task context. What the participants see as the purpose of the task, their cultural background, their affective state, and factors in the situational context may all influence the information that is obtained. One advantage of a case-study approach is that researchers can observe phenomena of interest in a variety of settings and tasks and compare the phenomenon under different conditions. For example, one might compare a student's writing in a contrived task and in an authentic task.

An infinite number of elicitation techniques exists. Which techniques are selected depends on the research questions and the case. The range of techniques used in the few studies reviewed above includes taped-recorded conversations, tape-recorded tutoring sessions, interviews with learners, interviews with learners' content teachers and professors, and think-aloud techniques. Other widely used techniques include interactive journal writing between researcher and student, composing tasks, discourse-completion written tasks (see Chapter 5), role-plays, translation tasks, and, of course, many types of tests. We will briefly discuss some considerations involved in conducting interviews and gathering verbal reports.

Interviewing. Interviews can vary along a continuum from highly *structured,* to *semi-structured,* to *unstructured.* The list of questions that an interviewer uses to conduct an interview constitutes an *interview guide.* In an interview guide for a highly structured interview, questions are fully specified, although open-ended, and the interviewer adheres fairly rigidly to the guide. In an unstructured interview, the guide provides only a general plan for the topics of the interview. The interviewer probes for additional information and follows leads that arise.

A good interview guide for a structured or semi-structured interview does more than simply list the questions to be asked. It may also contain suggestions for what to say at beginning and end of the interview regarding the purpose of the interview, for example. It provides questions to use for probing for additional information. It can be designed to reduce the amount of writing the interviewer must do, by listing typical response categories. It may also provide space for notes, although in my experience I have usually found it much more efficient to write notes on a separate pad of paper and number the notes to correspond with the guide.

Successful interviewing is both a skill and an art. It takes time, experience, and effort to learn to interview both efficiently and well. It is important to establish and maintain good rapport, to be able to control the pace and direction of the conversation as needed, and to know how to follow up on important issues. Different interview formats, such as a pair of interviewers with one respondent, or a group interview conducted by one interviewer, will flow more smoothly with careful planning and practice. After conducting an interview that is not tape-recorded, it is critical to go over the notes and fill in gaps that same day, for even after one day the interviewer's memory begins to fade and important information is lost.

Effective informal interviewing is a central data-collection technique for case studies that are ethnographic in orientation (see Chapter 6). Ethnographers use key informant interviews, life history interviews, and expressive autobiographic interviews. We will discuss interviewing further in subsequent chapters.[3]

Verbal Reports.   A different kind of elicitation technique that is very useful in L2 case-study research is obtaining students' verbal reports of their own thinking. These verbal reports can provide insights into students' cognitive processes (Ericsson & Simon, 1987). Think-aloud methods, verbal reports, and introspective/retrospective accounts have been used in research on composing processes (Flower et al., 1990; Hudelson, 1989; Lauer & Asher, 1988; Raimes, 1985; Zamel, 1983, 1987), on reading processes and strategies (Cohen, 1987; Goodman, 1989; Hosenfeld, 1984), on test-taking strategies (Feldmann & Stemmer, 1987), and on learning and communication strategies (Lennon, 1989).

Raimes (1985), for example, used a think-aloud procedure to trace the mental processes of university ESL students as they wrote a narrative essay. She asked students to think aloud into a tape recorder as they composed. Raimes first showed her students how to talk while composing and asked them to practice at home. After training, she conducted the study in class as part of regular class work. She asked students to write a narrative on an experience they had had that was unexpected: "Tell about something unexpected that happened to you"

(Raimes, 1985, p. 236). She then analyzed the taped record of their speech (called a protocol), using a coding system to determine the kinds of processes they used that could be discerned through their talking. These processes included planning, recursive processes at the sentence level, attention to errors, and attention to form. This example illustrates one way that introspection can be used.[4] Introspective reports can be analyzed using either quantitative or qualitative means or both.

While introspective techniques were not favored during the era of behaviorism, they gained favor as one means of providing data for cognitive research. Yet every data-collection method has its advantages and disadvantages. The disadvantages of verbal reports are several. Clearly, verbal reports of thinking do not provide direct observations of thinking processes. Rather, an assumption is made that verbal report data can be interpreted as accurately reflecting a sequence of generated thoughts and that these thoughts reflect underlying cognitive processes (Ericsson & Simon, 1987, p. 30). This assumption may not necessarily hold because students may not have access to these processes. Even if they do, they may mold their response to fit what they think the researcher wants to hear. Second, it cannot be assumed that the processes involved in composing aloud, for example, are the same as those involved in composing silently or composing in collaboration with a peer. The same is true for think-aloud reports while reading. Thus, conclusions about what students do while "thinking aloud" cannot necessarily be generalized to situations in which they act silently, collaboratively, or in some other way or in another language. The task contexts and language used for reading and writing can affect the kinds of processes and strategies that students use in reading and composing. Despite these cautions, however, a think-aloud situational context for reading or writing is interesting in itself, and a verbal report provides some insight into the processes that students use for particular tasks. (For discussions of verbal reports see Cohen, 1987; Ericsson & Simon, 1987; Faerch & Kasper, 1987a, 1987b; Flower et al., 1990.)

Collecting Existing Information. In addition to gathering data through naturalistic observations, elicitation, and interviews, researchers may gather a variety of other types of data that shed light on the research questions. In studies of learners, such information can include written work completed for classes, samples of writing, test data, data from school records, or information about the family or community. In his dissertation study of the literacy development of several successful Navajo students, Hartle-Schutte (1988) gathered school test data, not because he had faith in the validity of the information, but to compare the "official" scores to his own observations of each student's literacy activities and achievements. Gathering information from a variety of sources helped him gain a holistic view of his students.

In case studies of programs, such as bilingual, migrant, or ESL/EFL programs, researchers usually gather as many documents as possible about the program (such as proposals for funding, descriptions of the program, evaluation reports, curriculum principles, and materials) before and during site visits. These materials can provide much important background information, but because there is sometimes only a minimal match between what is written in such documents and what actually occurs in the program, accurate information must be gathered on-site.

Multiple Sources of Data for Triangulation. I once heard a senior researcher offer this advice to his graduate advisees: "Ask as few questions as possible, and gather as much information as possible about those questions." An important way to strive for rigor in a case study is through using multiple sources of data. *Triangulation* is the attempt to arrive at the same meaning by at least three different independent approaches. As Goetz and LeCompte (1984) point out, triangulation prevents the researcher from relying on initial impressions, it helps correct for observer biases, and it enhances the development of valid constructs during the study.

Analysis: A Search for Patterns

Analysis strategies vary widely depending on the purpose of the study and the types of data collected. Often, the general approach to data analysis in a case study is to examine the data for meaningful themes, issues, or variables, to discover how these are patterned, and to attempt to explain the patterns. Data analysis unually involves a continual process of looking for meaning by sorting reiteratively through the data.

In studies employing think-aloud data-collection techniques, as in the Raimes (1985) example presented above, protocol analysis involves systematically examining protocols to discover the processes that students use to accomplish writing tasks. Some researchers analyze spoken discourse to search for patterns of interest. For example, in Hawkins's (1988) study presented above, she analyzed student-teacher spoken discourse to search for examples of L2 learning through scaffolded interaction. Peyton and Seyoum (1989) also used discourse analysis to study teacher–student written interaction, although in their study they quantified variables to analyze patterns.

A high-quality analysis, whether quantitative, qualitative, or both, is one that (1) identifies important variables, issues, or themes; (2) discovers how these pattern and interrelate in the bounded system; (3) explains how these interrelationships influence the phenomena under study; and (4) offers fresh new insights.

The Case-Study Report

The writing of the report(s) is very important in case-study research. Many case-study writers attempt to produce a powerful and vivid account of what they have learned. The account might be spiced with interesting examples that allow the reader to really see and understand what occurred. In addition, the account may be powerful in that it tells a story or portrays scenes that touch the reader's emotions. Writers also use a variety of specific involvement strategies (Tannen, 1989) to bring the reader and the writer together. As a result, case-study reports can make very enjoyable reading when they are not only informative but also involving and entertaining.

But is an account just to be entertaining? Stake (1988) suggests that entertainment is not the purpose of a report. But by making it vivid, by creating suspense and evoking emotional responses, the writer appeals to more than one way of knowing. The writer gives the reader a vicarious cognitive experience. As Stake suggests, "This vicarious experience may be more easily integrated into a reader's existing experience than a quantitative record is" (Stake, 1988, p. 260). Tannen suggests that understanding and remembering are facilitated by the sense of involvement created through powerfully written discourse. How this notion may apply to learning from case-study accounts is an excellent topic for research.

CRITERIA FOR ANALYZING CASE STUDIES

As you read research that employs a case-study approach, you can use the questions below as a framework for assessing the study. Considering the answers to these questions will help you organize and build your understanding of the study.

1. What is the research question?
2. In what context was the research conducted?
3. Who were the participants in the study? How were they selected? What were their relevant characteristics?
4. What was the theoretical orientation of the researcher?
5. What was the role of the researcher?
6. What data-collection procedures were used? How much time was spent collecting data?
7. How were data analyzed? What were the findings?
8. What conclusions are drawn? Are they logically related to the descriptive data?
9. What is the contribution of the study to our knowledge of social or contextual factors in second language learning?
10. What are the stated implications for teaching?

SAMPLE CASE STUDY: A TALE OF TWO WRITERS

A study of two children's development as writers provides a valuable example of a case study (Hudelson, 1989). I selected this study because it illustrates (1) how the contexts in which ESL students engage in composing interact, (2) how these contexts can influence children's views of writing and the kinds of writing experiences they have, and (3) how children's own learning styles and personalities contribute to shaping their growth.

Hudelson explored individual differences in the development of two Spanish-speaking children as she observed and worked with them over an entire school year. She found that they differed in their approaches to the task of creating texts and that they developed in different ways and at different rates. More importantly, she found that what was expected in the regular classroom affected their views about writing at school.

1. What is the research question?

Hudelson's goal in the study was to investigate how the two children differed and the nature of their English writing growth in school. She formulated her question in a broad manner:

> My goal was to understand better the development of ESL writing in some native Spanish speaking children. (pp. 84–85)

The question is a significant one because writing development is an important aspect of overall L2 development that has been neglected in the past.

2 & 3. In what context was the research conducted? Who were the participants in the study? How were they selected? What were their relevant characteristics?

Hudelson observed two children and collected data in a bilingual second-grade classroom in a Dade County, Florida, public school. She chose to study Spanish speakers because she is fluent in Spanish and wanted to be able to use the children's native language as needed. In her report she provides a rich description of the children, their background, and the classroom. Here are just a few excerpts:

> Roberto was a "Marielito," a designation applied to the 125,000 people who left Cuba . . . from the port of Mariel . . . [he] had attended kindergarten in Cuba . . . [and] . . . had spent his first year in U.S. schools in a classroom populated solely by non–English-speaking Mariel children . . . Roberto was a quiet child . . . serious about school . . . [whose] . . . classroom style was to listen and to take everything in but not to volunteer an answer orally or commit something to paper unless he was sure that he had the right answer. His classroom teacher thought of Roberto as a good student. His ESOL teacher found him to be a child reluctant to participate orally. (p. 85)

Roberto's profile contrasts with that of Janice.

Janice was a student in the same classroom. In September she had just arrived from Puerto Rico with her mother. At first a seemingly shy girl homesick for Puerto Rico, Janice gradually became more outgoing. By the end of the school year she was a popular child, surrounded by others during activities. Initially Janice's style was to sit quietly, taking in everything and mimicking what others were doing. Later she became more talkative . . . She was clearly not the perfectionist Roberto was. She was not as reluctant as Roberto was to guess, to make mistakes. Her classroom teacher saw her as a satisfactory student. In ESOL she made rapid progress and moved at midyear . . . to a group that was progressing more quickly. By the end of the year, Janice was more comfortable with and more willing to use English than Roberto was. (pp. 85–86)

Hudelson describes how both Janice and Roberto received literacy instruction in three contexts: the regular classroom, Spanish-medium pullout instruction, and the ESOL classroom. She is critical of the approach to literacy instruction in both Spanish and English, characterizing it as "teacher directed and skills based." Here are a few excerpts from the description:

Roberto and Janice were both in a second-grade class, in which half the students were native Spanish speakers. . . . Their teacher, a native Spanish speaker, used English in classroom instruction . . . most of the Spanish speakers left the room for an hour of instruction in Spanish reading and writing . . . a phonics approach . . . The children did no original writing in Spanish . . . the LEP students, Roberto and Janice included, attended pullout ESOL classes three times a week. . . .

Janice and Roberto received English literacy instruction both in their classroom and in the ESOL class. . . . Daily activities, directed by the teacher, came only from text materials. The teacher evaluated the children on the basis of how well they performed on workbook tasks. Reading instruction focused almost exclusively on sounds, syllables, and words, rather than on connected text. The teachers did not ask children what they might want to read, nor did they ask children to create their own message. In fact, the teachers expressed the view that the children had to learn how to pronounce and write letters, words, and sentences before they could be asked to write on their own. (pp. 86–87)

The approach to writing taken by these teachers contrasts sharply with Hudelson's own theoretical orientation toward learning and teaching.

4. What was the theoretical orientation of the researcher?

Hudelson's theoretical orientation is that children's language and literacy develop more fully through active involvement in reading and writing activities that are authentic and meaningful to them. She describes the theoretical perspective taken in the study:

> The perspective taken is that children learn to read by reading and learn to write by constructing their own meanings in written form and by having other people react to what they have written. Proponents of whole language approaches to literacy . . . maintain that children are willing and even eager to write about topics of their own choice and that skill as a writer develops within the context of authentic, purposeful writing rather than through practicing isolated skills . . . numbers of educators have suggested that such learning environments are appropriate for second language (L2) acquirers, and that writing process strategies effective for NSs make sense in an L2. (p. 84)

One of her main interests, then, lay in exploring ways in which L2 writing development for these children is similar to writing development for monolingual English speakers learning to write in English (personal communication).

5. What was the role of the researcher?

In case studies, the researcher's role can range from a detached observer, to a participant observer, to an active change agent. Hudelson (1989) explains her role in the classroom and in the research. In addition, she explains how the role she had planned to play changed as she began observing the children and working with them.

> I served as a classroom volunteer, participant observer, and ESL tutor. . . . I had planned simply to document what I was seeing. However, a personal commitment to a whole language view of literacy resulted in my making direct efforts to encourage children's writing from this perspective on language development. (p. 85)

Because Hudelson's view of literacy development differed from that of the ESOL teacher, she asked for and was granted permission to experiment with some writing activities other than the exercises specified in the ESOL curriculum. Once or twice a month she worked with Janice and Roberto on these writing activities outside the classroom for an hour or more. She encouraged them to express themselves through drawing, to discuss their drawings in either language, and to write a little about them. After they wrote with her she asked them to read their writing aloud.

6. What data collection procedures were used? How much time was spent collecting data?

All of these sessions with the two children were audio-taped. Hudelson (1989) describes the procedures she used to gather information about the two children and their schooling.

> I spent one day a week observing and taking notes in the children's classrooms, helping children with school assignments, conversing with teachers, conducting regular audiotaped sessions with my tutees, and collecting reading and writing samples. (p. 85)

The study was conducted over a period of one school year. In addition, Hudelson made a brief follow-up visit the following school year to see Roberto and Janice in their third-grade classroom. A year is a sufficiently long period of time to gain access to a large amount of relevant data, to observe growth, and to observe factors that shape growth.

7. How were data analyzed? What were the findings?

Hudelson identified issues and looked for patterns that emerged in the two children's writing as the year progressed. These issues included how they viewed writing, how they approached the task of writing a text, the characteristics of their writing in relation to talking and drawing, their use of the L1 as a resource, and the amount and type of growth made (Hudelson, personal communication, October, 1989). She compared Roberto's patterns with those of Janice. First she describes how Roberto approached writing in English:

> (1) Roberto enjoyed drawing as a means of self-expression as well as a rehearsal for writing . . . (2) Roberto consistently created drawings that were more complex and complete than the writing that accompanied them . . . (3) Roberto was eager to share what he had drawn, and he created narratives about his creations . . . (4) Roberto often began in or switched quickly to Spanish as he created stories about his drawings. (5) After he provided a narration, he could be persuaded to write a little in English about what he had drawn. However, this did not happen voluntarily or as an integral part of the drawing . . . (6) Roberto consistently talked much more about his drawings than he wrote. Most of Roberto's meanings were carried by his pictures rather than by his writing. (pp. 89–90)

In case studies, authors often provide a number of examples that are typical of the phenomena being reported. Hudelson (1989) provides many examples of Roberto's writing. Here is a brief one:

> Roberto's cycle of drawing, sharing, and limited writing, accompanied by protestations about lack of knowledge of conventional forms, continued from January through May. In January he drew a vivid, multicolored picture of a fire and a fire engine. As he drew he told me, in Spanish, about a car that had been on fire in his neighborhood. When I asked him if he could write about what had happened, he wrote: *The car is in the faro* and read "The car is on fire." (p. 89)
> From February through April he wrote only phrases or lists of words. By the end of the school year he was still not creating more than single sentences or phrases to accompany his drawings. (p. 89)

This portrait of Roberto as an L2 writer is contrasted with a description of the changes in Janice's approach to writing and her growth. Janice moved more quickly from producing workbook- like sentences to creating texts. Hudelson (1989) describes her mid-year workbook-like writing:

> In December, after listening to Roberto explain his boat trip from Cuba to the United States, Janice drew a picture of a ship on some waves and a child next to the ship. But when asked to write something about what she had drawn, she created:

> | *Janice's Reading* | *Janice's Writing* |
> |---|---|
> | The cat is drinking | Do cat si durinking |
> | Dog sit Tiff is sitting | DogsiTiffsitting |

> Instead of writing something related to her picture, . . . Janice's writing strategy was to attempt to reproduce a text she had learned to copy in her workbook. While she used drawing as a vehicle for self-expression, she did not view writing in the same way. (p. 91)

Janice's development was similar to Roberto's during the first half of the year. Later, however, she moved beyond the stage of viewing writing as simply the accurate reproduction of workbook sentences. She began to interact more with Hudelson in Spanish about her writing, she began to add information to her writing in response to questions, and she used a variety of resources to get the words and spellings she wanted to use. "She used her Spanish to get information about how to say things in English. As Janice did this, she grew as a writer. In contrast, Roberto did not use oral input to add to his writing, nor did he ask for information about how to say something in English" (p. 93). By May, Janice used wordless picture books to create lengthy stories.

> Janice saw herself as an individual willing to take risks to construct meaning, a language user aware of mistakes but willing to make them, a bilingual who used her native language to ask for help with English. These behaviors were quite different from Roberto's. (p. 94)

When Hudelson visited Roberto the following fall in his third-grade class, however, he created two texts for her. Here she reports on this visit and on one of the texts:

> Roberto asked if I was going to take him out of the room so that he could draw and write. The teacher gave permission and we left the room. Roberto voluntarily narrated a wordless picture story to me in English and wrote and read to me a brief summary of some of the pictures in the story.

> | *Roberto's Reading* | *Roberto's Writing* |
> |---|---|
> | The duck is in the nest | The deuk is in the nest. |
> | She have many eggs in the | She have many eggs in |
> | nest. Father and Mother was | The nest. Father and |
> | happy and they and xxx and | Mather was happy and day |
> | happy | and natg and happy (pp. 96–97) |

Only after a full year was Roberto willing to risk producing a complete text in English. Even though he was still writing only spelling lists and book sentences in his class, he was willing to risk a text in the L2 writing environment that Hudelson had created.

8. *What conclusions are drawn? Are they logically related to the descriptive data?*

Hudelson first draws conclusions about how the contexts in which the children wrote—the regular classroom, the Spanish-medium instruction, and the ESOL pullout sessions—were related to their constrained views of writing. She then compares the growth each made working with her.

> Certainly the children's classroom writing experiences had an influence on their perceptions of writing and on their pieces. Initially the children viewed writing as copying, reproducing workbook material, or using spelling words to construct sentences. Both moved beyond this view. Each child responded to an environment quite different from that of the classroom, an environment that believed that ESL children could and should produce English texts while still learning the language. . . . In this environment Janice made more progress than Roberto. Janice probably would be classified as the "better" or more successful language learner. . . . (p. 94)

Hudelson also concludes that ESL children display individual differences in their L2 writing development. She attributes these differences in progress between Janice and Roberto to differences in their personalities, cognitive styles, and social styles. She summarizes how the two children differed in their approaches to language use and learning:

> Roberto's tentative, cautious, non-risk-taking behavior probably had an effect on his rate of progress both as a speaker and as a writer of English. Janice was more willing than Roberto to guess at answers, to use what she knew at a particular time, to make mistakes, to ask for information from sources outside herself. These characteristics probably contributed to her more rapid rate of progress as a user of English. (pp. 94–95)

In addition, she concludes that ESL children with varying characteristics respond differently to school language experiences and that, while teachers clearly have a powerful influence on children's learning, children take different paths.

> Finally, we must understand that children ultimately are in control of their own learning, including their learning of writing. (p. 96)

The reader can see that these conclusions are logically related to the data.

9. What is the contribution of the study to our knowledge of social or contextual factors in second language learning?

The study contributes to the body of research on individual differences in child second language learning and literacy development (Saville-Troike, 1989; Strong, 1983; Ventriglia, 1982; Wong Fillmore, 1976, 1983). Second, it provides a clear picture of the nature of these differences in the complex school context. The characteristics of the "bounded system" that this case study encompassed revealed relationships between the various contexts for writing and the children's views of writing. The vivid narrative report allows readers to see for themselves the interrelationships among the children, their teachers, the classrooms contexts, and development. It helps us see how language and literacy development involve personal, cognitive, and social processes. Two different children, even in the same settings, reacted differently to writing environments and tasks, but both did make progress.

Another way in which the study addresses contextual factors is that it illustrates specific ways that Janice and Roberto used their cultural background and their primary language, Spanish, as resources (see also Edelsky, 1986, 1989). Although it was not Hudelson's intent to address Spanish literacy development, it would be interesting to see how the children's Spanish writing developed and particularly how both their English and Spanish writing would have developed had they had more time in the type of high-quality environments that Hudelson created.

10. What are the stated implications for teaching?

Hudelson recommends that teachers view writing as an integral part of L2 development and that they provide ESL children with many writing opportunities, including writing different types of pieces for varying purposes and audiences. Teachers should give priority to helping children establish fluency and a willingness to write in their second language.

In addition to providing opportunities for writing, the role of the teacher is to give children "gentle but persistent encouragement to express themselves," to support them in their attempts to do so, and to accept their less than perfect work as part of a developmental process (Hudelson, 1989, p. 95). Teachers should create an atmosphere that encourages risktaking, while providing access to various types and levels of support, including the use of their primary language(s) and written materials in English.

Hudelson also suggests that teachers understand that drawing, and the oral narration and discussion that accompany drawing, are integral to the composing process. Drawing and talk about drawing can provide supportive scaffolding that promotes L2 development (see also Dyson, 1987).

In addition to these implications for creating environments that support writing, Hudelson suggests ways that teachers can serve as advocates for quality instruction for ESL children:

It [is] vitally important that we share our perspective on and our understandings of effective learning environments for second language learners. We need to share what we know and use examples from children such as Janice and Roberto to make our points. We need to become advocates for our ESL students to ensure them the best possible education. . . . We need to act on what we know, rather than "go along with" the prevailing classroom or district philosophy. (p. 96)

CONCLUSION

The case study is a very valuable approach to L2 research. While enjoying a strong tradition in child language research and a solid place in second language acquisition research, it has been viewed as nonrigorous by some and has had relatively low status in social science and educational research until recently. The major disadvantage of a case study, from the hypothetico-deductive perspective, is that one cannot generalize findings to other cases. Yet notions of generalization are problematic and are a topic of continual discussion and debate in all approaches to research.[5]

In L2 studies, the case-study approach is particularly useful for studying the kinds of issues illustrated in this chapter, such as learning processes and strategies, the nature of individual L2 written and oral development, and sociopsychological and affective aspects of classroom learning. The close and holistic look at a case in the context of the bounded system chosen for study can yield many rich insights about teaching and learning processes.

NOTES

1. Research methods are selected, created, and applied in the service of particular research questions and purposes. Therefore, the purpose of the "Uses" section in this and other methodological chapters is not simply to offer a traditional review of literature. Rather, it is to indicate some of the authentic purposes for which a research approach is used. Discussions of method can be dry and lifeless if decontextualized and not linked to real topics and authentic studies. This section, then, provides varied contexts for the discussion of methodology that follows. Readers can also use studies in this section as a kind of annotated bibliography, as a point of departure for additional readings.
2. See Freire and Macedo, 1987, for example.
3. For discussions of qualitative, interpretive, and/or ethnographic interviewing techniques for case studies see Agar, 1980; Denzin, 1990; Goetz and LeCompte, 1984, pp. 119–142; and Saville-Troike, 1989, pp. 123–129.
4. Faerch and Kasper (1987b) provide these criteria for the classification of introspective methods in L2 research:
   "1. Object of introspection:
      1a cognitive, affective or social aspects;

1b declarative v. procedural knowledge;
1c modality of language use (spoken v. written, receptive v. productive, combination, e.g., in translation);
1d continuous process v. specific aspect.
2. +/− related to concrete action.
3. Temporal relationship to action (simultaneous, immediately consecutive, delayed consecutive).
4. +/− informant training.
5. Elicitation procedure:
5a degree of structure;
5b +/− media support;
5c self-initiated v. other-initiated;
5d +/− interaction between informant and experimenter, between informants;
5e +/− integration with action;
5f +/− interference with action.
6. +/− combination of methods." (p. 11)
5. See, for example, Eisner and Peshkin, 1990 (pp. 171–242), and Shulman, 1988, for discussions of generalizability.

REFERENCES

Adamson, H. D. (in press). *Academic competence: Theory and Classroom Practice.* White Plains, NY: Longman.
Agar, M. (1980). *The professional stranger: An informal introduction to ethnography.* London: Academic Press.
Bailey, K. (1983). Competitiveness and anxiety in adult second language learning: Looking *at* and *through* the diary studies. In H. W. Seliger & M. H. Long (Eds.), *Classroom oriented research in second language acquisition* (pp. 67–103). Rowley, MA: Newbury House.
Bailey, K. (1985). Classroom centered research on language teaching and learning. In M. Celce-Murcia (Ed.), *Beyond basics: Issues and research in TESOL* (pp. 96–121). Rowley, MA: Newbury House.
Benson, M. (1989). The academic listening task: A case study. *TESOL Quarterly, 23,* 421–445.
Cohen, A. (1987). Using verbal reports in research on language learning. In C. Faerch & G. Kasper (Eds.), *Introspection in second language research* (pp. 82–95). Clevedon, England: Multilingual Matters.
Denzin, N. K. (1990). *Interpretive interactionism.* Newbury Park, CA: Sage.
Dyson, A. H. (1987). *Unintentional helping in the primary grades: Writing in the children's world* (Tech. Report No. 8). Berkeley: University of California, Center for the Study of Writing.
Edelsky, C. (1986). *Writing in a bilingual program: Había una vez.* Norwood, NJ: Ablex.
Edelsky, C. (1989). Putting language variation to work for you. In P. Rigg & V. G. Allen (Eds.), *When they don't all speak English* (pp. 96–107). Urbana, IL: National Council of Teachers of English.

Eisner, E. W., & Peshkin, A. (Eds.). (1990). *Qualitative inquiry in education: The continuing debate*. New York: Teachers College Press.

Enright, D. S. (1986). "Use everything you have to teach English": Providing useful input to young language learners. In P. Rigg & D. S. Enright (Eds.), *Children and ESL: Integrating perspectives* (pp. 115–162). Washington, DC: Teachers of English to Speakers of Other Languages.

Ericsson, K. A., & Simon, H. A. (1987). Verbal reports on thinking. In C. Faerch & G. Kasper (Eds.), *Introspection in second language research* (pp. 24–53). Clevedon, England: Multilingual Matters.

Faerch, C., & Kasper, G. (Eds.). (1987a). *Introspection in second language research*. Clevedon, England: Multilingual Matters.

Faerch, C., & Kasper, G. (Eds.). (1987b). From product to process: Introspective methods in second language research. In C. Faerch & G. Kasper (Eds.), *Introspection in second language research* (pp. 5–23). Clevedon, England: Multilingual Matters.

Feldmann, U., & Stemmer, B. (1987). Thin_____ aloud a_____ retrospective da_____ in C-te_____ taking: Diffe_____ languages—diff_____ learners—sa_____ approaches? In C. Faerch & G. Kasper (Eds.), *Introspection in second language research* (pp. 251–266). Clevedon, Avon, England: Multilingual Matters.

Flower, L., Stein, V. E., Ackerman, J. M., Kantz, M. H., McCormick, K. M., & Peck, N. D. (1990). *Reading to write: Exploring a cognitive and social process*. New York: Oxford University Press.

Freire, P., & Macedo, D. (1987). *Literacy: Reading the word and the world*. South Hadley, MA: Bergin and Garvey.

Goetz, J. P., & LeCompte, M. D. (1984). *Ethnography and qualitative design in educational research*. Orlando, FL: Academic Press.

Goodman, Y. M. (1989). *Retrospective miscue analysis: History, procedures and prospects*. Occasional Paper No. 19. Tucson: Arizona Center for Research and Development, Program in Language and Literacy, University of Arizona.

Gumperz, J. J. (1986). Interactional sociolinguistics in the study of schooling. In J. Cook-Gumperz (Ed.), *The social construction of literacy* (pp. 45–68). Cambridge: Cambridge University Press.

Hakuta, K. (1976). A case study of a Japanese child learning English. *Language Learning, 26,* 321–351.

Hakuta, K. (1986). *Mirror of language: The debate on bilingualism*. New York: Basic Books.

Hartle-Schutte, D. (1988). *Home environment characteristics of successful Navajo readers*. Unpublished doctoral dissertation, University of Arizona.

Hawkins, B. A. (1988). *Scaffolded classroom interaction and its relation to second language acquisition for language minority children*. Unpublished doctoral dissertation, University of California, Los Angeles.

Hosenfeld, C. (1984). Case studies of ninth grade readers. In J. C. Alderson & A. H. Urquhart (Eds.), *Reading in a foreign language* (pp. 231–249). London: Longman Group U.K.

Hudelson, S. (1989). A tale of two children: Individual differences in ESL children's writing. In D. M. Johnson & D. H. Roen (Eds.), *Richness in writing: Empowering ESL students* (pp. 84–99). White Plains, NY: Longman.

Johnson, D. M. (1987). The organization of instruction in Migrant Education: Assistance for children and youth at risk. *TESOL Quarterly, 21,* 437–459.

Jones, S. (1985). Problems with monitor use in second language composing. In M. Rose (Ed.), *When a writer can't write.* New York: Guilford Press.

Lakoff, G. (1987). *Women, fire, and dangerous things: What categories reveal about the mind.* Chicago: University of Chicago Press.

Lauer, J. M., & Asher, J. W. (1988). *Composition research: Empirical designs.* Oxford: Oxford University Press.

Lemke, J. (in press). Intertextuality and text semantics. In M. Gregory & P. Fries (Eds.), *Discourse in society: Functional perspectives.* Norwood, NJ: Ablex.

Lennon, P. (1989). Introspection and intentionality in advanced second-language acquisition. *Language Learning, 39,* 375–396.

McLaughlin, B. (1987). *Theories of second-language learning.* London: Edward Arnold.

Michaels, S. (1986). Narrative presentations: An oral preparation for literacy with first graders. In J. Cook-Gumperz (Ed.), *The social construction of literacy* (pp. 94–116). (Studies in Interactional Sociolinguistics 3) Cambridge: Cambridge University Press.

Nava, H., Reisner, E. R., Douglas, D., Johnson, D. M., Morales, M. F., Tallmadge, G. K., & Gadsden, V. L. (1984, August). *Descriptive analysis of Title VII-funded state education agency activities. Volume II: Nine case studies* (Report no. 7706–83–4690). Mountain View, CA and Arlington, VA: SRA Technologies.

Peyton, J., & Seyoum, M. (1989). The effect of teacher strategies on students' interactive writing: The case of dialogue journals. *Research in the teaching of English, 23,* 310–334.

Raimes, A. (1985). What unskilled ESL students do as they write: A classroom study of composing. *TESOL Quarterly, 19*(2), 229–258.

Rigg, P. (1985). Petra: Learning to read at 45. *Journal of Education, 167,* 129–139.

Rigg, P., & Allen, V. G. (Eds.). (1989). *When they don't all speak English: Integrating the ESL student into the regular classroom.* Urbana, IL: National Council of Teachers of English.

Saville-Troike, M. (1988). Private speech: Evidence for second language learning strategies during the "silent" period. *Journal of Child Language, 15,* 567–590.

Saville-Troike, M. (1989). *The ethnography of communication: An introduction* (2nd ed.). Oxford: Basil Blackwell.

Schmidt, R. W. (1983). Interaction, acculturation, and the acquisition of communicative competence: A case study of an adult. In N. Wolfson & E. Judd (Eds.), *Sociolinguistics and language acquisition* (pp. 137–174). Rowley, MA: Newbury House.

Schmidt, R. W., & Frota, S. N. (1986). Developing basic conversational ability in a second language: A case study of an adult learner of Portuguese. In R. R. Day (Ed.), *Talking to learn: Conversation in second language acquisition* (pp. 237–326). Rowley, MA: Newbury House.

Schumann, J. (1978). *The pidginization process: A model for second language acquisition.* Rowley, MA: Newbury House.

Shulman, L. S. (1988). Disciplines of inquiry in education: An overview. In R. M. Jaeger (Ed.), *Complementary methods for research in education* (pp. 3–23). Washington, DC: American Educational Research Association.

Smith, M. L., & Glass, G. V. (1987). *Research and evaluation in education and the social sciences.* Englewood Cliffs, NJ: Prentice Hall.

Stake, R. E. (1988). Case study methods in educational research: Seeking sweet water. In R. M. Jaeger (Ed.), *Complementary methods for research in education* (pp. 253–278). Washington, DC: American Educational Research Association.

Strong, M. (1983). Social styles and the second language acquisition of Spanish-speaking kindergartners. *TESOL Quarterly, 17,* 241–258.

Tannen, D. (1989). *Talking voices: Repetition, dialogue, and imagery in conversational discourse.* Cambridge: Cambridge University Press.

Urzua, C. (1987). "You stopped too soon": Second language children composing and revising. *TESOL Quarterly, 21,* 279–297.

Ventriglia, L. (1982). *Conversations of Miguel and Maria: How children learn a second language.* Reading, MA: Addison-Wesley.

Wong Fillmore, L. (1976). *The second time around: Cognitive and social strategies in second language acquisition.* Unpublished doctoral dissertation, Stanford University.

Wong Fillmore, L. (1983). The language learner as individual: Applications of research on individual differences for the ESL teacher. In M. Clarke & J. Handscombe (Eds.), *On TESOL '82* (pp. 157–174). Washington, DC: Teachers of English to Speakers of Other Languages.

Zamel, V. (1983). The composing processes of advanced ESL students: Six case studies. *TESOL Quarterly, 17,* 165–187.

Zamel, V. (1987). Recent research on writing pedagogy. *TESOL Quarterly, 21,* 697–715.

CHAPTER 5

Survey Research

What are the attitudes of Chinese students toward learning English? What foreign languages are taught in U.S. elementary and secondary schools? How do advanced students of ESL accomplish socially important speech acts? What is the nature of literacy instruction for adults? These are examples of the types of questions that researchers can explore using survey research methods.

A survey differs in important ways from a case study. In a case study the researcher looks closely at a particular case, such as a learner, a classroom, a program. Because case studies usually provide in-depth information, we may learn a great deal about the few cases under study, but we do not learn how similar those cases are to many others. In a survey, on the other hand, a researcher looks at many cases, but generally cannot examine each case in much depth. Rather, the purpose of a survey is to examine one or more variables for larger numbers of entities.

In this chapter we will examine the nature of and uses of survey research. Next we will discuss some of the key steps in designing a survey. Finally, we will propose a set of criteria for examining a survey and apply these to a sample study.

WHAT IS SURVEY RESEARCH?

The purpose of a survey is to learn about characteristics of an entire group of interest (a population) by examining a subset of that group (a sample). Many readers are familiar with the results of political surveys, although few of us have been asked for our opinion. Because it would not be feasible to survey the entire population of the United States, pollsters select a small sample that is designed to be similar in important ways to (representative of) the population as a whole. The results of the survey of the sample are then generalized to the population. A survey is usually defined, then, as a study of a large group through direct study of a subset of that group.[1]

USES OF SURVEYS

Survey methods have been used by second language, bilingual education, and foreign language researchers to study a wide variety of issues that impinge on language learning. These include the changing demographic context, the institutional settings in which L2 professionals function, the policies that affect learning and teaching, program administration, teacher preparation, attitudes of teachers and professors toward language varieties, classroom practices, target language norms, and student language use and growth. In this section we will look at findings from a collection of surveys to illustrate the types of research issues that have been addressed.

The Demographic Context

Survey methods are used to gather demographic information about language learners. For example, many surveys have been conducted to estimate the number of persons in the United States who are learning English as an additional language and in need of various language and/or literacy programs (Kaskowitz, Binkley, & Johnson, 1981; Waggoner, 1988). The results of such surveys are often controversial because they can affect policy decisions. They are used by professional organizations to lobby for language programs and by policymakers to establish and justify program policies.

After reviewing data from a number of demographic surveys, Olsen (1989) claimed that estimates of the numbers of limited-English-proficient (LEP) students from many of the surveys were unrealistically low. One reason is that adult students in high school completion programs (GED programs) have not been included. He reported his own analysis which indicated that, when both K–12 students and adult students were included in estimates, nearly 1 in every 18 persons nationwide who were in high school completion and preparation programs was identified and reported as LEP (p. 485). The results of continually updated and carefully scrutinized demographic surveys are important for describing the social contexts for language learning.

Languages in the Schools

While demographic surveys provide broad descriptive information about students' language and literacy characteristics, other surveys describe language programs offered in schools. What languages are taught in U.S. elementary and secondary schools? Rhodes and Oxford (1988) reported on a national survey of foreign languages in elementary and secondary schools conducted through the Center for Language Education and Research (CLEAR). This study, funded by the U.S. Department of Education, was motivated by a concern over a lack of foreign language study in schools. While the national sample consisted of 5% of the public and private elementary and secondary schools, only 52% of this sample responded. The results, as the authors correctly indicate, apply only to those who responded, not to the national population of schools.

A few results will give an indication of the nature of the findings. The most frequently taught languages in both secondary and elementary schools were Spanish, French, German, and Latin. Latin, in fact, was taught in more schools than were other important languages in the world such as Russian, Chinese, and Japanese. Most elementary programs were very limited in scope. Only 3% of the respondents offered programs, such as intensive FLES (foreign language in the elementary school) or immersion, aimed toward developing a fair degree of communicative competence. In addition, little articulation across levels was reported. The authors recommended that, to improve second language instruction, more intensive and rigorous programs beginning in the early grades and extending through high school are needed.

Applied Linguistics Course Content in Universities

In addition to providing information about language programs offered in the schools, surveys can provide descriptive data about the content of courses. In one such study (reported in Johnson, 1987), our research team surveyed the linguistics and applied linguistics curricula in university bilingual programs.

As part of the larger study of bilingual teacher preparation discussed later in this chapter, we surveyed a nationally representative sample of 328 required graduate courses with bilingual-education content. We gathered this information by making two- to three-day visits to each of 49 graduate programs. During the visits we conducted semi-structured interviews with professors of required courses and gathered course materials such as syllabi, reading lists, and tests. Later we used a 227-item "Framework of Competencies" to analyze the content of the courses.

The major goal of our analysis of the linguistics and applied linguistics curriculum was simply to describe what was being taught in these courses. We found that a relatively high percentage of programs emphasized two topics: the nature of language and language variation. Fewer programs required a focus on topics such as the functions of language, language attitudes, and discourse analysis. We recommended that, because the latter issues are important for bilingual education, they be included in the course content for teacher preparation.

In addition to describing course content, we compared master's programs to doctoral programs and compared federally funded to nonfunded programs to see if there were important differences across different types of programs. We found that over half of the master's programs required that students study contrastive analysis, while only 20% of the doctoral programs stressed this topic. Comparing Title-VII-funded to nonfunded programs, we found that while funded programs placed less emphasis on linguistics as a whole, particularly the formal aspects of language, they placed a somewhat stronger emphasis on functional, sociolinguistic, and cultural issues within the realm of linguistics. We viewed the strong sociocultural focus in the linguistics and applied linguistics curriculum as a positive aspect of the federally funded programs.

Foreign Language Writing Courses in Spanish

In a very different kind of study of course content, Harvey (1987) reports on his findings of a mail survey of foreign language writing courses. His goal was to survey instructional faculty in Spanish departments at universities, two-year colleges, and high schools to determine what types of writing courses were offered and what role computers were playing in instruction. He reported that composition courses were offered in many programs, that process approaches (which he defined as "prewriting, writing, and revising") were in use, and that in some sites students used word processing in special classrooms designated as "composition centers." While the topic of this survey may be interesting, the numbers the author reported have little meaning because of the low response rate. He mailed questionnaires to 1,678 faculty and teachers but only 10% responded. The author implies that the results are representative of university Spanish instructors nationwide, yet they can apply only to those who responded.

Professors' Reactions to L2 Writing

Written language production has been the topic of other surveys at the university level. Researchers have been interested in questions such as: How do professors in a U.S. university react to the writing of students who are not native speakers of English? Which errors do they consider most serious and how should this information inform the teaching of composition? Santos (1988) addressed these questions in a survey of 158 professors at one university. These professors, who volunteered to participate, came from departments in both the humanities/social sciences and the physical sciences. Each respondent read and rated a partially corrected composition written by either a Chinese or Korean student. They rated the papers on six 10-point scales, three scales to assess content (holistic impression, development, and sophistication) and three scales to assess language (comprehensibility, acceptability, and irritation). In addition, they rated individual sentences containing salient errors on the three language scales (comprehensibility, acceptability, and irritation).

In general, the professors gave the papers lower ratings on content than on language. They rated the sentences with errors as highly comprehensible, reasonably unirritating, but linguistically unacceptable. Groups of professors who were more "severe" in their judgments were younger professors, those in the physical sciences, and those who were themselves nonnative speakers of English (about 5% of the sample). Of the various types of errors (auxiliary verb, article, discourse cohesion, etc.) lexical errors were rated as the most serious. Santos suggested, therefore, that instructors of ESL writing should include in their courses a strong emphasis on vocabulary building and lexical selection and that such instruction should help ESL/EFL students receive more positive evaluations of their writing in academic courses.

The "Regular" Classroom Teacher's Perspective

The integration of ESL students into academic classes is an important topic of study not only in the university but also in the elementary school. Many ESL students in U.S. public schools spend most of their time in "regular" classrooms with teachers who have no training in L2 development (Rigg & Allen, 1989). Penfield (1987) was interested in how these regular teachers viewed the challenges of integrating ESL students into their classes. She administered a 15-item questionnaire of primarily open-ended questions to a sample of public school teachers who were attending required in-service workshops on ESL students in the regular classroom. The sample (called a "sample of convenience") was not designed to be representative of a specified population; rather, the author's purpose was to identify general areas of concern for regular teachers in their relationships with ESL students.

The results illustrate misconceptions and contradictions in their perceptions and their needs for training. The respondents listed math, spelling, and phonics as the "easiest" subjects to teach to ESL students, while they reported that learning how to integrate L2 development with academic content learning was their greatest training need. The most frustrating experience for them was their inability to communicate with ESL students and their parents, yet only 21% favored a bilingual education approach for students. The ESL students were often described as passive and introverted, and teachers often attributed their problems in school to parental attitudes and practices. Although respondents felt it was not their responsibility, as "regular" teachers, to promote L2 development, they did expect ESL teachers to teach not only English, but all content areas, and to provide native language instruction. Penfield (1987) concluded: "one of the most important functions of the ESL teacher may well be not merely to teach the

LEP student, but more significantly to provide inservice training of regular teachers" (p. 35).

The Learner

Turning our attention to the language learner, surveys can provide interesting insights into the issue of minorities and school achievement. Researchers have used survey data to study relationships between students' language characteristics and their educational aspirations and levels of achievement in literacy. Duran (1987), for example, reports on a national survey addressing characteristics of Hispanic students and their achievement in school. The High School and Beyond survey (Fernandez & Nielsen, in press, cited in Duran, 1987) included a nationally representative sample of 3,177 Hispanic high school seniors and 14,696 white, non-Hispanic high school seniors. Analyses of these data indicated that among those students from a "bilingual background" (vs. a "monolingual background") their self-judged proficiency in both English and the non-English language (usually Spanish) uniquely contributed to enhancement of their educational aspirations and achievement. In other words, as students' self-judged proficiency in the non-English language or in English increased, there was an increase in both students' educational aspirations and achievement test scores (Duran, 1987, p. 40).

Sociolinguistic Studies of Language Use

Sociolinguists interested in second language acquisition have conducted studies to provide information about the spoken language and language varieties that L2 learners are trying to learn. For example, a number of researchers have used a form of survey methodology to collect empirical data on speech acts such as compliments and compliment exchanges (Manes & Wolfson, 1981; Holmes, 1988; Wolfson, 1989).[2]

Manes and Wolfson (1981) concluded from a study of complimenting in everyday speech that compliments are highly formulaic. They found that three syntactic patterns accounted for 85% of their data. These patterns, accompanied by an example, were:

1. NP is/looks (really) ADJ   (e.g., "Your blouse is beautiful")
2. I (really) like/love NP   (e.g., "I like your car")
3. PRO is (really) (a) ADJ NP   (e.g., "That's a nice picture")

They also found that the semantic composition of the compliments was highly regular. The most commonly occurring adjectives were "nice," "good," "beautiful," "pretty," and "great." The topics of most compliments fell into two broad categories: appearance and/or possessions, and ability and/or accomplishments.

Holmes (1988) examined gender differences in complimenting and found that women gave compliments about appearance more than did men, and that men tended to compliment other men, but not women, on their possessions. In their responses to compliments, men tended to evade the compliment more than women.

Information about typical sociolinguistic usage from these studies is not only of theoretical interest but is also useful for teacher preparation and for syllabus design. As Wolfson (1989) states, "Analyses of sociolinguistic usage in American English are desperately needed in order that materials developers and language teachers have concrete, empirically based information upon which to plan instruction" (p. 79).

ISSUES IN SURVEY DESIGN

Doctoral candidates have sometimes chosen survey techniques for dissertations, viewing them as the simple way to do research (Haller, 1979, cited in Smith & Glass, 1987). Yet there are important technical issues involved in constructing adequate and useful surveys. Many of the surveys in the educational literature as well as in the foreign language and TESOL literature, although they may address interesting questions, are lacking in technical adequacy.

In designing a survey, the researcher must make a series of careful decisions about how the study will be carried out. The detailed plan that results is the *research design*. Important issues to be considered in developing a survey research design are: determining the purpose of the study; stating the research question(s); specifying the population and drawing a sample from the population; deciding on the methods of data collection, developing instruments, and training data collectors or interviewers; collecting data; analyzing the data; and addressing nonresponse. Understanding the steps and how they are interrelated will help you assess and construct your own meaning from the reports of surveys that you read. We will examine these steps in a general manner here and then in the context of a sample study.

Defining a Population

The first step, after stating the research question(s), is to define a population. The *population* is the entire group of entities or persons to which the results of a study are intended to apply. The population of interest can vary widely depending on the research question and the purpose of the study. The population might be a set of schools, for example. Consider the research question posed by Rhodes and Oxford (1988): What languages are taught in U.S. elementary and secondary schools? To answer this question as it is worded, one would need to define the population of interest as all elementary and secondary schools in the United States and to select a sample from that group.

A population may also be a group of persons such as students or teachers. Consider the following research question: What are the attitudes of "regular" classroom teachers in this state toward the teaching of ESOL? To answer this question the researcher would need to define the population as all "regular" teachers in the state. If she decided that it would not be feasible to survey the entire group, she could sample from that group or she might choose to reword the question to delimit the population to all "regular" teachers within several districts. In Penfield's (1987) survey she studied regular teachers attending certain in-service training sessions.

In addition to entities and persons, a population of interest may be a set of instances of language use, such as conversations or written texts (written assignments, oral narratives, conversational exchanges, journal entries) or speech acts (requests, apologies, compliments, suggestions). Consider, for example, this research question: What types of written texts do international students in U.S. graduate schools produce in response to assignments in university content courses? To answer this question the researcher might want to limit the population of written texts to those for certain subjects within one institution. She could then survey this entire population if it is feasible to do so, or she might draw a sample from this population.

Sampling

Sampling is a crucial methodological issue in survey research. Because it is usually not feasible to survey the entire group of interest (the population), researchers usually select a subgroup (a sample). The key principle to understand about sampling is that the way that the sample is selected affects the conclusions that can be drawn about the results. The sample selected for study must be similar to the population of interest in important ways if the results of the study are intended to apply to (be representative of) that population.

Let us imagine, for example, that you were interested in the attitudes toward L2 writing of a population you defined as all international undergraduate students in a particular U.S. university. For purposes of practicality and convenience, however, you decided to study only freshmen, and only those freshmen who were enrolled in two sections of a particular ESL composition course. You could not, then, draw conclusions about all "international undergraduate students" at the university. Rather, you could only draw conclusions about the students that you studied. Why is this so? Students in other classes might have very different characteristics and different attitudes.

Many studies employ samples of convenience or of volunteers. A *sample of convenience,* as in the example above, contains elements or persons selected because of their accessibility. A *volunteer sample* consists of persons who volunteer to participate in a study. These two types of samples are called *nonprobability samples.* An important question to ask when reading studies that use such samples is: How might the group in the sample differ from the population it is intended to represent? Because the sample group may differ in systematic and important ways from the population of interest, we could not "statistically infer" that the findings for the sample are similar to the findings for the population. We could, however, make judgments about how the results might generalize to the population. "Any generalization from a nonprobability sample to its population must be made on the basis of a reasoned comparison of the sample with the population. That is, the inference is judgmental rather than statistical" (Smith & Glass, 1987, p. 228).

The purpose of the research should determine sample selection procedures. If it is not the purpose of the researcher to generalize to a population, then it is not necessary to sample from a population. The results, then, apply only to the group studied, and inferences made based on the findings must be judgmental. This does not mean that a survey based on a convenience sample is not valuable. Its value often lies not so much in its quantitative generalizability but in identifying important issues or trends. It may also serve as a pilot study to prepare for a larger study.

The purpose of most surveys, however, is to draw conclusions about large numbers of entities or persons by studying a subset of them. Therefore, you should understand the basic procedures involved in sampling. You should know that there are long-established and carefully developed procedures for sampling (one good and readable source is Fowler, 1984). Researchers conducting surveys put careful thought into devising a sampling plan that will produce a sample that is adequately representative of the population to which they wish to apply their results. These sampling procedures should be explained in any reports of the research. Readers can then decide for themselves if the sample is adequately representative of the population.

The first step in sampling, after defining the population of interest, is to define a *sampling frame*. The sampling frame is a list of the set of people (or entities) in the population who actually have a chance of being selected. The next step is to select a sample that is *representative* of that sampling frame. There are several ways to select representative samples.

Probability sampling, as opposed to *nonprobability sampling* is called, involves selecting a sample so that we know the probability that each element has of being selected. *Simple random sampling,* for example, is one technique designed to ensure that the essential characteristics of the sample being studied are like those of the population from which the sample is drawn. Each element has the same chance of being selected.

Stratified sampling involves dividing the population into strata (levels) and selecting samples from within each level. Let us say, for example, that we wish to study an aspect of the L2 writing strategies of intermediate-level students of English. If we were to select a simple random sample, we might not include a sufficient number of students of different language backgrounds. Japanese students might use strategies that differ from those of Spanish-speaking students, for example. In addition, the strategies of low-intermediate students might differ from those at the high-intermediate level.

To obtain a sample that includes each category of students, we would include two strata (levels) of the proficiency variable (low-intermediate and high-intermediate) and three strata for the variable of language background (Japanese, Spanish, other). We would divide students into these six subgroups and then sample from within each subgroup. The proportion of students from each subgroup could be proportional to their numbers in the defined population (a proportional sample) or we could draw larger samples from certain groups. Stratified sampling ensures that there will be a sufficient number of students of each important type and thus allows us to make comparisons across types.[3]

Using probability sampling procedures, such as random and stratified sampling, allows researchers not only to make inferences to the population of interest but also to specify how precisely (accurately) the sample represents the population. We will see an illustration of these concepts when we turn to the sample study.

Methods of Collecting Survey Data

Another important step in designing a survey is deciding what means of collecting information will be most effective. The most prevalent data-collection methods are questionnaires, interviews, and direct observations of language use. In addition, many other types of information can be gathered including test results, compositions, or reactions to L2 oral or written-language data. Let us briefly review some key considerations in developing and using questionnaires, interviews, and direct observation for surveys.

Questionnaires. Perhaps the most common method of data collection in L2 survey research is the questionnaire. Questionnaires can range from short 5-item instruments, for example, to long documents that require one or two hours to complete. They can be designed to be administered by mail, in person, or by phone. Computer-assisted telephone interviewing (CATI) is a poor choice because people tend to hang up on the impersonal computer interviewer. Telecommunication systems, such as electronic mail, offer additional means of administering questionnaires. The major reason that questionnaires are widely used in survey research is that they require less time, and therefore less expense, than do interviews or observations.

Questionnaire construction is not nearly as simple as it may appear! For this reason it is often sensible to use good instruments or items that have been developed based on sound theory and carefully assessed in previous studies. Building on previous work not only helps improve the quality of instruments but allows researchers to relate the findings of similar studies to one another. For example, the program of social-psychological research on attitudes and motivations carried out by Clement (1987), Gardner (1989), and others uses question-naires that have evolved through many studies.

What makes a good questionnaire item? In addition to building on theory and previous research, the following principles provide some general guidelines. Items should be written in clear, nontechnical language that is easy to understand; items should not contain negative phrasing that is difficult to process (for example, "Which of these is not a disadvantage?"); and they should contain only one idea per item. For potentially confusing items, it is important to give the respondents an example that illustrates how they should answer the question. When reading reports of surveys, always look at the actual items that were used in the study. Generally authors include at least some items either in an appendix or in the body of the report.

Items in questionnaires can be *open-ended* in format, allowing respondents to reply in their own words, or *closed,* requiring the respondent to select one from among a limited number of responses. While closed question formats, such as multiple choice, are useful for obtaining quantitative information and are easier to analyze, open-ended questions can be useful for gathering qualitative information and for discovering new variables in responses. Open-ended questions are particularly useful in the early phases of questionnaire development because what is learned from these responses can be incorporated into closed items.

The discourse structure of questionnaires is important to consider as well. For example, some experts suggest moving from general questions to more specific questions. Branching is sometimes called for when certain items do not apply to a respondent (for example, "If you answered 'no' to question 10, skip to question 16").

While it may seem obvious that the respondent must be able to understand the language of the questionnaire, countless researchers have given students questionnaires and tested them in languages or varieties that were not fully comprehensible to the students. The results, then, are not valid because the instruments did not assess what they were intended to assess. The students' level of literacy must also be considered. If there are questions about a person's ability to read and understand a questionnaire, it can be given verbally.

The most crucial step in questionnaire development, one that should never be omitted, is careful pilot-testing. Questionnaires should be tried out with respondents who are similar to those who will respond in the study. It is inevitable that problems will be detected. Problem items should then be revised and pilot-tested again.

Interview Guides and Interviewing. Many of the principles of questionnaire development also apply to the development of instruments for use in interviews. We discussed a number of issues involved in interviewing in the chapter on case studies. Although interviews are very time-consuming for survey research, and therefore more expensive to use as a data-collection method, they have several clear advantages over mailed questionnaires. First, mailed questionnaires usually yield low response rates, while response rates from interviews can be quite high. The trade-off is that sample sizes for interviews must usually be smaller. Another advantage is that in an interview, respondents are more likely to answer all the questions presented because of their personal involvement with the interviewer. A third and very important advantage is that the interviewer can obtain more meaningful information because he or she can rephrase questions that are not clear to the respondent, probe for additional relevant information, and follow leads. When several interviews are conducted with the same respondent, the rapport that builds can lead to more meaningful information.

Observing and Collecting Language Data. Some of the L2 survey research focuses on language, both the target language that learners are acquiring and learner language. Observing naturally occurring oral language is not a widely used data-collection technique in L2 educational research because it is so time-consuming. More commonly, surveys involve collecting existing language data such as tests or student writing or eliciting data through written means.

Collecting language data is a basic procedure in quantitative sociolinguistic survey research, however. Data collection may involve eliciting language through interviews (see, for example, Poplack, 1989) that may be quite short or may include up to several hours of conversation. Collecting completely natural language samples is a common technique used in sociolinguistic research on speech act production (Holmes, 1988, p. 446; Wolfson, 1989, p. 110). In Holmes' (1988) study of complimenting in New Zealand, for example, data collectors recorded a sequence of about 20 compliment exchanges in the order they heard them without selection or censorship. They recorded the exact words used in the compliment exchange, both compliment and response, along with relevant details about the context, and the relative status of the interlocutors.

Discourse Completion Tests. Second language researchers interested in describing the sociolinguistic and pragmatic competence of language learners have used a procedure called the Discourse Completion Test (DCT) (Blum-Kulka, 1982; Blum-Kulka, House, & Kasper, 1989; Blum-Kulka & Levenston, 1987; Eisenstein & Bodman, 1986; Olshtain & Cohen, 1983; Wolfson, 1989). In this elicitation procedure students are given a written description of a situation and asked to respond either by role-playing or by writing down what they would say in such a situation.

For example, to elicit requests, the following situations have been presented (Blum-Kulka & Levenston, 1987):

- A student asks his roommate to clean up the kitchen, which the other left in a mess.
- A student asks a teacher for an extension for finishing a seminar paper.

To elicit an apology, the following situations have been used (Blum-Kulka & Levenston, 1987):

- A driver in a parking lot backs into a car.
- A student borrows her professor's book, which she promised to return that day, but she forgot to bring it.

The written instrument (the DCT) may consist of either scripted dialogues or descriptions of situations. Wolfson (1989) explains that "the dialogues are introduced by a brief description which gives the context in which the dialogue is supposed to occur and specifies the conditioning factors considered most relevant" (p. 143). However, one problem with this method is that what one would say depends on many situational factors such as role relationships (tenor), topic, or formality. Each respondent constructs the situation somewhat differently in his or her own mind. This technique can be used for a descriptive survey approach to research as well as for other approaches, such as case studies and experiments.

Testing Language Performance. A large-scale testing program can be considered a type of survey using testing as a method of data collection. The California Assessment Program (CAP), for example, through matrix sampling, has gathered data on students' (including ESL students) ability to write on several topics (Cooper & Breneman, 1989). The purpose of the testing program is to assess all students in the state of California by sampling a subset of them. Similarly, testing programs, such as the TOEFL, TWE, and SPEAK programs, survey the linguistic performance of thousands of students, although the purposes are for assessment, admission, or placement.

Data Analyses

In reading reports of survey research you may expect to find four types of data analysis.

Descriptive Analyses. First, descriptive analyses of the results of a survey are often reported in frequencies (the actual number responding in a certain way) and percentages. These *descriptive statistics* are numbers that summarize the data. For example, a result of a survey of L2 reading strategies might be reported in this way: "Only 30% of the low-intermediate-level students reported that they tried to guess words from context when reading in the L2."

Taking an authentic example, Duran, Enright, and Rock (1985, cited in Duran, 1987) surveyed over 700 self-identified Hispanic freshmen in four-year colleges to determine their language characteristics. They found that most of the students (about 70%) came from backgrounds where Spanish was spoken and 85% identified English as their most proficient language.

In addition to the use of frequencies and percentages, results of surveys can be reported as means (averages) and other measures of central tendency, and measures of variability (such as standard deviations).

Correlational Analyses. Descriptive results such as these are interesting in themselves and may be the only analyses presented. However, once key descriptive results are determined, researchers can further explore important questions by using correlational techniques to analyze relationships among variables.

For example, in their survey of Hispanic freshmen, Duran and colleagues (Duran, 1987) were interested not only in the students' basic language characteristics but also in the students' ratings of their own academic skills, their SAT scores, and the relationships between these variables. They developed a set of questions to examine students' perceptions of their ability to use English for academic purposes. They asked students to rate their academic English skills in all four modalities (writing, reading, oral understanding, speaking). The items asked students to rate (on a scale of 1 to 5) how well they could perform academic literacy tasks such as: "organize my writing to meet instructor's expectations," "understand vocabulary terms I read," and "understand classroom lectures." They found that responses to these questions were significantly associated with SAT verbal scores. This means that students who rated themselves as more proficient in these areas were those who scored higher on the standardized test. Duran (1987) suggests that these results illustrate the importance of self-knowledge of academic literacy skills. This example shows just one way that survey research may incorporate correlational analyses.

Analyses of Precision of Estimates and of Nonresponse. A third type of data analysis that you may expect to find in survey research is an analysis of the precision (accuracy) of the results. *Precision* refers to the accuracy with which the results from the study of the sample represent the results for the population. We will examine this issue in the context of the sample study. Finally, an additional type of analysis to look for in a survey, one that is rare in L2 studies, is an analysis of the possible detrimental effects of nonresponse. We will look at the issue of nonresponse briefly here and explore it further in the sample study later in the chapter.

Bias Due to Nonresponse

It is important in survey research to assess the degree to which nonrespondents introduce bias into the sample data. What does this mean? Suppose, for example, that you conducted a questionnaire survey of L2 speakers' subjective reactions to the use of politeness strategies. Let us imagine that you received responses from all of the women but from none of the men. You would then need to consider how the answers from the men might differ from those of the women. If you reported results based only on the women's responses, these results might be biased in certain ways. What could you do to determine if bias is a problem? You could make efforts to obtain responses from the males in your sample and examine how the responses of the men differed from those of the women.

In written reports of surveys, researchers should provide at least some information about those who do not respond so that readers can assess whether nonrespondents may have differed significantly from respondents. Authors should provide some evidence that the responses were not significantly biased due to nonresponse. Smith and Glass suggest that "when response rates are less than 90 percent even after follow-up, the researcher should perform nonresponse bias checks" (1987, p. 235). If it appears that response rates might be low, surveys would be more valid and useful if researchers reduced their sample size somewhat and put more energy into obtaining higher response rates.

CRITERIA FOR ANALYZING SURVEYS

When reading reports of survey research, you can assess the study using the questions listed below. Your answers to these questions will help you decide how to interpret the results, how much confidence you can have in the numerical results that are reported, and what can be learned from the research.

1. What is the research question?
2. In what context was the survey conducted?
3. How was the population defined?
4. What sampling procedures were used? How representative is the sample?
5. How were variables observed or measured?
6. What procedures were used to collect data?
7. What attempts were made to increase response rates? What response rates were achieved?
8. Was there nonresponse bias?
9. What analyses were performed?
10. What were the results and what conclusions are drawn? Are generalizations about the results appropriate?
11. What is the contribution of the study to our knowledge of social or contextual factors in L2 learning or teaching?
12. What are the stated implications?

SAMPLE SURVEY: EMPLOYMENT OF GRADUATES OF BILINGUAL EDUCATION PROGRAMS IN COLLEGES AND UNIVERSITIES

To illustrate how a survey is conducted, we will examine a national survey of graduates of bilingual programs in colleges and universities conducted for the U.S. Department of Education (Johnson, 1985). I have selected this study because, methodologically, it was a carefully designed survey with relatively good response rates. In addition, the study addresses an important question regarding the effects of federal efforts to improve the education of language-minority students through teacher preparation. The findings of the survey documented that a high percentage of program graduates were successful in finding jobs in which they served the target population—students limited in English proficiency. These graduates served students either directly through teaching or indirectly through leadership positions or teacher preparation.

1. What is the research question?

The objective of the survey was to obtain data on the employment of graduates of bachelor's, master's, and doctoral degree programs one to three years after completing their programs. The major question of interest was: What proportion of these graduates subsequently participate in the field of bilingual education and in what capacities? In addition, we were interested in a broad array of secondary questions about their work, such as: What subjects do the graduates teach? What languages do they use on the job? What kinds of students do the teachers serve?

2. In what context was the survey conducted?

Three types of contexts are relevant because each contributed to shaping the research. These include the policies of the federal government with regard to supporting the preparation of bilingual educators, the larger study of which this survey was a part, and the institutional context in which the study was conducted.

Policy Context for the Survey. There have been severe shortages of teachers qualified to address adequately the educational needs of limited-English-proficient students. As a result, significant amounts of federal education funds have been directed toward preparing bilingual education teachers and producing masters and doctoral graduates with expertise in bilingual education who could then prepare additional teachers. Specifically, Title VII of the Elementary and Secondary Education Act (ESEA) provided funds both for university programs and for student fellowships and stipends. The overall intent of the funds was to reduce the shortage of qualified professionals and to provide a more meaningful and higher-quality education to students who are not proficient in English.

The U.S. Department of Education funded this survey of graduates because the department was interested in determining to what extent the funds actually contributed to improving the education of students of limited English proficiency. The department wanted to know whether program graduates worked in the field of bilingual education after completing their programs. Such employment would represent one measure of the effectiveness of the Title VII program and would indicate that the money was having the intended effect. Thus the major research questions were determined by the government, while researchers posed many more specific questions.

Research Context. While the policy context determined the major research questions, the research context affected the survey design. This survey of graduates was part of a much larger study. The U.S. Department of Education funded a 30-month comprehensive study of bilingual education training programs in colleges and universities. The major purposes of this overall study were to (1) provide a description of programs, and (2) estimate the extent to which graduates of such programs contributed to the national supply of bilingual teachers.

In the first phase of the study, a nationally representative sample of 56 two- and four-year colleges and universities was selected for study. A team of two researchers visited each institution to collect descriptive information on the programs. The results of this portion of the study provide comprehensive descriptions of bilingual doctoral, master's, and bachelor's programs, addressing the following topics: program context, management and organizational structure, faculty, students, curricula, course content, and instruction.[4]

Two major studies were conducted in the second phase of the overall study to address the second objective: (1) the graduate survey (discussed here), and (2) a study of the need for and the supply of bilingual education teachers nationwide.[5] The latter was part of an ongoing series of federally funded studies that addressed the changing need for bilingual teachers.

The need to carry out the survey of graduates within the larger study of university programs affected the sampling plan, as we will see below.

Institutional Context. The study was conducted in a professional research firm rather than in a university setting. After a process of evaluating the merits of competing proposals, the Department of Education contracted with RMC Research Corporation, a private firm, to conduct the study. The research team consisted of 11 persons, with several members of the team working full-time for over two years on the project. The team included a statistician who worked with us on the technical aspects of sampling and data analysis as well as a consulting ethnographer who offered guidance on the qualitative aspects of data collection and analysis for the wider study. This setting for conducting research allows a great deal of continual interaction among researchers, which improves the quality of a study. The major audiences for the reports were, first, the sponsor, and second, researchers involved in similar work. Results were disseminated to the wider community primarily through conference presentations and later through journal articles.

3. How was the population defined?

In survey research, the population of interest is the group to which researchers want to generalize; that is, the group to which the results apply. In this study, our target population was the national pool of all graduates of bilingual bachelor's, credential, master's, post-master's, and doctoral programs during a three-year period.

4. What sampling procedures were used? How representative was the sample?

The sampling procedures used in this study were fairly complex but their logic is not difficult to understand. Because we wanted to generalize our findings to the population defined above, it was important to devise a sampling plan that would allow such generalization. We selected graduates in the second stage of a two-stage sampling plan.

The First-Stage Sample. First, for the overall study, we sampled 56 colleges and universities to examine their bilingual education programs. This was the "first-stage sample." This sample was representative of the national population of colleges and universities with bilingual education programs.[6]

The Second-Stage Sample. Within these colleges and universities, we asked directors of the bilingual education programs to provide lists of program graduates for each of three academic years: 1977–1978, 1978–1979, and 1979–1980. We divided these graduates into two groups: those who completed programs designed to train bilingual education teachers and those who completed programs designed to prepare bilingual education teacher trainers. These lists formed the sampling frame. We then sampled 809 teacher graduates for a mail survey and 168 trainer graduates for a phone survey. This was the "second-stage sample." Because the procedures for selecting a sample from the teacher group and from the trainer group differed, they are discussed separately below.

Sample of Teachers. We defined the teacher population as those students who completed a program leading to certification or endorsement and/or a degree in bilingual education at the bachelor's or master's level.

One way to select a sample would be to chose a random sample from the entire group. We felt, however, that graduates' answers to questions might differ depending on factors such as:

1. the language group they intended to serve (Spanish speakers vs. speakers of a language other than Spanish),
2. the year in which they graduated,
3. whether the state had bilingual education (BE) certification, or
4. the type of program from which they graduated (bachelor's program, master's program, BE certification-only program).

For example, it might have been easier to secure a position in bilingual education for those graduates with master's degrees, who knew Spanish, and who were in states that required bilingual education certification (see variables 1, 3, and 4 above).

Therefore, rather than selecting a random sample, we divided the pool of teacher graduates into subgroups according to these four variables (strata) and used what is called a *stratified sampling design*. This means that we created a sampling matrix (a grid) of 36 cells (2 × 3 × 2 × 3) and selected a sample of teachers from each cell.[7] Selecting teachers from each of these subgroups assured that there would be sufficient numbers from each group to draw conclusions about that group.

How large should a sample be? The size of a sample depends primarily on two concerns: (1) financial resources and time available for the study, and (2) the level of precision (accuracy) desired in deriving population estimates. The larger the sample, the more accurate the results can be; but surveying large samples is expensive and time-consuming.[8]

In consultation with our statistician, we determined the level of precision desired and the sample size that would be needed to reach that level of precision. We decided that to be able to make accurate estimates of the national population we needed to sample 809 (75%) of the graduates we had identified from lists. This sample represented about 13% of the 6,462 bilingual education teachers who graduated nationwide in the three-year period.

Here I explain the level of precision (accuracy) that is obtained with a sample of this size:

> The sample drawn was large enough so that, in general, one can be 95 percent confident that if 50 percent of the sample has a certain characteristic, the true percentage of the population having that characteristic lies between 40 and 60. (Johnson, 1985, p. 61)

In conclusion, this level of precision indicates that the sample size is large enough to be adequately representative of the population of bilingual teacher graduates.

Sample of Teacher Trainers. We classified graduates as "trainers" if they had graduated from a doctoral program or from a post-master's program. We also classified those master's program graduates who had received a Title VII fellowship as trainers because the intent of the federal fellowship was to prepare teacher trainers.

Of the 226 trainer graduates from the 56 colleges and universities, program directors were able to provide names and addresses for only 168 (74%). Because the number from which to sample was small, we surveyed all 168 trainer graduates. This number represents 33% of the national population (Johnson, 1985, p. 62).

5. How were variables observed or measured?

The measurement instruments that the research staff used to gather data on the variables of interest were questionnaires administered both by mail and through telephone interviews. For teacher graduates, we developed a 16-page question-naire consisting of 44 questions. For trainer graduates, we developed a 22-page, 42-item questionnaire that we administered in telephone interviews.

Questionnaire Construction. Questionnaire construction involved a number of steps: reviewing relevant literature and previous related research; submitting the instruments to an advisory panel of experts for review; pilot-testing them with actual bilingual program graduates; and carefully revising them. Finally, the forms had to be approved ("cleared") by an agency of the federal government that attempts to reduce the response burden of federal studies.

Content. The major topics addressed in the questionnaires included: field of employment, type of job, subjects taught, language use on the job, language(s) spoken by students, and salary. Many other related topics were included as well. In addition, the questionnaires included items that would allow us to construct a general profile of survey respondents, including questions about their self-rated language proficiency, and optional questions regarding age, ethnicity, and gender.

Branching. A questionnaire of this type requires a complex and carefully planned branching structure. For example, we asked graduates who were not employed a series of questions about the reasons for their lack of employment and about their plans. Similarly, we asked graduates who were employed within a "BE-related field" a set of questions that differed from those we asked of graduates employed in a "non-BE-related field." Careful pilot-testing is crucial to be sure that the branching structure functions as planned.

6. What procedures were used to collect data?

We surveyed teachers by mail and teacher trainers by phone. Teacher graduates received a copy of the questionnaire, a letter from RMC Research Corporation describing the purpose of the survey and requesting their participation, a supporting letter from the director of the federal bilingual education office, and a self-addressed stamped envelope for return of the completed questionnaire.

Trainer graduates received similar letters, advising that within the next few weeks they would be telephoned for a brief interview by a member of the research staff. In addition, trainer graduates received a stamped postcard asking them to confirm or supply their current telephone number. Careful training and continuous communication among telephone interviewers to resolve any problems were important parts of the data-collection process. To assure anonymity, we did not use graduates' names; rather, each individual was identified by a unique six-digit code.

7. What attempts were made to increase response rates? What response rates were achieved?

In this study a great deal of emphasis was placed on obtaining acceptable response rates so that results would adequately represent the defined national population. Our research team used a five-wave procedure to obtain high response rates:

> To achieve the highest possible response rates, five attempts were made to obtain responses from teacher graduates. . . . After the initial questionnaire was mailed to teacher graduates, a second set, or wave, of questionnaires was sent to those who did not respond to the first wave. For the third and fourth waves, the teacher questionnaire was reduced to 10 questions to increase the response rate. (Johnson, 1985, p.63)

Even after these four attempts, the response rates had not reached acceptable levels:

> After four waves, the response rate was 64 percent for those teachers in the sample preparing to work with Spanish-speaking pupils and 75 percent for the teachers preparing to work with speakers of a language other than Spanish. . . . After two attempts to locate trainers, a 67 percent response rate was achieved. (p. 63)

It was then necessary to take additional measures to raise the response rates:

> To increase response rates for both teachers and trainers, a special telephone follow-up of nonrespondents was undertaken. Of a total of 328 teacher and

trainer nonrespondents, 228 (182 teachers and 46 trainers) were randomly selected for follow-up. . . . These telephone interviews provided responses from an additional 78 teachers and 14 trainers, bringing the final response rate up to 76 percent for both teachers and trainers. (pp. 63–64)

What response rate is considered adequate? There is no agreed-upon standard for a minimum acceptable response rate, because what is acceptable depends on a number of factors. Fowler (1984) suggests 75% as a rule of thumb, but even with a 75% response rate, it is important to consider whether nonresponse bias is a serious problem. Let us now turn to this issue.

8. Was there nonresponse bias?

A common flaw in survey research, particularly in L2 and foreign language survey research, is to ignore sources of error other than sampling. As we saw above, nonresponse can be a major source of error if those who do not respond differ in important ways from those who do. For example, those BE teacher graduates who held positions as BE teachers might have been more likely to respond and to respond immediately than those graduates who were unable to find employment. For this reason, it is important to achieve high response rates and to compare the responses of those who respond immediately to the responses of those who respond later or only after follow-up measures are implemented.

In this study, questionnaires were coded by wave so that we could analyze bias according to wave. The procedure and the results of the analysis were explained in this way in the formal report:

Bias due to response wave and nonresponse was studied by comparing those who responded to the initial mailing (the first wave), those who responded to subsequent waves (2, 3, and 4), and those contacted in the follow-up study of nonrespondents (wave 5). Teacher data were analyzed for bias across the five waves by comparing responses on key questions. There was little or no bias among waves 1, 2, 3, and 5. While wave 4 was significantly biased ($p < .05$) toward fewer teachers in the field of BE, the magnitude of the bias and the number of cases were small. The results indicated that the sample was not likely to be biased due to nonresponse. Therefore, subsequent analyses were run with all waves combined. (Johnson, 1985, p. 64)

Our study of response bias, then, allowed us to conclude that the results were not likely to be biased due to nonresponse.

9. What analyses were performed?

The analyses of data in our study included not only the assessment of response bias described above but also the analysis of the survey respondents' answers to questions. We performed separate analyses for teacher data and trainer data. We analyzed data primarily by calculating frequencies and means and by comparing these among groups. For example, data were compared for program type, year of graduation, state certification status, and language group.

10. What were the results and what conclusions are drawn? Are generalizations about the results appropriate?

While there are many more results than can be discussed here, the primary purpose of the survey was to determine the graduates' employment status. We will, therefore, discuss results for employment, as well as for language teaching and use, and some characteristics of the graduates.

Teachers' Employment. We found that 77% of the teacher graduates were working with limited-English-proficient (LEP) students, either directly in bilingual education programs or in other kinds of programs designed to serve LEP students. Eighty-two percent were employed in some type of teaching position. This second result compares very favorably with data from other researchers (Metz & Crane, 1980; Graybeal, 1981) who reported that only about 55% of the general population of teacher graduates obtained teaching positions within a year of graduation.

The vast majority of teachers in BE-related positions worked with Spanish-speaking students (94% of the teachers). Of other language groups, relatively large percentages of teachers worked with speakers of Vietnamese (12% of the teachers) and Cantonese (9% of the teachers).

To explain why some graduates were not employed, we had included a branch of questions regarding reasons for lack of employment. The most common reason given was that there was "no opening." This reason was selected by 37% of the respondents to this question.

Teacher Trainers' Employment. Of the graduates prepared to train teachers, 83% had obtained positions that involved serving LEP students, and 77% of these were in either training or other leadership positions. Interestingly, none of the graduates in the sample had obtained a position as a researcher or evaluator.

Teaching English. Another finding of interest was that 70% of teacher graduates working in a BE-related field taught ESL. For 48% of the elementary teachers and 58% of the secondary teachers, the teaching of ESL was a "primary responsibility" of their jobs.

Language Use on the Job. We found that graduates did not use the native language of their students as much as they used English. Opponents of bilingual education have been concerned that not enough English is used in the programs. Yet only 12% of BE teacher graduates employed in a BE-related field reported using a language other than English for more than 60% of the workday. This finding is consistent with data from other studies (Halcon, 1983; Tikunoff, 1983) that have demonstrated that English has often been used substantially more than the native language of the LEP pupils in bilingual classrooms.

Gender and Trends in Ethnicity. Responses to questions on gender and ethnicity allowed us to examine the characteristics of graduates. By including graduates from three successive years, we were able to detect trends in the data. A disturbing trend was a decrease in Hispanic students.

> The overwhelming majority of the graduates were female—80 percent of the teachers and 78 percent of the trainers. For all three years combined, 60 percent of the teacher graduates and 61 percent of the trainer graduates were Hispanic, while 31 percent of the teacher graduates and 29 percent of the trainer graduates were white, non-Hispanic. It is interesting to note that over the three-year period the percentage of white, non-Hispanic teacher graduates increased slightly (26 to 31 to 36) while the percentage of Hispanics decreased (69 to 61 to 51 percent). (Johnson, 1985, p. 64)

We found important differences in salaries according to gender. For example, the salaries of male doctoral graduates were substantially higher than those of female doctoral graduates. We could not draw conclusions about the reasons for this discrepancy; this was not a major research question, and we had not gathered the relevant information.

11. & 12. What is the contribution of the study to our knowledge of social or contextual factors in L2 learning or teaching? What are the stated implications?

The nature of federal policies and the effects of those policies and associated funding on institutions, on teachers, and ultimately on students are important topics of research for those interested in language learning and dual language instruction (Lessow-Hurley, 1990). This survey of graduates, and the larger study of college and university programs of which it was a part, contributes to our knowledge of how policy, an important contextual factor, impinges on various aspects of schooling in bilingual settings. The preservice preparation of teachers in colleges and universities and their subsequent activities in their jobs clearly affect students' learning experiences.

This survey established that large percentages of teacher graduates of Title VII-funded programs were successful in securing jobs in which they served students who were learning English as an additional language. Similarly, large percentages of "trainer" graduates were found to be serving the intended population. These results indicated that federal funding was having the impact that policymakers had intended.

The survey data, when interpreted in light of data collected in the broader study, also provided information about a lack of congruity between two contexts—the content of teacher preparation courses and the nature of the teacher graduates' work with students. I explain this incongruity and a resulting implication as follows:

> While 70 percent of the BE teacher graduates reported that they taught ESL and about half considered the teaching of ESL to be one of their primary duties, data from the first phase of the study revealed that only about 61 percent of the bachelor's programs required a course in teaching a second language. Many of the courses that were offered placed primary emphasis on methods designed for teaching adults rather than children. Because 82 percent of BE bachelor's graduates and 70 percent of master's graduates secured positions as elementary teachers, it would appear desirable to revamp many ESL methods courses to address the needs of children. (Johnson, 1985, p. 75)

These results provide one example of how problems in the course content of university programs can ultimately impact K–12 students.

CONCLUSION

Well-conducted surveys have a number of advantages. The main advantages is their breadth. That is, when they involve large samples they can be very useful for providing a broad view of issues. For example, the much publicized demographic data of the 1980s was influential in promoting interest, among the general population of educators, in issues of cultural diversity, second language learning, and bilingualism. Surveys, then, can be particularly useful for capturing the essence of trends and are useful for planning. Similarly, sociolinguistic surveys add to our knowledge of language variation and language use in society.

Even though surveys may address important questions and be methodologically sound, they have a number of limitations. First, surveys are not intended to yield conclusions about cause-and-effect relationships, as are experiments. Second, as with any research, no survey is value-free or theory-free. This means that it is crucial to assess what might have motivated the study, how results are used, and how the way questions are worded might shape answers. Third, quantitative surveys are generally not useful for illuminating processes in L2 development, as case studies can be. Finally, by sacrificing depth and thoroughness for breadth and representativeness, surveys usually cannot provide a rich picture of the complex and interacting social, cultural, linguistic, and cognitive factors that are important in language learning and teaching situations. Ethnographic approaches are more valuable for these purposes, as we see next.

NOTES

1. It should be noted that, while this is the prototype definition of survey research, there are variations. For example, a survey might contain one question asked of a large number of respondents, such as a census question. In addition, survey research may overlap with case-study research. That is, survey *methods* could be used to gather data on a single entity that is the *focus* of a case study. Consider this example. In a case study of a school, a researcher might decide to survey the entire teaching staff (i.e., the entire population of teachers) using a written questionnaire. In addition, the researcher might survey a sample of teachers through interviews. Data gathered through various methods, including the surveys, would be used to address questions asked about the case.

2. While Wolfson (1989) and Holmes (1988) describe the data-collection technique as "ethnographic," the study is closer to a survey using nonprobability sampling procedures and collecting naturalistic data. An ethnography is a contextually rich description of a cultural setting and/or events.

3. Systematic sampling procedures are used in quantitative sociolinguistic research. Poplack (1989), for example, describes in detail the procedures used to select a sample for a sociolinguistic study of language-contact phenomena, particularly the effects of English on French, in five neighborhoods in the Ottawa-Hull area in Canada. This data base is "far larger than other corpora of spoken French . . ." (p. 429).

4. The results of this portion of the study are reported in Binkley, Johnson, Stewart, Abrica-Carrasco, Nava, and Thrope, 1981; Johnson, 1987; Johnson & Binkley, 1987.

5. Results of the second phase are reported in Kaskowitz, Binkley, and Johnson, 1981; and Johnson, 1985.

6. A detailed description of the sampling methodology and sample representativeness is provided in Binkley and others, 1981, Vol. I.

7. Some cells were empty because of the nature of the relationship among stratification variables. For example, there can be no graduates of BE certification programs in states without BE certification.

8. Sampling error is greatest at 50% and decreases as the percentage of the sample having a certain characteristic approaches zero or 100% (Fowler, 1984).

REFERENCES

Binkley, J. L., Johnson, D. M., Stewart, B. L., Abrica-Carrasco, R., Nava, H. G., & Thrope, B. (1981). *A study of teacher training programs in bilingual education. Volume I: Program descriptions.* RMC Report No. UR-474. Mountain View, CA: RMC Research Corporation.

Blum-Kulka, S. (1982). Learning how to say what you mean in a second language: A study of the speech act performance of learners of Hebrew as a second language. *Applied Linguistics, 3,* 29–59.

Blum-Kulka, S., House, J., & Kasper, G. (1989). *Cross-cultural pragmatics: Requests and apologies.* Norwood, NJ: Ablex.

Blum-Kulka, S., & Levenston, E. A. (1987). Lexical-grammatical pragmatic indicators. *Studies in Second Language Acquisition, 9,* 155–170.

Clement, R. (1987). Second language proficiency and acculturation: An investigation of the effects of language status and individual characteristics. *Journal of Language and Social Psychology, 5,* 271–290.

Cooper, C., & Breneman, B. (1989, Fall). California's new writing assessment. *The Quarterly of the National Writing Project and the Center for the Study of Writing, 11,*(4), 9–14, 22.

Duran, R. P. (1987). Factors affecting development of second language literacy. In S. R. Goldman & H. T. Trueba (Eds.), *Becoming literate in English as second language* (pp. 33–55). Norwood, NJ: Ablex.

Eisenstein, M., & Bodman, J. (1986). "I very appreciate": Expressions of gratitude by native and non-native speakers of American English. *Applied Linguistics, 7,* 167–185.

Fowler, J. J. (1984). *Survey research methods.* Beverly Hills, CA: Sage.

Gardner, R. C. (1989). Attitudes and motivation. In R. B. Kaplan (Ed.), *Annual Review of Applied Linguistics* (Vol. 9, 1988) (pp. 135–148). Cambridge: Cambridge University Press.

Graybeal, W. S. (1981). *Teacher supply and demand in public schools 1980–1981.* NEA Research Memo. Washington, D.C.: National Education Association.

Halcon, J. J. (1983) A structural profile of basic Title VII (Spanish-English bilingual bicultural education programs. *NABE Journal 7,* 55–73.

Harvey, T. E. (1987). Second-language composition instruction, computers and first-language pedagogy: A descriptive survey. *Foreign Language Annals, 20,* 171–175.

Holmes, H. (1988). Paying compliments: A sex-preferential politeness strategy. *Journal of Pragmatics, 12,* 445–465.

Johnson, D. M. (1985). Results of a national survey of graduates of bilingual education programs. *TESOL Quarterly, 19,* 59–77.

Johnson, D. M. (1987). Linguistics and applied linguistics curricula in graduate programs in bilingual education. *Hispania, 70,* 900–907.

Johnson, D. M., & Binkley, J. L. (1987). Management and organizational structure in university bilingual education programs: A national survey of title VII. *NABE Journal, 11,* 95–115.

Kaskowitz, D. H., Binkley, J. L., & Johnson, D. M. (1981). *A study of teacher training programs in bilingual education: Volume II: The supply of and demand for bilingual education teachers.* RMC Report No. UR-487. Mountain View, CA: RMC Research Corporation.

Lessow-Hurley, J. (1990). *The foundations of dual language instruction.* White Plains, NY: Longman.

Manes, J., & Wolfson, N. (1981). The compliment formula. In F. Coulmas (Ed.), *Conversational routine* (pp. 115–132). The Hague: Mouton.

Metz, A. S., & Crane, J. L. (1980). *New teachers in the job market.* Washington, D.C.: National Center for Education Statistics.

Olsen, R. E. W-B. (1989). A survey of limited English proficient student enrollments and identification criteria. *TESOL Quarterly, 23,* 469–488.

Olshtain, E., & Cohen, A. (1983). Apology: A speech act set. In N. Wolfson & E. Judd (Eds.), *Sociolinguistics and language acquisition* (pp. 18–35). Rowley, MA: Newbury House.

Penfield, J. (1987). ESL: The regular classroom teachers's perspective. *TESOL Quarterly, 21*, 21–39.

Poplack, S. (1989). The care and handling of a mega-corpus: The Ottawa-Hull French Project. In R. W. Fasold & D. Schiffrin (Eds.), *Language change and variation* (pp. 411–444). Amsterdam/Philadelphia: John Benjamins.

Rhodes, N. C., & Oxford, R. L. (1988). Foreign languages in elementary and secondary schools: Results of a national survey. *Foreign Language Annals, 21*, 51–69.

Rigg, P., & Allen, V. (Eds.). (1989). *When they don't all speak English: Integrating the ESL student into the regular classroom.* Urbana, IL: National Council of Teachers of English.

Santos, T. (1988). Professors' reactions to the academic writing of nonnative-speaking students. *TESOL Quarterly, 22*, 69–90.

Smith, M. L., & Glass, G. V. (1987). *Research and evaluation in education and the social sciences.* Englewood Cliffs, NJ: Prentice-Hall.

Tikunoff, W. (1983). *Significant bilingual instructional features study.* San Francisco: Far West Laboratory.

Waggoner, D. (1988). Language minorities in the United States in the 1980's: The evidence from the 1980 census. In S. L. McKay & S. C. Wong (Eds.), *Language diversity: Problem or resource* (pp. 69–108). New York: Harper & Row/Newbury House.

Wolfson, N. (1989). *Perspectives: Sociolinguistics and TESOL.* New York: Harper & Row/Newbury House.

CHAPTER 6

Ethnographic Research

What sociocultural knowledge do students from diverse linguistic and cultural backgrounds need in order to understand and benefit from instruction in school? How do patterns of classroom interaction and communication differ across cultures? How do these differences relate to language learning? What is the hidden curriculum in L2 adult literacy classes? These are questions that researchers using ethnographic approaches might ask.

In this chapter we will address ethnographic research, specifically ethnographically oriented research that is relevant to the learning of additional languages and cultures in formal institutional settings. After introducing characteristics of ethnographic research, we will review several studies and their findings. We will then discuss issues in methodology. Finally we will use a set of guidelines to examine an ethnographic account of the cultural adjustment of Asian Indian immigrants to a rural U.S. community and school.

WHAT IS ETHNOGRAPHY?

Because ethnographic approaches have gained wider acceptance in research in second language acquisition and teaching, there has been a great deal of discussion about what constitutes "real ethnography." The views of ethnography discussed in this chapter are drawn from work by scholars such as Agar (1980), Goetz & LeCompte (1984), Gumperz (1986), Heath (1982a), Hymes (1982), Jacob (1987), Rosaldo (1989), Saville-Troike (1989), Spindler and Spindler (1987), Spradley (1980), Watson-Gegeo (1988), and Wolcott (1988). There are two general focuses of ethnographic study that are particularly relevant to the field of second language acquisition and teaching. These are educationally oriented ethnography (Spindler & Spindler, 1987; Wolcott, 1987) and the ethnography of communication (Heath, 1983; Hymes, 1972; Saville-Troike; 1989).

The Ethnography of Schooling

Spindler, an anthropologist specializing in the ethnography of schooling, has defined *educational ethnography* as "the study of any or all educational processes, whether related to a 'school' or not" (1982, p. 2). He has defined *the ethnography of schooling* as the study of "educational and enculturative processes that are related to schools and intentional schooling," including aspects of school-related life such as peer groups (1982, p. 2). Because this research tradition informs us about both enculturation and acculturation processes, it is important for gaining a fuller understanding of all that is involved in learning an additional language and culture. It is also important in understanding ways to make educational experiences more culturally sensitive and appropriate.

The Ethnography of Communication

The *ethnography of communication* combines anthropological and sociolinguistic perspectives to address the study of communicative behavior as it functions in the context of culture (Saville-Troike, 1989). Work in this field centers on what a speaker needs to know to communicate appropriately in a speech community and on how such knowledge is learned and used. By extension, it might inform us about what a writer needs to know to communicate appropriately and effectively in a discourse community. Analyses focus on the system of communicative events in a speech community and how social meaning is conveyed through these events. The products of such studies include ethnographic descriptions of how communication functions in diverse communities (Heath, 1983; Saville-Troike, 1989). As Saville-Troike (1989) stresses, ethnographers of communication base their work on the assumption that language must be viewed as a social phenomenon:

> The ethnography of communication takes language first and foremost as a socially situated cultural form, while recognizing the necessity to analyze the code itself and the cognitive process of its speakers and hearers. To accept a lesser scope for linguistic description is to risk reducing it to triviality, and to deny any possibility of understanding how language lives in the minds and on the tongues of its users. (p. 3)

This field, initiated by Hymes, is important for second language studies because it not only defines what it is that learners must learn as they are socialized into a new language and culture, but it also provides a way of relating second language acquisition (which can be viewed as L2 socialization) to acculturation.

The purpose of ethnographic research is to describe and interpret the cultural behavior, including communicative behavior, of a group. Ethnographic research may have many characteristics in common with nonethnographic case-study research, but the crucial differences lie in (1) the anthropological grounding and cultural emphasis in ethnographic work and in (2) the group focus. The ethnographer studies the cultural system of a group and provides a rich description and cultural interpretation of communicative and other behavior, attitudes, and values. Ethnographies, like case studies, may focus on particular cases or on a limited cultural setting, such as a classroom or a school. For a case study, the bounded system includes contexts that are relevant to the research questions, but not necessarily cultural contexts. However, for an ethnography, cultural context is crucial. For some researchers, cultural context may be defined as the school or "classroom culture," while for others, cultural context must extend into the home, community, and wider society. The other key difference lies in the ethnographer's focus on the cultural group rather than on the individual. While the goal of a case study may be to describe differences in the L2 writing development of two individuals (as in the Hudelson sample study in Chapter 4), the goal of an ethnographic study is cultural explanation. The shared values and behaviors of the group are of interest rather than differences in individuals due to factors such as personality, ability, or cognitive style.

Cultural anthropology is the mother discipline of ethnography (Heath, 1982a), although sociologists have made important contributions as well. Ethnography is considered the field arm of anthropology (Spindler, 1982, p. 2). Data-collection procedures, termed "fieldwork" by anthropologists, include watching and asking (observing and interviewing). Most often the ethnographer is a participant observer, an outsider who stays on the scene, perhaps as much as a year or more, to learn about the group. This might mean studying a far-off village somewhere or a different culture right at home. Unlike experimental research in which researchers manipulate conditions, ethnographers study phenomena in their natural state and as unobtrusively as possible. Ethnographers themselves are the major data-collection instruments. That is, they rely more on themselves than on tests and questionnaires, if these are used at all. Unlike survey and experimental researchers who specify research questions in advance, ethnographers develop and refine their questions as they learn in the field.

In summary, although other approaches to research may involve similar field techiniques, many visits or long stays at the research site, and good descriptive accounts, they are not ethnographies unless they involve holistic study of cultural phenomena and cultural interpretation of behavior. Interestingly, many respected ethnographers are very cautious and selective about applying the terms "ethnographic" and "ethnography" to their own studies.

With this brief introduction to ethnographic approaches to research, let us look next at some ethnographic studies to see the types of questions that are asked, the sociocultural contexts that are studied, and the cultural interpretation offered.

USES OF ETHNOGRAPHIES

Among the most important uses of ethnographic research for L2 learning has been to inform us about the ways that students' cultural experiences in home and community compare with the culture of the schools, universities, and communities where they study, and the implications of these differences for second language and culture learning. This kind of information helps explain how cultural assumptions and values can shape interactions, can cause cross-cultural miscommunication, and can lead to differing attitudes toward the learning situation and differing approaches to learning.

Much of the ethnographic work has focused on younger language learners. Unfortunately, there is surprisingly little ethnographic work on the language learning and cultural adjustment of adolescents and adults relative to the many experimental and correlational studies. We have much yet to gain by employing ethnographic approaches to understanding second and foreign language learners in high schools, colleges, and varied adult educational and workplace settings.

Cultural Discontinuities for Native Americans

There is a growing body of cultural descriptions of home–school discontinuities that Native American children in the U.S. experience (Philips, 1972, 1983; Mohatt & Erickson, 1981). A study by Macias (1987) adds to this body of work. He describes some of the discontinuities experienced by Tohono O'odham (formerly Papago) children as they entered preschool. New school experiences for them included an emphasis on individual verbal performance in front of an audience, teacher-controlled rather than autonomous activities, and strange foods and games. In his report, the author details how Tohono O'odham teachers in the Papago Early Childhood/Head Start Program successfully mitigated these discontinuities to ease the Indian children's transition from home to school in culturally sensitive ways.

Contrasting Acculturation Patterns

The research of Ochs and Schieffelin (Ochs & Schieffelin, 1984; Schieffelin & Ochs, 1986) and others has illustrated ways that language socialization differs across cultures and how socialization patterns are linked to cultural values, attitudes, and beliefs. This work is important because socialization at home relates to L2 development in school settings.

Willett (1987) conducted an interesting ethnographic study of two young children who had just arrived in the United States and were acquiring English in a preschool. The girls, both children of graduate students, were Jeni, from Korea, and Alisia, from Brazil. Willett studied the girls as a participant observer in her own daughter's nursery school. She spent five months observing every day for 30 minutes and participated for about four hours each week for four months. She also gathered data through interviews with the girls' parents and teachers. Willett was interested in the girls' interaction patterns in the preschool, how the patterns might have been culturally shaped, and how they may have affected both the learning strategies that the children used and what they learned of English.

She found that the two girls approached social participation, second language use, and learning in very different ways, which reflected their respective cultural values. Jeni, the Korean, began speaking English soon. She sought out interactions with adults and was able to nominate topics with them, elicit talk, and manipulate their speech. She tended to ignore her peers, however, and did not join their spontaneous activities. Jeni's pronunciation was poor, compared to Alisia's, and she made little use of formulaic phrases. On the other hand, Jeni made rapid progress in semantic and syntactic development relying heavily on a "one-word-at-a-time approach."

The Brazilian girl, Alisia, unlike Jeni, was initially devastated to discover that she was not socially competent with her peers. She did not talk for about three months, but was busy observing the interactional patterns of the children and joining in nonverbally. When she did begin to use English (starting with a highly appropriate "Please pass the bananas") her pronunciation and intonation were native-like and she used a variety of formulaic chunks appropriately. She was not a risk-taker, but careful to be sure that she knew a phrase well before using it. This strategy allowed her to interact effectively with peers.

Willett concluded that the girls' interaction styles reflected the respective values of their sociocultural environments at home. One of the major contrasts she drew was between the emphasis on peer sociability in the Brazilian family and on Confucian values and one-on-one learning interactions with adults in Korean culture. She suggests that Jeni's superior syntactic development may have resulted from her adult interactions, while Alisia's appropriate use of formulaic routines and her excellent pronunciation may have resulted from her peer interactions.

The importance of Willett's study is that it extends language socialization work into second language acquisition in school settings. It illustrates how culturally shaped language socialization patterns from home can affect both how children interact in the L2 and what they learn.

Literate Behaviors at Home

Vasquez (1988) conducted an ethnographic study of literate behaviors in Mexican American families. Building on work by S. B. Heath and J. Langer, Vasquez distinguishes literate behaviors from literate skills. Rather than indicating the ability to separate and manipulate discrete elements of a text (such as vocabulary, grammar, or topic sentences), literate behaviors are defined as the ability to talk about the meaning of a printed text, to discuss, interpret, analyze, and create extended language. Literate behaviors are print-inspired but separable from the printed text. Vasquez (1988) was interested in how these oral abilities were used in the homes of four Mexican immigrant children. She further defined literate behaviors, for her study, as "oral strategies that demonstrate the ability to talk about the meaning of an oral text" (p. 2). She found four patterns of oral literate behaviors in homes: (1) a retelling, which may be a retelling of a *cuento* (a family story, folklore), of something the speaker heard, or of a personal experience; (2) an extension, which is an extended stretch of discourse prompted by an oral or visual form of a text such as a symbol, a word, or a picture; (3) a reconstruction, which is constructed by family members as they interpret the meaning of an oral text (such as a medical prescription) or as they interpret the meaning of a written text (such as an amnesty application); and (4) comparisons, which consist of comments about attitudes, preferences, or social conditions in relation to some immediate issue.

Analyzing the contextual features of the four patterns, Vasquez found fluid and variable participation patterns and no particular restraints on children's participation. She concluded that these oral language activities were cooperative, collaborative, and egalitarian.

One value of this type of research is that it illuminates the ways children of a particular cultural group interpret and construct meaning, abilities that are valued in academic settings. Knowledge about how literate behaviors are used and developed in the homes of different cultural groups (we might call this "language and literacy socialization") can inform educators so that they can better build on their students' intellectual strengths.

Bilingual Education and Quechua Language Maintenance

In addition to studying learners, classrooms, and families, researchers have used ethnographic methodologies to examine bilingual education programs in their sociocultural contexts. Scholars have long recommended that the sociolinguistic situation of the community should be a crucial factor in the design of bilingual and multilingual education programs.

Hornberger (1987a, 1987b) illustrates the importance of this notion in her study of a bilingual education project in Peru. The study is multidisciplinary, drawing on theoretical notions from cultural anthropology, the sociology of language, educational policy, bilingual education, and language planning (Ruiz, 1984). Through a two-year ethnographic and sociolinguistic study, Hornberger investigated relationships between bilingual education and Quechua language maintenance in highland Puno, Peru. Specifically, she studied how two Quechua communities in the area used and valued Spanish and Quechua both in their community life and in their schools. One of these communities was implementing a Spanish-Quechua bilingual program, while the other was providing Spanish-only schooling. Data were gathered over the two-year period through various kinds of both participant and quantitative observation and through interviews ranging from informal to formal.

One of the key findings was that the bilingual program in the school Hornberger studied was successful in terms of increased student participation in learning, improved teaching techniques, and positive classroom relations. The national bilingual education project as a whole, however, failed for a number of reasons, including problems of teacher transfer, resistance to the use of Quechua for schooling, and inconsistencies between the orientations of official national language policies and those of the bilingual education project. Hornberger points out that the findings have relevance beyond the Peruvian context because they illustrate that the shape and fate of bilingual education programs in schools do not depend simply on pedagogical effectiveness, but also on political, social, and cultural factors.

Cultural and Occupational Adjustment of Vietnamese Adults

Each of the studies discussed up to this point has addressed the experiences of children. The vast majority of the L2 research on older learners is descriptive, correlational, or experimental. Yet relationships between the cultural adjustment of adults and language learning are important both for developing richer theories of second language acquisition and for improving teaching. This topic merits much more attention than it has received. Let us examine an ethnographic study of the cultural adjustment of Vietnamese adults, even though it does not link cultural adjustment to language learning, as the Willette study does.

Finnan (1987), a cultural anthropologist, conducted a study of Vietnamese refugees. She was interested in examining the role of the ethnic community in contributing to the adults' development of an occupational identity in the U.S. context, specifically in the Santa Clara Valley in the late 1970s when the electronics industry was in a boom period.

As a nonstudent participant observer, Finnan attended a six-month job training program designed to prepare electronics technicians, and conducted interviews with Vietnamese adults. She concluded that not only did the Vietnamese adults mold their new sense of self to fit the role of electronics technician, but they formed an image of the job that was consistent with their self-image. Even though most were highly educated and overqualified for technician-level jobs, they viewed the requirements of the job as appropriate for their level of English proficiency. But because they also viewed themselves as educated, hard-working, ambitious, and diligent, they considered the job an effective way to enter the electronics industry and to gradually advance to higher levels. The Vietnamese students remained excited about becoming electronics technicians in spite of instruction that was poor and not sufficiently challenging. She also found that men trained for the technician jobs while many of the women trained for lower-level assembly positions.

Finnan concluded that the Vietnamese community played a powerful role in channeling its members into this type of job by providing supports and by projecting a positive image of the job as challenging, clean, skilled, middle class, and full of potential. The influence of the ethnic community on the development of an occupational identity seemed to be greater than other influences such as personality or aptitude in occupational decision making. (See Tollefson, 1989, for a review of other types of research related to the resettlement of Southeast Asian refugees in the United States.)

The few studies reviewed here provide an indication of the types of questions that ethnographers address, the contexts they attend to, and the kinds of conclusions they draw based on cultural interpretation. We will now turn to research methodology.

DOING ETHNOGRAPHIC RESEARCH

In this section we will review some of the key issues involved in conducting ethnographic research. An understanding of these issues will help you define the nature of ethnographic research and better understand reports of such research. As there is controversy about what counts as ethnography or ethnographic (van Lier, 1988), we will address characteristics on which there is some consensus, centering our discussion around some criteria for good ethnography suggested by George and Louise Spindler (1987), which constitute an operational definition of anthropological ethnography applied to the study of education. We will also point out some of the controversies and alternative approaches. The topics we will address are research questions, the role of theory, ethnographic purpose, field techniques, contexts and holism, analysis, cultural interpretation, and the written ethnographic account.

The Dynamic Nature of Research Questions

Ethnographic studies are guided by research questions, as are all studies. There are key differences, however, in the life of these questions between differing approaches to research. As in much case-study research, ethnographic research questions have a dynamic nature that contrasts sharply with the predetermined and fixed nature of questions in studies in the hypothetico-deductive paradigm. Researchers conducting correlational, quantitative survey, and experimental studies spell out their questions and hypotheses in detail in advance and carefully adhere to them throughout the study. They do modify and refine their questions, but primarily for subsequent studies.

Ethnographic researchers pose broad questions at the onset of the study, but they refine, refocus, and append them in the field as the study progresses. Why is this so? Some of the issues that are important to study, important because they will help answer the broad research questions, will only come to light in the field and could not have been foreseen. One purpose of initial fieldwork, then, is to develop more specific questions.

> Hypotheses emerge *in situ,* as the study goes on in the setting selected for observation. Judgment on what may be significant to study in depth is deferred until the orienting phase of the field work has been completed (Spindler & Spindler, Criterion II, 1987, p. 19).

A defining characteristic of ethnography, then, is that questions and hypotheses emerge on site; they are not all spelled out in advance. This is also a characteristic of other case studies, but is essential for ethnographic research.

The Role of Theory

If new and refined questions emerge as the study progresses, then what is the role of theory in guiding the study? As Watson-Gegeo (1988) explains in her discussion of ethnographic methodology, "The role of theory in guiding observation and interpretation in ethnography seems to be poorly understood outside anthropology. Ethnographers do not claim that they come to a situation like a 'blank slate,' with no preconceptions or guides for observation. Theory is important for helping ethnographers decide what kinds of evidence are likely to be significant in answering research questions posed at the beginning of the study and developed while in the field" (p. 579). Ethnographic researchers, then, are knowledgeable about the relevant theoretical literature before beginning a study.

> We assume that the researcher will have searched the literature and defined the "problem" before beginning fieldwork, however much the problem may be modified, or even discarded, as field research proceeds (Spindler & Spindler, Criterion II, 1987, p. 19).

What kinds of theoretical literature are most relevant for ethnographic studies of second language and culture learning? Concepts and theories of social and cultural processes and structures are basic. These processes include language socialization (Schieffelin & Ochs, 1986), inference in conversation and reading (Gumperz, 1982), and Bruner's notion of scaffolding (Cazden, 1988; Hawkins, 1988). Concepts of structure at various levels include cultural schemata and scripts for school (Floyd & Carrell, 1987; Saville-Troike & Kleifgen, 1986), participation structures in classroom and community (Philips, 1972, 1983), and classroom discourse structures (Cazden, 1988; Varonis & Gass, 1985). Common foci of analysis for communication are literacy events (Anderson, Teale, & Estrada, 1980; Heath, 1983, p. 386), literate behaviors (Vasquez, 1988), speech events (Hymes, 1972; Saville-Troike, 1989), lessons, conversational and written interactions, or texts. Notions of situational context based on the work of Halliday and Hasan (1985), Hymes (1972), and others are relevant. At a more detailed level, ethnographers may analyze specific communicative acts or speech acts, and lexico-grammatical features.

The most relevant theories of second language acquisition are those that address social and cultural processes, language attitudes, and social-psychological motivations (Schumann, 1986; Gardner, 1986; Saville-Troike, 1989; Spolsky, 1989). Also important are theories regarding relationships between cultural processes and L2 academic achievement (Ogbu, 1987; Cook-Gumperz, 1986; Erickson, 1986). Theories of culture are basic to anthropologically oriented ethnographic research (see Shweder & LeVine, 1984, for a review). Spindler and Spindler, for example, propose a dynamic view of culture:

> A transcultural, comparative perspective is present, though frequently as an unstated assumption. That is, cultural variation over time and space is considered a natural human condition. All cultures are seen as adaptations to the exigencies of human life and exhibit common as well as distinguishing features. (Criterion VII, 1987, p. 19)

For research on children, Schultz and Theophano (1987) caution against "adulto-centric" notions of culture and emphasize the notion that children are culture transformers and creators (see also Rosaldo, 1989).

While theoretical notions help guide ethnographic inquiry, a goal of many ethnographers is to develop theory through the course of the research. How does this occur? As Watson-Gegeo explains, "The ethnographer shifts the focus of observation to include phenomena and interactions outside the scope suggested by prior theory, both to correct for what may be missing from or misleading in prior theory and to search for interactions, patterns of behavior, and other phenomena significant to and perhaps unique in the situation under study" (1988, p. 579).

Ethnographic Purpose

The most important goal of ethnographic inquiry is to discover the insider's view of reality—the *emic* view. Emic refers to "culturally based perspectives, interpretations, and categories used by members of the group under study to conceptualize and encode knowledge and to guide their own behavior" (Watson-Gegeo, 1988, p. 580). A basic but controversial assumption of ethnography is that it is indeed possible to see and understand the insider's view of reality.

The purpose of fieldwork, then, is to provide a comprehensive and accurate picture of a cultural setting and to explain the implicit cultural knowledge of the participants.

> Sociocultural knowledge held by social participants makes social behavior and communication sensible. Therefore, a major part of the ethnographic task is to elicit that knowledge from informant-participants in as systematic a fashion as possible. (Spindler & Spindler, 1987, Criterion V, p. 19)
>
> Some of the sociocultural knowledge affecting behavior and communication in any particular setting being studied is implicit or tacit, not known to some natives and known only ambiguously to others. A significant task of ethnography is therefore to make what is implicit and tacit to informants explicit. (Spindler & Spindler, 1987, Criterion VIII, p. 19)

By attending to actions and events in the ongoing flow of social discourse, the ethnographer attempts to construe what they mean to the participants (Geertz, 1973).

Field Techniques: Watching and Asking

To accomplish these purposes, researchers rely primarily on participant observation and interviewing. They also gather various written and nonwritten resources.

> The native view of reality is attended through inferences from observation and through the various forms of ethnographic inquiry (including interview and other eliciting procedures). (Spindler & Spindler, Criterion IV, 1987, p. 19)

A brief digression is needed here regarding the subjects of ethnographic study. The anthropological term "native" refers to the participants in the social setting being studied. We will use the term "participant" because it is neutral, without the pejorative connotations of "native." Traditionally, anthropologists have gone as far away from home as possible to study a less "civilized" culture in an "exotic" (meaning unfamiliar, far-away) village. As Saville-Troike points out, "anthropology has reflected Western ethnocentric distinctions between conquered colonial (or internal neo-colonial) groups and their conquerors" (1989, p. 108). More recently, however, researchers have also studied cultural settings closer to home, and minorities have studied other minorities or have studied their own culture, attempting to "make the familiar strange." Still, with some exceptions (Saville-Troike, 1988a, 1988b, for example) there are few ethnographic studies of upper-class, immigrant L2 learners or of adult language learners who are temporary residents in a host country. Thus the reality of the "natives" or "participants" is usually that of a socially subordinate group.

Participant Observation.   Participant observation is the ethnographic researcher's primary data-collection technique. To try to see reality from the participants' point of view requires that the researcher spend a great deal of time on-site. A few short visits are never adequate. For example, three two-day visits to a school over a year's time is not sufficient to develop a deep understanding of a situation from an insider's point of view. Nor does simply sending research assistants out to the site provide the researcher with firsthand understanding. Rather, a long-term stay is necessary.

> Observation is prolonged and repetitive. Chains of events are observed more than once to establish the reliability of observations. (Spindler & Spindler, Criterion III, 1987, p. 19)

While most writers on ethnographic methodology agree that participant observation is almost always required, some consider participant observation the key feature of ethnographic inquiry. Hammersley, an educational sociologist, and Atkinson, a sociologist, in their book *Ethnography: Principles in Practice* (1983), view ethnography not as a paradigm (that is, an alternative to experimental and other paradigms), but as one of the many research methods used by social scientists interested in educational phenomena. They point out that there are diverse ideas about the defining features of ethnography, but that, for them, ethnography is participant observation. Anthropological ethnographers tend to disagree, however, placing major emphasis not on data-collection techniques but on cultural and/or sociocultural interpretation.

Whether participant observation is the key feature of ethnography or simply a necessary but not a sufficient condition for quality ethnographic research, most agree that it is a crucial approach to data gathering. Saville-Troike (1989) points out, however, that while participant observation is generally required in studying communication, in some situations observation without participation is appropriate. It would often not be appropriate to participate, for example, in certain meetings or with children at play.

Role Options and Conflicts.   Participant observation means that the ethnographer both observes and participates in the cultural setting. In what specific ways, however, can one both observe and participate at the same time in an L2 institutional setting? Clearly, the roles for participation may be somewhat limited by situational constraints and by the researcher's characteristics and skills. One avenue is to work or volunteer as a part-time teacher, classroom aide, or tutor. A part-time role is more feasible than a full-time role because too much responsibility leaves too little time for watching, asking, and notetaking. Role options may be broader in some language institutes, however, and might involve functions such as advising, placement, assessment, supervision, or curriculum development that would provide normal, expected access to many situations. Wolcott (1988) distinguishes among being an *active participant,* a *privileged observer,* and a *limited observer,* urging researchers to be active participants rather than passive observers—the usual role for researchers in schools.

The language abilities of researchers are crucial in much L2 ethnographic research. The ethnographer must know the language of the group under study (Heath, 1982a). For example, to get the insider's view of how a child who does not yet speak English feels about learning a new language and culture requires that the researcher communicate with the child in his or her native language.

In reading ethnographic reports it is important to consider how the roles of participant and of observer are enacted and related and how they evolve over time. As readers, you should also consider whether the researcher had the language abilities to communicate fully with participants, and then think about how researcher roles and skills may have affected both what was observed and how observations were interpreted.

Interviewing. While ethnographic research is *naturalistic,* in that people and phenomena are studied in their naturally occurring environments, ethnographic field techniques go beyond observing to various kinds of interviewing. What counts as interviewing? Wolcott states: "I include as an interview activity anything that the fieldworker does that intrudes upon the natural setting and is done with the conscious intent of obtaining particular information directly from one's subjects" (1988, p. 194). Interviews may include key informant interviews, life history interviews, or expressive autobiographic interviews. They can range from structured and formal to informal.

A key informant is "an individual in whom one invests a disproportionate amount of time because that individual appears to be particularly well informed, articulate, approachable, or available" (Wolcott, 1988, p. 195). For example, in evaluating bilingual education programs we often found that project directors were excellent key informants because they not only knew the most about the project in its historical and present-day contexts but also were the most available for lengthy semiformal interviewing at the school district site and informal interviews over lunches and dinners. Most principals and superintendents were not good informants because they had little knowledge of the goals or practices of the bilingual programs.

What makes an interview ethnographic? The emic goals of the interview, rather than techniques, make it ethnographic. Spindler and Spindler explain how general interviewing strategies lead to emic goals.

Since the informant (any person being interviewed) is one who knows and who has the emic, native cultural knowledge the ethnographic interviewer must not predetermine responses by the kinds of questions asked. The management of the interview must be carried out so as to promote the unfolding of emic cultural knowledge in its most heuristic, natural form. This form will often be influenced by emotionally laden preoccupations that must be allowed expression. (Spindler & Spindler, Criterion IX, 1987, p. 19)

The specific techniques for interviewing must be developed as the ethnographer learns.

Instruments, codes, schedules, questionnaires, agenda for interviews, and so forth, should be generated *in situ* as a result of observation and ethnographic inquiry. (Spindler & Spindler, Criterion VI, 1987, p. 19)

Developing interview guides and other elicitation strategies, then, is a recursive process, proceeding along with ongoing fieldwork and data analysis.

Written Resources. Ethnographers also gather a variety of written materials or documents such as diaries, letters, or samples of students' writing. In L2 research these written sources can also include program proposals, planning documents, reports, curriculum materials, attendance records, and written information from parents. Assuring participants anonymity is an important ethical consideration in this process.

Although ethnographic approaches are categorized as qualitative research, this does not mean that quantitative data are not used or should not be used. Ethnographers gather primarily qualitative data, but may also find certain kinds of quantitative data useful in gaining a holistic understanding. In the studies reviewed in this chapter, you can see that researchers gathered test scores, community demographic data, and quantitative language-use data.

Nonwritten Sources. Ethnographers also gather nonwritten data of various types. Videotapes of classroom interaction, audiotapes of student and teacher language use, photos, artifacts (things), children's drawing and art, maps of the setting, and films are all used in L2 ethnographies.

Any form of technical device that will enable the ethnographer to collect more live data—immediate, natural, detailed behavior—will be used, such as cameras, audiotapes, and videotapes, and field-based instruments. (Spindler & Spindler, 1987, Criterion X, p. 20)

The great advantage of videotapes is that they reveal nonverbal aspects of communication, although it is important to consider that the camera operator's perspective may not coincide with the researcher's or participants' perspective

(Saville-Troike, 1989). The laptop computer is a more recent addition to the choices of field equipment (Fetterman, 1989).

Multiple Ways of Finding Out. The ethnographer never relies on only one means of gathering information. Rather, a variety of techniques are used in combination over a lengthy time period so that information obtained in different ways and from different sources can be compared. Researchers are then able to *triangulate,* that is, to bring together all the information that pertains to a research question. The value of triangulation is that it reduces observer or interviewer bias and enhances the validity and reliability (accuracy) of the information.

To conclude this section on field techniques, it is important to stress that using any or all of these techniques does not make a study ethnographic, nor does triangulation make a study ethnographic. Although fieldwork is the *sine qua non* of ethnography, "field techniques in-and-of-themselves cannot an ethnography make" (Wolcott, 1987, p. 38). It is important to distinguish between educational researchers who draw on ethnographic approaches in doing descriptive studies and researchers informed by anthropology who do ethnography in formal educational settings (Heath, 1982a; Wolcott, 1988, p. 202). The key difference is that the ethnographer attends to the broad cultural context in gathering information, interpreting, and reporting an account. What counts as "cultural context," however, can be interpreted in a variety of ways.

Holism: Attending to Contexts

Ethnographers of many persuasions agree that attention to context is a crucial characteristic of good ethnographic inquiry.

> Observations are contextualized, both in the immediate setting in which behavior is observed and in further contexts beyond that context, as relevant. (Spindler & Spindler, Criterion I, 1987, p. 18)

Differences of opinion arise, however, over the types of contexts that are relevant, their scope, and how "cultural" they are. At this point the distinction between macroethnographic and microethnographic research is important.

Microethnographic studies involve the analysis of small-scale events and processes such as dyadic communication in classroom lessons and in other communicative interactions (Au, 1980; Erickson, 1986). These are not considered true ethnographies by some scholars if they do not involve the study of broader cultural factors and interpretation in light of these factors (see Goetz & LeCompte, 1984, pp. 17, 23 for a discussion). Rather, in these studies the relevant contexts that help to interpret the meaning of the interactions are often narrower. They might include, for example, other interactions during the same or related lessons (Enright, 1986), interactions in other subject areas (Hawkins, 1988; Diaz, Moll, & Mehan, 1986), the "culture" of the classroom as a whole, other school programs, and the school or university culture.

Macroethnographic studies address larger-scale events and processes in relation to classroom communication and L2 learning, such as the culture of the home, the cultural values of the community, and political processes. For example, Philips' (1972, 1983) study of the Warm Springs Indians' interaction patterns is macroethnographic because she examined both school interactions and community interactions, showed how they differed, and explained Indian students' patterns of school participation in terms of cultural norms. The insights from this study ring true for readers from a variety of cultural backgrounds whose cultural norms for classroom participation differ from those in the culture in which they are studying. Another fine example is Heath's book-length study comparing the ways of talking at home and at school in two cultural communities (Heath, 1983).

Ethnographers continually attend to context. Whether context includes either the micro- or macrocontexts in which the interaction is embedded or both, accounting for (explaining) communicative interaction in classrooms requires linking its meaning or its implications to relevant contexts (Watson-Gegeo, 1988). Wolcott uses a photographic metaphor to help us envision how one attends to the object of investigation in its context: "One's focus moves constantly between figure and ground—like a zoom lens on a camera—to catch the fine detail of what individuals are doing and to keep a perspective on the context of that behavior" (1988, p. 203).

The Diachronic Perspective. At least three dimensions are involved in viewing research as micro or macro, however: space (the size and "geographic" location of units), causality (processes), and time. DeWalt and Pelto (1985) suggest that the concepts of micro and macro cannot be defined as absolute but have meaning only in terms of the interrelationshps of the units, processes, and time frames under consideration The time or *diachronic* dimension can be viewed in two ways. First, it can refer to the duration of fieldwork. Clearly, sufficient time in the field is necessary to observe substantial changes in L2 development or acculturation. Second, it can refer to historical context. Few studies in formal educational contexts, however, attend to the historical cultural context. Heath (1982a) suggests that ethnographers should draw on the anthropological tradition of ethnohistorical research to study the social past as well as the social present. The Gibson study (1987a, 1987b, 1988) reviewed below takes a dynamic view of culture, giving some attention to the historical context of the Asian Indian group she studied and making predictions about their future. Hornberger's (1987a, 1987b) work also has a diachronic dimension because it addresses how societal phenomena, such as language policies, change over time.

Ethnographic Analysis

Four concepts are important in gaining a preliminary understanding of ethnographic analysis. Analysis is recursive, grounded in the data, comprehensive, and interpretive.

Recursive. We have seen that analysis is an ongoing process in ethnographic research. That is, only after researchers analyze information gathered in initial fieldwork do they make further decisions about what is important to investigate and develop additional field procedures to gather the information. Analysis, fieldwork, and writing are intertwined as the study progresses and becomes more focused.

Grounded in the Data. Unlike correlational studies in which the researcher analyzes data using predetermined categories, in ethnographic inquiry, each situation must be understood in its own terms (Watson-Gegeo, 1988, p. 579). Analysis, therefore, requires developing categories and concepts that make sense and have functional relevance to the participants in the setting. These categories and concepts—developed inductively, in context, and from the ground up—are refined and used in analysis.

Ethnographers analyze data by looking for cultural and communicative patterns. "In essence, ethnography is the background tapestry—busily detailed, seemingly chaotic; however, upon closer look, it reveals patterns, and with repeated scrutiny, it may reveal yet other patterns (Heath, 1982a, p. 45). In Willett's study, for example, these patterns included interaction patterns, family cultural values, and linguistic production. Discovering these patterns and the relationships among them can lead to the development of grounded theory. Saville-Troike explains how grounded theory is developed. "The descriptive model which results from such analysis is then used to generate theoretical propositions that account for the data, or as a base against which to evaluate the adequacy of other theories. The theory then provides hypotheses to be tested against additional data collection and analysis" (1988b, p. 250).

Comprehensive. In evaluating ethnographic reports, it is important to look for evidence that the analysis of the data is comprehensive. As Watson-Gegeo points out:

> One of the greatest weaknesses in many published studies is their reliance on a few anecdotes used to support the researcher's theoretical point of view or conclusions, but chosen by criteria usually not clarified for the reader. . . . When illustrative examples are presented in an ethnographic report, they should be the result of a systematic selection of representative examples, in which both variation and central tendency or typicality in the data are reflected. Anything less caricatures rather than characterizes what the ethnographer has observed and recorded. (1988, p. 585)

From Description to Interpretation. Many ethnographers agree that the most important characteristic of ethnography is its concern with cultural interpretation (Geertz, 1973; Wolcott, 1987, 1988, p. 218). "It is not ethnography unless it uses some model of social or cultural process in both the gathering and interpretation of data" (Spindler & Spindler, 1987, p. 2).

For example, the study of migrant education referred to elsewhere in this book (Chapters 2 and 8) shares certain characteristics with ethnographic research. We used most of the field techniques described here; we used both qualitative and quantitative methods, and we visited sites a number of times; important questions and hypotheses emerged as the study progressed; we attended to various levels of context, and triangulation was an important strategy in data collection and analysis. But this study was not ethnographic because evaluation, not cultural explanation, was its primary goal and researchers did not engage in long-term participant observation at the sites. Wolcott (1988) reminds us that "the essence of ethnography derives from its anthropological concern for cultural interpretation rather than for how one looks or even what one looks at" (p. 217).

Cultural interpretation involves "thick" rather than "thin description," according to Geertz (1973). *Thick description* requires interpreting the meaning that particular social actions and events have for the actors. Geertz's (1973) interpretation of a Balinese cock fight is a fine and classic example of thick description in anthropology. The Willett study (1987) provides a good example of cultural interpretation in an L2 classroom study because she explains the contrasting L2 learning patterns and interaction styles of the Brazilian and the Korean girls by linking them to cultural norms.

Stereotyping or Generalizing? As my students have read ethnographic accounts, some have objected strongly to cultural generalizations, suggesting that they are stereotypes. Where does one draw the line between appropriate cultural generalizing and stereotyping? One key to knowing just how much generalization is warranted lies in gathering a great deal of information and triangulating. Overgeneralization can also be avoided by sticking close to the data, by being tentative in making inferences about how culture is reflected in behavior (Wolcott, 1987), and by considering the research unfinished (Heath, 1983, p. 13; Rosaldo, 1989).

The Written Account

The product of a full ethnographic study is an ethnography, very often a book. Researchers may report parts of a study or its key findings in journal articles or in book chapters, however. What is most striking about these short reports to readers accustomed to experiments and quantitative studies is that data-collection methods are sometimes not discussed, analysis methods are rarely explained, and reliability and validity, standards so important to defend in quantitative approaches, are usually not addressed. Rather, the space is devoted to rich or thick description, the heart of the ethnographic endeavor. As with other large or lengthy studies, one must turn to the book-length document to obtain a full picture of the study.

Much discussion has arisen about how to write accounts. One controversy centers on how much interpretation the writer should provide. Some hold the view that by providing sufficient descriptive and interpretive information, the account should "give readers an adequate basis for reaching independent interpretations of their own" (Wolcott, 1988, p. 219). This notion, also suggested for case studies by Stake (1988), has appeal because it is consistent with theories of reading as a process of constructing meaning, and makes sense particularly when the reader has a great deal of relevant experience and knowledge. Current discussions about how to write accounts are important for readers, because the way writers identify the position from which they are writing affects how we interpret (Rosaldo, 1989).

Controversy also abounds regarding whether ethnographers are stepping out of their roles as ethnographers when they recommend change. Some believe that to make recommendations for changes in educational institutions is not an appropriate role (Wolcott, 1988, p. 219). The Spindlers' view (1987, p. xii) is that ethnographers of anthropological persuasion are "more concerned with what *is* than what *ought* to be," but that "interpretive ethnography" requires interpretation and speculation, and "implications for change are close to the surface." Fetterman (1987), on the other hand, illustrates how findings can have direct effects on policy. Similarly, Carrasco (1981) and Moll and Diaz (1987) have effectively illustrated how ethnographic findings from classroom and community, especially when linked to instructional theories, can have clear and important implications for practice in L2 and bilingual classrooms.

CRITERIA FOR ASSESSING ETHNOGRAPHIC REPORTS

Building on our discussion of ethnography thus far, as well as on guidelines proposed by other scholars, we can construct the following set of question to consider in reading reports of ethnographic research. While you cannot expect that all of these issues will be addressed in the brief reports that appear in book chapters or journal articles, it is likely that all will be addressed in a book-length report.

1. What are the goals of the ethnography? What is the research problem?
2. In what contexts was the research conducted?
3. What is the group or case under study?
4. What conceptual and theoretical frame works inform the study?

5. What field techniques were used? For how much time? In what contexts? What were the roles of the ethnographer?
6. What analysis strategies were developed and used? What levels and types of context were attended to in interpretation?
7. What recurrent patterns are described?
8. What cultural interpretation is provided?
9. What is the contribution of the study to our knowledge of sociocultural factors involved in schooling in a second language and culture?
10. What are the stated implications for teaching?

SAMPLE ETHNOGRAPHIC STUDY: CULTURAL ACCOMMODATION OF ASIAN INDIAN IMMIGRANTS

We will now examine an interesting report using these criteria as a guide. The study (Gibson, 1987a, 1987b, 1988) is an ethnographic investigation of the social and cultural adjustment and academic performance of working-class Asian Indian immigrants in a rural U.S. high school.[1]

Much research has focused on relationships between sociocultural factors and academic learning, and a variety of theories have been proposed to account for school failure or success for certain cultural groups. These explanations have included cultural and linguistic deficit theories, linguistic mismatch theories, cultural difference theories, internal colony theories, castelike minority and variable response theories, secondary cultural discontinuity theories (see reviews by Cook-Gumperz, 1986; Erickson, 1986; Gumperz, 1986; Jacob & Jordan, 1987; Ogbu, 1987). Yet we know very little about relationships between cultural adjustment and academic participation for many cultural groups. What are the consequences of assimilation for success in school, for language learning, and for community harmony? Ethnographic research can provide insights about acculturation goals and patterns, and their potential consequences for a particular cultural group at a specific time in a particular setting.

Gibson's study focused on students and their families who migrated to the United States from the Punjab region of India, an area with Islamic influence and a less rigid caste system. Through a two-year study of 44 Punjabis and 43 local high school students, Gibson found that on the whole Punjabi students persisted and did relatively well in school in spite of language and cultural differences. After studying school performance and participation as well as community and family attitudes, she concluded that their strategy for cultural adjustment was one of accommodation without assimilation. In fact, she found that some of the cultural attitudes, beliefs, and practices that were most at odds with local customs were precisely those that promoted the Punjabi teenagers' success in school.

1. What are the goals of the ethnography? What is the research problem?

One purpose of the ethnography was to study tensions between local students, whom Gibson termed "Valleysiders," and the Punjabi immigrant students. Early in the report Gibson describes the impetus for the study from the point of view of the district:

> The impetus for the research was the local school district's need for information about the Punjabi community and the problems faced in school by Punjabi youth. Standardized tests administered by the district . . . had revealed a serious disparity between the academic achievement of Punjabi high school students, as a group, and the rest of the student body. District officials were concerned, furthermore, by mounting tensions between "Valleysiders" (my term for Valleyside's white majority) and Punjabis, both in school settings and in the community at large. (Gibson, 1987a, pp. 281–282)

The author then distinguishes between the Punjabi students who were doing well academically and those who were less proficient in English and receiving an inferior education.

> Second generation Punjabi students, together with those who had arrived in Valleyside as small children, in spite of facing cultural, linguistic, and social difficulties in school, did quite well academically. Recent immigrants fared less well. Although most recent arrivals persisted in school through 12th grade, they never broke out of a remedial track. (Gibson, 1987a, p. 282)

The major purpose of the study, then, was to examine the Punjabis' performance and experiences at high school and to determine how their cultural background was related to their academic performance and school social life. The researcher compared the Valleysider majority group, whose performance she characterized as "rather mediocre," with the Punjabi minority group. This cross-cultural, comparative perspective is a characteristic of much ethnographic research.

2. In what contexts was the research conducted?

Two types of context are important for this study, both the research context and the settings in which the study was conducted. The research was funded as a collaborative endeavor by the National Institute of Education from 1980 to 1982. Gibson explains the project:

> The project was a collaborative effort, involving a Punjabi community organization, the school district, parents, students, and community members. . . . The collaborative and comparative nature of the project was

reflected in the makeup of the research team which included two Punjabi Sikhs, one male and one female, and two white Americans, both female. (1987a, p. 282)

Because a goal of ethnography is to understand cultural phenomena from the insiders' perspective, the ethnolinguistically mixed composition of the team is a positive feature of this study. Such collaboration should result in cross-cultural comparisons that are more valid and, thus, findings should be more credible to both communities.

Gibson (1987a) describes the geographical setting for the research such that the community and school remain anonymous:

> The setting for the study is a small agricultural town in California's Central Valley where Punjabi immigrants constitute about 13% of the total student population. I call the town "Valleyside." . . . About 70% of the population were Valleysiders, 12% Punjabis, 12% Mexican Americans, and 4% other minorities. (pp. 281, 283)

The author describes the town and the attitudes of Valleysiders and Punjabis toward their life there. We learn that peaches, pears, prunes, walnuts, and almonds were the principal crops in this agricultural community. The Valleysider parents, whose median income was about $30,000, enjoyed the rural atmosphere of the town in spite of its provincial nature and the increasing difficulty of earning a living from a small farm. Many ran businesses or worked in other public- and private-sector jobs. Most were generally satisfied with these jobs, seeing few opportunities for advancement.

The Punjabis who came to Valleyside had been owners of small farms in the Punjab region of India. After migrating, many worked initially as laborers in fruit orchards but eventually bought their own small farms or worked in factories in nearby cities. Because the future for farming appeared bleak, however, Punjabi children looked to careers other than farming. The attitudes of many Valleysiders toward the Punjabis were hostile. But, as Gibson notes:

> In spite of the prejudice, most Punjabis were positive about life in America. They, like their Valleysider neighbors, valued the personal freedoms of this country and the economic opportunities they believed it offers. (1987a, p. 286)

Gibson's description of the community and its economic situation provides contextual information that relates to both groups' goals for schooling.

3. What is the group or case under study?

The groups under study were the Punjabis and their Valleysider counterparts. To obtain a comprehensive picture of the Punjabi high school students, the researchers decided to study seniors at the end of their studies. They sampled all

44 Punjabi high school seniors. Of the Valleysider seniors, 46 were sampled at random and 43 of these, along with their parents, participated in the study.

Gibson provides further information about the native language, religious background, and regional identity of the Punjabis in the study:

> Although Sikhs constitute the overwhelming majority of Valleyside's Asian Indian population there are also a few Hindu and Moslem families living in the area. Like the Sikhs, they too, are Punjabis. Punjabi is their mother tongue, Punjab their homeland. While differing in religious beliefs, their cultural heritage is in most ways similar to that of the Valleyside Sikhs. Punjabi, thus, is a regional identity. (1987a, p. 281)

Note that while this is a case study of Punjabi Sikh farm families, the case is a cultural group in a particular cultural context. It is in this way that anthropologically oriented ethnographic studies differ from other types of case studies.

4. What conceptual and theoretical frameworks inform the study?

The cultural concepts that play a key role in the study are cultural discontinuity, cultural differences, cultural adaptation patterns (including accommodation and assimilation), and success theory. These notions are explained for the particular group under study. The author positions her study within the international comparative literature addressing relationships between minority (or immigrant) status and school performance (Gibson, 1987b).

An important theoretical stance she takes is the view that situational variables, as well as cultural and structural (or contextual) variables, must be considered in explaining variation across groups in school performance. Gibson explains:

> To understand these variations in the school performance of immigrant minorities, we need to look not only at the social structure of the host society and the cultural background of the minority group, but also at the minority group's situation in the host society, including its perceptions of the opportunities available and the historical context of its relationship to the dominant group. (1987b, p. 272)

We can also assume that the transcultural, comparative perspective described by Spindler and Spindler (1987) is present as an unstated assumption. The view that cultural variation over time and space is a natural human condition is evident in Gibson's findings about how the Punjabis have adapted their values and in her inferring that they would continue to adjust their strategies to changing conditions. That is, Gibson does not view their cultural patterns as static and unchanging.

5. What field techniques were used? For how much time? In what contexts? What were the roles of the ethnographer?

This was a two-year study that involved participating in and observing school and community affairs, interviewing students, parents, teachers, and examining documents and school performance data. Gibson (1987a) describes the data-collection procedures:

> Members of the research team were able to participate in and observe community and school affairs over a 2-year period. Interviews with the Valleyside High seniors, their parents, and their teachers form the heart of the project's data base. Almost all interviews were tape recorded and later transcribed. Those conducted in Punjabi were translated into English. The analysis draws, additionally, from student and teacher questionnaires, student themes, school documents, and academic performance data for some 600 Punjabi, Mexican American, and Valleysider students, grades 9 through 12. (p. 282)

6. What analysis strategies were developed and used? What levels and types of context were attended to in interpretation?

Gibson does not describe analysis procedures in the book chapter (1987a) or journal article (1987b). However, these reports reveal the levels of context that were attended to in interpretation. These were family, community, school social life, school classes, and school programs such as ESL and remedial tracks. As with many ethnographic reports published as journal articles and book chapters, hers are devoted to description and interpretation, rather than to methods of data collection and analysis.[2]

7. What recurrent patterns are described?

The reports address success theory and academic performance for both groups, barriers to success in school for Punjabis, and the relationships between community forces and school performance. We will summarize some key findings and provide excerpts that illustrate recurring patterns.

Valleysider Success Theory. The author paints a picture of Valleysiders' attitudes toward gaining a high school education. Students tended to take only the courses they needed to get by, placing much value on outside activities and jobs. Gibson (1987a) provides this example as typical:

> One Valleysider student explained that he had not taken any math course beyond 1st-year algebra because he did not feel the more advanced courses would prove useful in the future. The "peak" of his education, he reported, had

come in 10th grade, when he had taken algebra 1, biology, and English 2.
After that his interest and energies had turned away from school to an
after-school job, musical interests, and activities with friends. Following high
school he hoped to support himself through a lawn maintenance business.
(p. 287)

Most parents wanted their teenagers to graduate from high school, to enjoy their
high school years, and to be prepared to work for a living. A university degree
was not a goal as it was not seen as an essential step to success. Rather, high
value was placed on social skills, initiative and drive, and working at part-time
jobs to develop independence and self-reliance. Valleyside teenagers, both girls
and boys, were encouraged to be very independent by their senior year.

> The ability to get along in society was stressed by teachers as well as parents,
> many of whom placed social criteria for success ahead of academic ones.
> (p. 289)

Note that the ethnographer attempts to report what is typical while also providing
the reader with a sense of the range of variability in the data. The major focus,
though, is on characteristics that are socially shared by the cultural group.

Punjabi Success Theory. Valleysider views of what was required for success
contrasted sharply with those of the Punjabi community. Punjabi parents wanted
their children to be prepared to support themselves, but they did not stress
financial and social independence during adolesence, as the author explains.

> All Punjabi parents expect the younger generation to defer to elders for
> direction and approval. Adolescence, from the Punjabi perspective is a time
> when young people need especially strong parental supervision and guid-
> ance . . . after they had studied and were married, they would be able to
> shoulder reponsibility for their own decisions. (pp. 290–291)

Teenagers, especially girls who were highly restricted, were expected to
behave properly to uphold family honor so that successful marriages could be
arranged.

> Arranged marriages and the value placed on maintaining family honor are
> central to the Punjabi Sikhs' system of cultural maintenance. Valleyside
> Punjabis saw it as their duty to choose a mate for each of their children. . . .
> For Punjabis arranged marriages do not conflict with "standing on your own
> feet." Through careful selection Punjabi parents felt that they not only could
> secure their child's future, but their own. (pp. 291–292)

The author then describes a link between family values and school behavior:

Schooling came first, ahead of housework, jobs, and most especially social activities. "The main thing is to study," one mother said, "nothing else" . . . [Children] were urged to acquire the skills and credentials necessary for competing in mainstream society, but warned at the same time to do nothing that would shame their families. "Dress to please the people," Punjabis frequently said, "but eat to please yourself." Accommodation without asssimilation was their strategy. (p. 292)

As a result of parental pressure to take responsibility for learning, second-generation Punjabis, and those who arrived from India before the fourth grade, fared very well in high school. Punjabi males, for example, had better attendance, did more homework, earned better grades, and graduated at higher rates than did Valleysider males. Two-thirds aspired to a four-year college degree in areas such as electronics, computer science, and engineering. They believed that a strong command of English would help them achieve their goals.

The picture was not so good for those students who arrived from India after the fourth grade. Nearly 90% of this group were weak in English throughout high school and their overall education was not high quality. They were kept in ESL classes too long for reasons (both social and legal) other than their level of English proficiency, and were then tracked into low-level classes that they found less than challenging. Nearly all succeeded in graduating, however.

8. What cultural interpretation is provided?

Punjabis stressed strict parental supervision (especially for girls), strong prohibitions and sanctions against any actions that would dishonor the family, parental arranging of marriages, strong community ties, a serious attitude toward a solid academic education, and economic success through hard work on the part of the individual. Gibson reports that the community valued education more in the U.S. context than they had in the Punjab because it was believed to be important for obtaining good jobs.

The author contrasts these cultural values with those of the local Valleysiders. While they viewed a diploma as essential, they placed a relatively higher value on acquiring social competencies and tended to view academics less seriously. The author concludes that the Punjabis' theory of success was based not only on their cultural background but also on their current response to perceived opportunities in U.S. society. Adolescents were encouraged to fit in to school life to the extent necessary to achieve and prepare for employment, but not to become like Americans. Gibson (1987a) explains:

Educated Punjabis who have become economically successful, while also maintaining strong ties to the community, serve as role models for the younger generation and reinforce the overall Punjabi Sikh strategy of accommodation without assimilation. Sikhs are not merely accommodative, however. If a time comes when accommodation proves ineffective, it may be anticipated that Valleyside Sikhs will turn to other means. (p. 306)

You can see how the researcher, through prolonged study of the students in their cultural setting, has "assigned" (Wolcott, 1987) cultural interpretations to patterns of behavior and attitudes that she and the research team observed. These cultural interpretations draw not only on cultural background but also on cultural responses to the current context.

9. What is the contribution of the study to our knowledge of sociocultural factors involved in schooling in a second language and culture?

The first contribution of this study is that it illustrates that stereotypical statements about how certain cultural groups achieve in school should be avoided. Despite much correlational evidence that socioeconomic status (SES) is related to academic success (Gumperz, 1986), such findings should not be generalized across groups or across time. Low SES in a previous cultural setting or in the present cultural setting, as this Punjabi study illustrates, is not necessarily associated with low achievement.

Second, this kind of ethnographic study can contribute to developing more adequate theories about the relationships between acculturation and L2 learning. The much cited 1978 version of Schumann's acculturation theory stated that the more one acculturates the better one learns the language. This kind of research illustrates that simple theories about the relationships between language learning (and, by extension, academic success in that language) lack explanatory adequacy. They do not account for the complex reality of a cultural group's accommodation patterns.

Finally, these findings have important implications for teacher attitudes toward cultural maintenance. The attitude of Valleyside teachers toward the Punjabi students was that full assimilation was inevitable and desirable, and that the Punjabis should try to blend in socially. Yet even if the Punjabis held this goal, racial differences would preclude true "blending," and the consequences might not be so favorable. Gibson observes: "Few seem to recognize that the racial difference would remain, or that the changes they asked for would undermine the very strength of the Punjabi family system and community" (1987a, p. 308). The important point is that many of the Punjabi values that Valleysiders saw as most different were precisely those that promoted school success. Wolcott suggests that we learn to see culture as "a system of mutual expectations about what ought to be" (1988, p. 204). The teachers' expectations about what ought to be for the Punjabi students were not necessarily in the best overall academic and social interest of the Punjabi students.

10. What are the stated implications for teaching?

Gibson (1987a) concludes her report with this advice to educators:

The issue for educators is not whether immigrants change their way of life, or how fast, but whether schools foster an instructional and social climate that helps students to pursue their educational and vocational goals. If teachers and administrators continue to believe that cultural assimilation is the single and simple quid pro quo for school success, we shall make little progress in promoting equal educational opportunities for minority students. . . . To improve academic performance we need to identify and to create learning environments encouraging to just those values and attitudes of Punjabis and other immigrants which support their success in the American system of public education. (p. 309)

More generally, ethnographic research can help educators learn to understand and value their students' cultural traditions. At the same time, it can motivate us as we help all our students develop cross-cultural perspectives.

CONCLUSION

Ethnographic research involves the naturalistic study of social and cultural phenomena in context. The products of ethnographic research are descriptions and cultural interpretations of communicative and interactional phenomena. While theories and concepts of social and cultural processes inform the studies, additional research questions, hypotheses, and strategies for collecting information are developed as the study progresses. Most ethnographic research involves a long period of participant observation, of watching and asking. Knowledge of the languages of the participants, combined with careful study of their cultural setting, allows the researcher to understand the meanings of phenomena from the participants' perspective. In this way, ethnographic research is "experience-near" rather than "experience-distant" (Geertz, 1984).

Second language research in formal contexts has traditionally relied on too few approaches, too few ways of knowing and understanding. The great contribution of ethnographic approaches is their attention to context. The growing use of ethnography is exciting not only because it offers grounded insights not usually available through approaches of the hypothetico-deductive type, but also because it opens new ways for both teachers and students to be more involved in constructing knowledge that will ultimately improve practice.

NOTES

1. The discussion here is based on a book chapter (Gibson, 1987a) and on a journal article (Gibson, 1987b). Readers can turn to the book-length report (Gibson, 1988) for a complete account.
2. See note 1.

REFERENCES

Agar, M. (1980). *The professional stranger: An informal introduction to ethnography.* Orlando, FL: Academic Press.

Anderson, A. B., Teale, W. B., & Estrada, E. (1980). Low-income children's preschool literacy experience: Some naturalistic observations. *The Quarterly Newsletter of the Laboratory of Comparative Human Cognition, 2*(3), 59–65.

Au, K. H. (1980). Participation structures in a reading lesson with Hawaiian children: Analysis of a culturally appropriate instructional event. *Anthropology and Education Quarterly, 11,* 91–115.

Carrasco, R. (1981). Expanded awareness of student performance: A case study in applied ethnographic monitoring in a bilingual classroom. In H. T. Trueba, G. P. Guthrie, K. H-P. Au (Eds.), *Culture and the bilingual classroom: Studies in classroom ethnography* (pp. 153–177). Rowley, MA: Newbury House.

Cazden, C. B. (1988). *Classroom discourse: The language of teaching and learning.* Portsmouth, NH: Heinemann.

Cook-Gumperz, J. (Ed.). (1986). *The social construction of literacy.* Cambridge: Cambridge University Press.

DeWalt, B. R., & Pelto, P. J. (1985). Microlevel/macrolevel linkages: An introduction to the issues and a framework for analysis. In B. R. DeWalt & P. J. Pelto (Eds.), *Micro and macro levels of analysis in anthropology.* Boulder, CO: Westview Press.

Diaz, S., Moll, L., & Mehan, H. (1986). Sociocultural resources in instruction: A context-specific approach. In California State Department of Education (Ed.), *Beyond language: Social and cultural factors in schooling language minority students* (pp. 143–186). Los Angeles: California State University, Evaluation, Dissemination and Assessment Center.

Enright, D. S. (1986). "Use everything you have to teach English": Providing useful input to young language learners. In P. Rigg & D. S. Enright (Eds.), *Children and ESL: Integrating perspectives* (pp. 115–162). Washington, D.C.: Teachers of English to Speakers of Other Languages.

Erickson, F. (1986). In Wittrock, M. C. (Ed.), *Handbook of research on teaching* (3rd ed.) (pp. 119–161). New York: Macmillan (American Educational Research Assoc.).

Fetterman, D. M. (1987). Ethnographic educational evaluation. In G. Spindler & L. Spindler (Eds.), *Interpretive ethnography of education: At home and abroad* (pp. 81–106). Hillsdale, NJ: Lawrence Erlbaum.

Fetterman, D. M. (1989). *Ethnography step by step.* Newbury Park, CA: Sage.

Finnan, C. R. (1987). The influence of the ethnic community on the adjustment of Vietnamese refugees. In G. Spindler & L. Spindler (Eds.), *Interpretive ethnography of education: At home and abroad* (pp. 313–330). Hillsdale, NJ: Lawrence Erlbaum.

Floyd, P., & Carrell, P. (1987). Effect on ESL reading of teaching cultural content schemata. *Language Learning, 37,* 89–108.

Gardner, R. (1986). *Social psychological aspects of second language learning.* London: Edward Arnold.

Geertz, C. (1973). Thick description. In C. Geertz, *The interpretation of cultures.* New York: Basic Books.

Geertz, C. (1984). "From the native's point of view": On the nature of anthropological understanding. In R. Shweder & R. LeVine (Eds.), *Culture Theory: Essays on mind, self, and emotion* (pp. 123–136). Cambridge: Cambridge University Press.

Gibson, M. A. (1987a). Punjabi immigrants in an American high school. In G. Spindler & L. Spindler (Eds.), *Interpretive ethnography of education: At home and abroad* (pp. 281–310). Hillsdale, NJ: Lawrence Erlbaum.

Gibson, M. A. (1987b). The school performance of immigrant minorities: A comparative view. *Anthropology & Education Quarterly, 18,* 262–275.

Gibson, M. A. (1988). *Accommodation without assimilation.* Ithaca, NY: Cornell University Press.

Goetz, J. P., & LeCompte, M. D. (1984). *Ethnography and qualitative design in educational research.* Orlando, FL: Academic Press.

Gumperz, J. J. (1982). *Discourse processes.* Cambridge: Cambridge University Press.

Gumperz, J. J. (1986). Interactional sociolinguistics in the study of schooling. In J. Cook-Gumperz (Ed.), *The social construction of literacy.* Cambridge: Cambridge University Press.

Halliday, M. A. K., & Hasan, R. (1985). *Language, context, and text: Aspects of language in a social semiotic perspective.* Victoria, Australia: Deakin University.

Hammersley, M., & Atkinson, P. (1983). *Ethnography: Principles in practice.* London: Tavistock Publications.

Hawkins, B. A. (1988). *Scaffolded classroom interaction and its relation to second language acquisition for language minority children.* Unpublished doctoral dissertation, University of California, Los Angeles.

Heath, S. B. (1982a). Ethnography in education: Defining the essentials. In P. Gilmore & A. A. Glatthorn (Eds.), *Children in and out of school: Ethnography and education* (pp. 33–55). Washington, DC: Center for Applied Linguistics.

Heath, S. B. (1982b). Questioning at home and at school: A comparative study. In G. Spindler (Ed.), *Doing the ethnography of schooling.* New York: Holt, Rinehart & Winston.

Heath, S. B. (1983). *Ways with words.* Cambridge: Cambridge University Press.

Hornberger, N. H. (1987a). Bilingual education and Quechua language maintenance in highland Puno, Peru. *NABE Journal,* 117– 140.

Hornberger, N. H. (1987b). Bilingual education success, but policy failure. *Language in Society, 16,* 205–226.

Hymes, D. (1972). Models of the interaction of language and social life. In J. J. Gumperz & D. Hymes (Eds.), *Directions in sociolinguistics: The ethnography of communication* (pp. 35–71). New York: Holt, Rinehart & Winston.

Hymes, D. (1982). What is ethnography? In P. Gilmore & A. A. Glatthorn (Eds.), *Children in and out of school: Ethnography and education* (pp. 21–32). Washington, DC: Center for Applied Linguistics.

Jacob, E. (1987). Qualitative research traditions: A review. *Review of Educational Research, 57,* 1–50.

Jacob, E., & Jordan, C. (Eds.). (1987). Explaining the school performance of minority students [Special Issue]. *Anthropology & Education Quarterly, 18*(4).

Macias, J. (1987). The hidden curriculum of Papago teachers: American Indian strategies for mitigating cultural discontinuity in early schooling. In G. Spindler & L. Spindler (Eds.), *Interpretive ethnography of education: At home and abroad* (pp. 363–380). Hillsdale, NJ: Lawrence Erlbaum.

Mohatt, G., & Erickson, F. (1981). Cultural differences in teaching styles in an Odawa school: A sociolinguistic approach. In H. T. Trueba, G. P. Guthrie, & K. H-P. Au (Eds.), *Culture and the bilingual classroom: Studies in classroom ethnography* (pp. 105–119). Rowley, MA: Newbury House.

Moll, L. C., & Diaz, S. (1987). Teaching writing as communication: The use of ethnographic findings in classroom practice. In D. Bloome (Ed.), *Literacy and schooling* (pp. 55–65). Norwood, NJ: Ablex.

Ochs, E., & Schieffelin, B. B. (1984). Language acquisition and socialization: Three developmental stories and their implications. In R. Shweder & R. LeVine (Eds.), *Culture theory: Essays on mind, self, and emotion* (pp. 276–320). Cambridge: Cambridge University Press.

Ogbu, J. (1987). Variability in minority responses to schooling. In G. Spindler & L. Spindler (Eds.), *Interpretive ethnography of education: At home and abroad* (pp. 255–278). Hillsdale, NJ: Lawrence Erlbaum.

Philips, S. U. (1972). Participant structures and communicative competence: Warm Springs children in community and classroom. In C. B. Cazden, V. P. John, & D. Hymes (Eds.), *Functions of language in the classroom* (pp. 370–394). New York: Teachers College Press.

Philips, S. U. (1983). *The invisible culture: Communication in classroom and community in the Warm Springs Indian Reservation*. White Plains, NY: Longman.

Rosaldo, R. (1989). *Culture and truth: The remaking of social analysis*. Boston: Beacon Press.

Ruiz, R. (1984). Orientations in language planning. *NABE Journal, 8,* 15–34.

Saville-Troike, M. (1988a). Private speech: Evidence for second language learning strategies during the "silent" period. *Journal of Child Language, 15,* 567–590.

Saville-Troike, M. (1988b). From context to communication: Paths to second language acquisition. In D. Tannen (Ed.), *Linguistics in context: Connecting observation and understanding* (pp. 249– 268). Norwood, NJ: Ablex.

Saville-Troike, M. (1989). *The ethnography of communication: An introduction* (2nd ed.). Oxford: Basil Blackwell.

Saville-Troike, M., & Kleifgen, J. (1986). Scripts for school: Cross-cultural communication in elementary classrooms. *Text, 6,* 207–221.

Schieffelin, B. B., & Ochs, E. (1986). *Language socialization across cultures*. Cambridge: Cambridge University Press.

Schultz, J., & Theophano, J. S. (1987). Saving place and marking time: Some aspects of the social lives of three-year-old children. In H. T. Trueba (Ed.), *Success or failure?: Learning and the language minority student* (pp. 33–38). New York: Newbury House/Harper & Row.

Schumann, J. H. (1986). Research on the acculturation model for second language acquisition. *Journal of Multilingual and Multicultural Development, 7,* 379–392.

Shweder, R., & LeVine, R. (Eds.). (1984). *Culture theory: Essays on mind, self, and emotion*. Cambridge: Cambridge University Press.

Spindler, G. (1982). *Doing the ethnography of schooling*. New York: CBS College Publishing.

Spindler, G., & Spindler, L. (Eds.). (1987). *Interpretive ethnography of education: At home and abroad*. Hillsdale, NJ: Lawrence Erlbaum.

Spolsky, B. (1989). *Conditions for second language learning*. Oxford: Oxford University Press.

Spradley, J. P. (1980). *Participant observation*. New York: Holt, Rinehart & Winston.

Stake, R. E. (1988). Case study methods in educational research: Seeking sweetwater. In R. M. Jaeger (Ed.), *Complementary methods for research in education* (pp. 3–23). Washington, DC: American Educational Research Association.

Tollefson, J. W. (1989). Educating for employment in programs for Southeast Asian refugees: A review of research. *TESOL Quarterly, 23,* 337–343.

van Lier, L. (1988). *The classroom and the language learner*. London: Longman.

Varonis, E., & Gass, S. M. (1985). Non-native/non-native conversation: A model for negotiation of meaning. *Applied Linguistics, 6,* 71–90.

Vasquez, O. A. (1988, November). *Ethnographic perspectives on literacy in a minority setting*. Paper presented at the Annual Meeting of the National Council of Teachers of English, Saint Louis.

Watson-Gegeo, K. (1988). Ethnography in ESL: Defining the essentials. *TESOL Quarterly, 22,* 575–592.

Willett, J. (1987). Contrasting acculturation patterns of two non–English-speaking preschoolers. In H. T. Trueba (Ed.), *Success or failure?: Learning and the language minority student* (pp. 69–84). New York: Newbury House/Harper & Row.

Wolcott, H. (1987). On ethnographic intent. In G. Spindler & L. Spindler (Eds.), *Interpretive ethnography of education at home and abroad* (pp. 37–57). Hillsdale, NJ: Lawrence Erlbaum.

Wolcott, H. F. (1988). Ethnographic research in education. In R. M. Jaeger (Ed.), *Complementary methods for research in education* (pp. 187–249). Washington, DC: American Educational Research Association.

CHAPTER 7

Experimental Research

Does teaching students to use the reading strategies that successful L2 readers use help improve their comprehension? Are small-group, cooperative methods more effective than traditional, teacher-fronted methods for L2 learning? Which models of bilingual education are most effective for all students? How does the task context affect writing processes? These are examples of questions that L2 researchers using experimental approaches might ask. Each question could be examined using an experimental approach because each asks about the effect of an activity on some aspect of learning. In this chapter we will examine the experimental approach to research, particularly as it is used to examine issues in learning in formal institutional and classroom contexts.

Experimental research is briefly defined in the first part of the chapter. In the following sections some uses of experiments are discussed and the major features of experimental design are explained. We will then consider criteria for assessing experimental studies and use these criteria to explore a sample study. The sample is a study of the effects of functional second language tasks on Spanish-speaking students' English use and growth.

WHAT IS EXPERIMENTAL RESEARCH?

The experiment, in all its various forms, has been and remains one of the major approaches to L2 research. It is widely used by second language acquisition researchers and applied linguists (Barnett, 1986; Cook, 1986, 1988; Hatch & Lazaraton, 1990; Tarone, 1988), educational researchers (Porter, 1988), sociolinguists (Fasold, 1984), and is particularly favored by psychologists, psycholinguists, educational psychologists, and some program evaluators (Tallmadge, 1977).

In an experiment, the researcher's goal is to establish a cause-and-effect relationship between two phenomena. The researcher aims to establish that one variable, the *independent variable,* causes changes in another variable, the *dependent variable.* This can be shown as:

independent variable → affects →dependent variable

For example, a researcher may wish to determine whether the explicit teaching of cultural background information to university ESL students will increase their comprehension of certain texts (Floyd & Carrell, 1987).

A classroom experiment of this type involves selecting a sample of students, randomly assigning them to experimental and control groups, providing the experimental group with a carefully planned instructional "treatment" (note that language such as "treatment" comes from the sciences) while providing the control group with an alternative treatment, and, finally, assessing how well each group performs on the dependent variable.

The most essential characteristic of an experiment is that the researcher manipulates the independent variable; that is, the researcher designs and sets up the experimental and control treatments. In addition, the essential characteristic of a *true experiment* is that subjects are randomly assigned to the experimental and control groups. The purpose of random assignment is to assure that the students in the treatment (experimental) group are as similar as possible to those in the control group so that if the results differ, these differences can be attributed to the different treatments rather than to differences between the two groups of students.

There are many variations on the experiment and many forms of quasi-experimentation (Cook & Campbell, 1979). Instructional experiments that require randomly assigning subjects to treatment and control conditions are often not possible or legal in classroom, school, and university settings. In spite of the impracticality or undesirability of conducting tightly controlled instructional experiments in many authentic educational settings, a number of studies, with varying levels of control have been carried out. Most L2 experiments, however, involve asking students to carry out tasks in lab settings or in simulated classroom environments.

USES OF EXPERIMENTS

Second language researchers have investigated a wide variety of issues in classroom L2 learning through experimentation. People often want to know if one task, one teaching method, one type of learning environment, or one program is more effective than another. In this section we will review findings from a collection of classroom-based and other experiments to illustrate just a few of the issues that researchers have addressed.

A Writing Experiment

A great deal of interest has arisen in research on L2 writing and composition in the last decade (see reviews in Hudelson, 1989; Johnson & Roen, 1989; Zamel, 1987). Discussions have focused on issues such as the similarities and differences in writing processes in a first or additional language, the nature and effectiveness of highly interactive approaches, the value of teaching rhetorical structure, the nature and timing of teacher and peer responses to L2 writers, and cultural factors.

Robb, Ross, and Shortreed (1986) conducted an experiment to examine the role of teacher response in efficiently promoting growth in English writing by Japanese students. They asked this research question: "What is the most effective and practical feedback strategy in an EFL context characterized by extremely large teacher-to-student ratios and little contact time?" (p. 85). To investigate the issue they conducted an experiment in which they randomly assigned 134 Japanese college freshmen to four sections of English composition. Each section employed a different method of providing teacher feedback on compositions. The four feedback methods ranged from correcting all lexical, syntactic, and stylistic errors and asking students to do likewise in their revisions (they called this the "most salient method"), to marking the number of errors per line in the margin and asking students to correct what they could (the "least salient method").

The researchers found very few differences in the accuracy, fluency, or complexity of students' writing across the four groups after about 35 hours of instruction. They concluded that "highly detailed feedback on sentence-level mechanics may not be worth the instructors' time and effort even if . . . students claim to need and use it" (Robb, Ross, & Shortreed, 1986, p. 91). They suggest that one reason for this finding is that "EFL writers can assimilate only a small proportion of corrective feedback into their current grammatical system . . ." (p. 89). Ross, Shortreed, and Robb published an article in 1988, reporting on a study they conducted to further investigate these issues. Important limitations on the value of these studies are that the techniques used for feedback may be very different from those used in current writing courses and the measures used to assess growth were very narrow.

A Cooperative Learning Experiment

Cooperative learning has been a major movement in L2 classrooms and bilingual education (California State Department of Education, 1982; Kagan, 1986). It has also been resisted on grounds of impracticality and ethnocentrism for some cultural settings. How effective are cooperative approaches compared to more traditional, whole-class approaches? Bejarano (1987) addressed this question in a large cooperative learning experiment conducted in Israel. Based on social-psychological and educational work by Sharan, Aronson, Slavin, and others, Bejarano adapted cooperative learning theories and methods to ESL classrooms in Israel and studied their effects on the L2 acquisition of 665 seventh-grade students. Two methods of cooperative interaction were examined. Both methods (one called Student Teams Achievement Divisions and the other called Discussion Groups) involved group work. Classes using these methods were compared to classes using a "whole-class" method. Teachers were assigned at random to one of the methods. After 4½ months of instruction, the results indicated that the two cooperative learning methods were more effective than the whole-class method for promoting listening comprehension, but no differences in reading improvement were detected. An experiment such as this does not provide much information about the processes involved in these two types of cooperative learning. Rather, the study answers questions about the effects of the methods on student language performance after several months.

A Learning Strategy Experiment

We have seen in previous chapters that significant work has been carried out in exploring L2 learning strategies (O'Malley & Chamot, 1989; Oxford, 1990; Wenden, 1987). We have also seen that researchers have used correlational approaches to examine the relationships between using certain learning strategies and L2 growth (Politzer & McGroarty, 1985; McGroarty, 1989).

Through classroom experiments, other researchers have examined the effects of the explicit teaching of certain strategies on students' L2 learning and performance. O'Malley and his colleagues (1985), for example, found that high school students' linguistic performance in giving oral reports showed significant improvement as a result of instruction in the specific strategies needed to carry out the task.

Reading Experiments

The value of teaching specific reading strategies is a topic of research as well. Barnett (1988) examined the effects of teaching reading strategies on two student outcomes: (1) use of these strategies, and (2) general L2 reading comprehension. She studied 264 fourth-semester college students who were learning French as a foreign language. One group of students (4 classes) were explicitly taught reading strategies such as guessing from context, while the remainder of the students (15 classes) were not given strategy instruction. This was not a true experiment, since intact classes were used; that is, there was no random assignment of students to experimental or control classes. Barnett found that students in the group receiving strategy instruction were better able to predict parts of a passage by guessing from context. They did not, however, perform better in general reading comprehension at the end of the course, as measured through the number of propositions (ideas) recalled from a passage they read.

Other reading experiments have focused on discourse structure and cultural background knowledge (Carrell, 1987). Carrell (1985), in research with university ESL students, found that explicitly teaching top-level rhetorical organization of expository texts resulted in improved ability to recall information in the texts. Floyd and Carrell (1987) found, through another experiment, that presenting cultural background information improved students' recall of texts. As Connor (1987) suggests, multiple approaches to studying L2 reading are desirable, but the experiment has tended to dominate as the most common method in ESL/EFL and foreign language research on adult learners.

Experiments in Negotiated Interaction

Pica, Young, and Doughty conducted a line of research on the benefits of negotiated interaction for L2 acquisition. In a small experiment (1987) simulating a classroom environment, they compared two ways of modifying linguistic input to determine which resulted in greater comprehension. They examined 16 intermediate adult ESL students' comprehension of instructions for placing objects on a board under two conditions. In the first condition a native speaker (NS) of English read a linguistically premodified script of instructions to the subjects. Input premodifications included reducing syntactic complexity, increasing the number of words per instruction, and repeating content words. In this condition subjects could not interact with the NS who was reading the instructions. In the second condition, however, subjects were read an unmodified version of the instructions and were encouraged to interact and negotiate meaning with the NS to achieve comprehension.

Pica and colleagues (1987) found that, as predicted, greater comprehension resulted from the discourse modified through interaction; that is, subjects in the second condition were able to place more items correctly on the board. More importantly, they found that redundancy in input was an important factor contributing to comprehension, but syntactic complexity made little difference in comprehension.

Experiments in Cognitive Aspects of Grammar

Experimentation involving elicitation, grammatical judgments, or grammatical manipulations can be useful for studying cognitive and linguistic phenomena that would not be apparent in natural speech or writing. Some work in SLA theory, for example, is centered on examining the roles of universal grammar (UG) and L1 knowledge in L2 learning (see reviews in Cook, 1988; Ellis, 1985; Gass, 1989; McLaughlin & Harrington, 1990; Rutherford, 1987). White (1986), for example, conducted a study of the pro-drop parameter with Spanish-speaking Latin Americans and French speakers from Quebec. Spanish is a pro-drop language while English and French are non-pro-drop languages. White found that the French-speaking learners of English judged null-subject sentences (such as *Is very busy) as less acceptable than did Spanish learners of English. Interpretation of such work involves attempting to determine how linguistic knowledge is represented in the mind.

This limited sampling of studies illustrates just a few of the types of questions that researchers have addressed using experimental designs, and it has focused primarily on instructional and task experimentation. In each experiment the researchers manipulated conditions. That is, they selected subjects, assigned them to one of two or three different treatments, or had them perform tasks that they had designed. They then measured the effects of the treatments or tasks on one or more outcomes. We will now look at the logic and goals of experimental design. An understanding of these procedures will help you better evaluate experiments.

EXPERIMENTAL DESIGN CONSIDERATIONS

How would you conduct a comparative experimental study? Let us imagine that you work as an administrator or teacher in a large institution that provides a variety of language courses. Suppose you have developed what you consider to be an outstanding new approach to teaching English literacy to adults who are speakers of other languages. You wish to illustrate the effectiveness of the program and obtain funding from a governmental or private agency. This agency, however, requires "hard evidence" that a program is successful, more successful than other programs, before it will award funds. You decide, therefore, to conduct an experiment to illustrate that your literacy program is effective.

The new teaching/learning approach you developed would be your experimental treatment, and the existing teaching approach would be the alternative (control) treatment. Your first step in setting up a true experiment would be to select a group of, let us say, 90 adults and randomly assign them to three experimental classes and to three control classes. You would assess students to determine their literacy levels. Students in the experimental classes would then experience the new program and those in the control classes would go through the existing program. You would carefully monitor and describe the implementation of the two programs. After a period of six months, you would assess students to determine which program was more effective in developing literacy. The steps you would follow in setting up this hypothetical experiment are represented in Figure 7.1.

Step	Procedure	Symbol
1.	Select subjects	R-S or No R-S
2.	Assign subjects	R-A or No R-A
3.	Administer pretest	O1
4.	Implement and monitor treatment	X1 vs. X2
5.	Administer posttest	O2

Note: R-S = Random Selection; R-A = Random Assignment; O = Observation/Testing; X = Treatment/Instructional intervention

Figure 7.1. Steps in Sample Experiment

As you can well imagine, you would run into numerous obstacles in attempting to set up such an experiment. Consider for a moment what some of the problems are that you would have to address and which of these you expect would be surmountable. For example, how would you select the 90 subjects? Could you randomly assign them to different classes? What obstacles might preclude random assignment? How would you pretest subjects to assess their literacy in English and the other language(s) they know? Would teachers be willing to adhere to guidelines for the differing instructional methods? How would you know if the classes were taught as you planned? Do you think attrition would be a problem between pretest and posttest? How do you think these issues would affect your study and the conclusions you could draw? These questions must be addressed in both planning and evaluating experiments.

True instructional experiments conducted in formal settings can be very valuable, but they are relatively rare for a number of reasons. First, it is not often possible or desirable to randomly assign students to two differing treatments. Indeed, in some situations it would be not only unethical but illegal to deny students access to an instructional program that is considered effective simply for purposes of experimental study.

Consider another possibility for forming a control group. Suppose that you accepted only two-thirds of the applicants who wished to enter the adult literacy program because you wished to compare, after one year, those who went through the new program (the treatment group) and those who experienced the existing program (the control group) to a third group of students, those who were left to develop their English literacy on their own through natural and other processes (a so-called no-treatment group). The results of such a study might be interesting, but most professionals would consider it unethical to deny admittance to a program to one group of students who very much want to study. While this design may sound far-fetched to some readers, it has been used in misguided attempts to establish the experimental condition of "no-treatment." Random assignment, either to different treatments (one of which is viewed as inferior in some way) or to a "no-treatment" condition, one of the requirements of a true experiment, is not a reasonable possibility in many situations. A more sensible plan is to study closely and compare two approaches that are both considered quite good. Also, both small-scale, short-term classroom experiments and experiments with tasks offer ways to test out differing approaches to promoting learning. Let us examine in more detail major design issues in comparative experimental research.

The Research Question and Hypotheses

The basis of the design for the true experiment came to the social sciences from agriculture and from psychology (Smith & Glass, 1987). Campbell and Stanley's *Experimental and Quasi-experimental Designs for Research* published in 1966 and the subsequent *Quasi-Experimentation: Design & Analysis Issues for Field Settings* by Cook and Campbell (1979) have been highly influential guides in education research. For many years the true experiment was considered the ideal model of rigorous research. Later, various forms of quasi-experimentation were outlined and valued as useful in field settings. More recently there is a more balanced emphasis on using varying approaches to research, and experiments are less revered than they once were. What is important is that the approach that is used be suitable for its purpose.

Interestingly, though, the questions that motivate experiments are much like the questions teachers ask and want answers to. For example, teachers often pose questions such as: What prereading activities are most effective in promoting student comprehension? Let us consider how this question would need to be specified for an experiment.

Because this general question could be studied in many ways, the experimenter must make a series of decisions that involve narrowing the question. First, what prereading activities are of interest? These could involve teacher-selected and teacher-presented activities such as schema construction or activation activities or vocabulary preparation. Alternatively, they might involve student generated activities or they might build on a preceding, related task. The researcher makes a choice about which activities to study and which to exclude from the study.

Similarly, there are many ways to define and assess comprehension. Comprehension might be defined as the immediate recall of ideas demonstrated through written recall. It might be defined as delayed ability to identify rhetorical structure or vocabulary. Or it might be defined as the ability to use information in a text to accomplish a related writing task. The experimenter must make a decision about how to define comprehension operationally so that it can be measured for the study.

The experimenter, then, converts the very general question that guides the study into a more specific question or statement. This specific formulation is a *hypothesis*. In the hypothesis the experimenter states how the two alternative prereading activities (two "levels" or "values" of the independent variable) will affect comprehension (the dependent variable). The hypothesis might initially be stated in this way:

> Teaching rhetorical structure results in better comprehension of main ideas than does teaching vocabulary.

This hypothesis would be specified even more precisely as decisions are made about how to define and measure constructs. The hypothesis is then tested in the experiment and either rejected as false or accepted as true. Hypothesis testing is a central feature of experimental approaches.

Independent and Dependent Variables

In the example above, prereading activity is considered the independent variable. Recall that a *variable* is a characteristic that can vary. The *independent variable* is the characteristic that is hypothesized to have an effect on comprehension. This independent variable has two *values* or *levels*. The first is teaching rhetorical structure and the second is teaching vocabulary. The *dependent variable* (also called *outcome* or *criterion*) is the variable that will be affected by the independent variable; that is, it is the goal of instruction that will be studied. In this example, the dependent variable is comprehension of main ideas. Often, experiments are more complex, involving more variables (see Hatch & Lazaraton, 1990).

Many kinds of independent and dependent variables are examined in comparative L2 experiments. The independent variable might be program, task, feedback or response technique, type of strategy instruction, or type of linguistic input. The dependent variable might involve various aspects of comprehension and production, the use of processes and strategies, and affective outcomes as well. The experimenter attempts to eliminate or to control the effects of other extraneous variables that might influence results.

In summary, we can define an *experiment* as one formal way to determine how a specific set of actions or conditions (the independent variable) causes changes in some behavior (the dependent variable).

The Population, the Subjects, and the Researcher

Population. We have seen that in survey research most researchers select a sample for direct study with the intention of generalizing results to the larger population of interest. One important way to assess the quality of a survey is to determine whether there is adequate basis for generalizing to the population. Similarly, in experiments, most researchers have goals for generalization. That is, experimenters intend to conclude that the hypothesis is either true or false for a defined population (Porter, 1988). In rare cases they may sample from the population of interest. Most often, however, samples of convenience or volunteer samples are more feasible. We will return to these issues below in discussing limits on generalization.

Subjects. As in correlational and in other quantitative research, the persons selected for study in experiments are referred to as "subjects," not participants. This is merely conventional terminology from psychology and other disciplines and not intended to be dehumanizing. It is, however, associated with the notion of distance between experimenter and subjects that relates to experimental goals of objectivity, validity, and reliability. Experimenters are almost always less involved with their "subjects" than is the ethnographer engaged in participant observation who is attempting to understand "from the native's point of view" (Geertz, 1984).

The Role of the Researcher. The typical role of the experimental researcher, then, differs widely from that of the ethnographer. Experimenters set up and control situations, but they then usually back into an observer role. They are clearly not "detached," because they must control and monitor the treatments, supervise observations, testing, measurement, scoring, and so on. But, unlike ethnographers, they usually do not participate in the activities they are studying. And unlike methodological discussions of ethnographic methods, in most such discussions of experimental research the role of the researcher is simply not mentioned. In experiments, the researcher manages instruments, while in ethnography the researcher is the instrument.

Experimental design requirements do constrain the researcher's role in certain ways. Specifically, the researcher's participation in procedures such as observation, testing, and rating is necessarily limited because of internal validity requirements that observers, testers, and raters be "blind" to the hypotheses of the study so that they will not be biased toward or against a particular group. These design requirements are aimed at establishing cause. When strictly adhered to, they not only place some constraints on the researcher's participation in the setting but they also preclude certain types of collaborative teacher-researcher arrangements.

Causality and Control

In the chapter on correlational research, we emphasized that evidence of correlational associations between variables does not imply that one variable caused the other. For example, in correlational research on the relationships between motivation and L2 proficiency it is difficult to say for groups of learners whether (1) motivation causes higher levels of proficiency, (2) higher levels of proficiency lead to increased motivation, or (3) motivation and proficiency affect each other in a continuously interactive manner. Nevertheless, researchers do make causal claims about these issues and readers tend to discuss the issues using causal terms. As Porter (1988) points out, "In educational research, even when the word 'cause' is not used explicitly, it may still be that cause is the interpretation. This is equally true for the researcher and for the individual readers of a research report" (p. 395). Even questions such as "How can teachers better support learners?" and "How can we create richer learning environments?" may be essentially causal in implication, if they express teachers' interest in how their actions ultimately affect students. It is important, then, to be familiar with the logic of experimental research, how it attempts formally to establish causality, and to be well aware of its limitations. The research approach we are focusing on here is the true experiment, an idealized type, with some discussion of quasi-experimental approaches. It is not crucially important to be able to classify research into a specific category, as new categories are continually created. The point is, no matter what the approach, you should be able to assess the validity of the claims that researchers make based on what they did, so that you will have a stronger basis for constructing meanings from the studies.

The Study of Planned Change. It is useful to think of an experiment as a study of planned change. Unlike naturalistic research in which phenomena are studied in their naturally occurring environments, an experiment, by definition, involves manipulating the situation. The experimenter, who wishes to compare two conditions, designs the conditions and sets them up. For example, in the Robb, Ross, and Shortreed (1986) experiment referred to earlier in this chapter, the researchers compared the effects of variations in responses to student writing in EFL classes in Japan. They did not study existing classes with existing, naturally occurring variations in teacher feedback. Rather, they designed differing response guidelines, asked the teachers to implement them, and examined their effects on student writing.

Random Assignment. Random assignment is considered a key feature of the *true experiment,* while experiments without random assignment of persons to conditions are considered *quasi-experiments.* The purpose of random assignment of subjects to conditions is to give each subject an equal chance of participating in any one of the experimental conditions. This is done to ensure that the groups are as similar to one another as possible. The larger the sample, of course, the more likely that the groups will be similar.

Consider the example of the adult literacy program. Suppose that rather than randomly assigning students to the two alternative programs, you used intact classes and implemented the new program in three classes and the existing program in the other three classes. After six months you assessed the students on measures of literacy and found that the mean scores for the treatment group were significantly higher than the mean scores for the control group. Can you then conclude that the new program is the cause of these observed differences? You cannot draw this conclusion, because the students in the treatment group might have differed in systematic ways from those in the control group. For example, those in the treatment group might have had a stronger L1 literacy background or they might have been more highly motivated. Although the treatment group outperformed (learned more than) the control group, you do not know if the difference was due to the new instructional program or if it was due to differences between the two groups of students. You could not conclude that the new program was more effective than the existing program on the basis of your experiment.

This problem of *nonequivalence* of groups is a threat to the validity of the study. To conduct an experiment that can establish causality, the researcher controls not only the treatment (the planned changes) but also the assignment of subjects to treatment and control groups. Random assignment helps ensure that the groups will be similar and that the differences in results can be attributed to the treatment.

Internal and External Validity

In interpreting and evaluating an experiment, two general goals of experimental design should be considered: internal validity and external validity. An experiment has a high degree of *internal validity* if one can claim that the treatment was the cause of the observed difference in the dependent variable. The notion of *external validity* involves generalizability. We will consider each of these goals.

Internal Validity. An experiment is designed to establish a cause-and-effect relationship; that is, the researcher's goal is to be able to conclude that observed differences between groups on the dependent variables are attributable to the treatments, not to other causes. Campbell and Stanley posed the question of internal validity in this way: "Did in fact the experimental treatments make a difference in this specific experimental instance?" (1966, p. 5). To explore this issue, the next question to ask is: What other factors might have caused the results? Statements about possible *alternative causes* and effects are *rival hypotheses*. In the adult literacy example, we might develop rival hypotheses that the superior performance of the treatment group was due to their stronger motivation or to their stronger L1 literacy background rather than to the instructional program.

Experiments are designed so that after the experiment is terminated, it will be possible to rule out alternative hypotheses about the causes of the results. This is accomplished by building certain controls into the design. The purpose of controls is to help ensure that differences in the results of the study will be due to differences in the two treatments, rather than to other factors. These controls help improve the internal validity of the study. The more alternative explanations for the results that the researcher can eliminate through controls, the more internally valid an experiment is.

What are some types of control? The first and most obvious control is the presence of a control group. Random assignment of subjects to treatment and control groups is another kind of control. It controls the characteristics of the subjects across groups by equating them (to a certain degree) and reducing problems of nonequivalence. Another general principle of control is to ensure that nothing except the planned treatment being studied is different for the two groups. That is, all other conditions—such as teacher, curriculum, environment, materials, and so on—should be exactly the same for both groups. As you can imagine, tight controls are easier to achieve in a laboratory setting, but more difficult and less desirable to achieve in a field setting. So, while tightly controlled laboratory experiments are more rigorous, they are less interesting because they differ so greatly from real-world conditions. Field experiments are more interesting because they take place in authentic settings, but they are generally less rigorous by experimental standards.

To conclude, an experiment has a high degree of internal validity if one can claim that the independent variable is the only reasonable cause of the differences observed in the dependent variable. Conversely, if there are many plausible rival hypotheses about causes of the results, the experiment has little internal validity.[1]

Generalization. Another important question to consider in interpreting experiments is: To what other persons in what other situations or settings would the results apply? Specifically, would the results hold for speakers of different languages? For learners of different ages? Would the same results be obtained in a different cultural setting or in a different country? In a different type of institution? How would the results have differed if the task were set up differently?

In reading reports of experiments, you have probably noted the generalizations that authors make. They often explicitly state, or simply imply, that the results are applicable or valid for other people in other contexts. On the other hand, many authors are careful to state that the results are not necessarily valid for different situations. Most authors make some statements about the external validity (generalizability) of the study. Campbell and Stanley originally posed the external validity question in this way: "To what populations, settings, treatment variables, and measurement variables can this effect be generalized?" (1966, p. 5). The extent to which cause-effect relationships are generalizable is considered one indicator of the quality of an experiment (Campbell & Stanley, 1966; Porter, 1988). Generalizability of findings is considered important because one goal in conducting experiments is to contribute to general knowledge.

The sort of statistical generalization to a population that is typical of surveys is usually not done in experiments. Rather, the author provides a discussion of generalizability and readers make their own judgmental inferences. Many readers overgeneralize, however, even on the basis of very little information. Therefore, the more complete the description of the study setting, the subjects, the treatment or task conditions, the measures, and the procedures, the stronger basis readers have for assessing the similarities of these factors to those in other situations. Readers can then judge for themselves how valid the study is for other settings.

Second language experimental research has been notorious for statements that overgeneralize findings. Readers should be particularly careful not to make inappropriate generalizations to other persons, other cultural groups, other settings, other task conditions, other channels/modalities, and other outcomes. Let us briefly consider a study that illustrates this point.

Hansen-Strain (1989) found that among students of similar language proficiency levels, students from oral cultural traditions (Samoan and Tongan) performed differently on measures of language proficiency than did students from literate traditions (Chinese, Japanese, Korean). One finding was that the Polynesian students showed greater command of English relative clauses when tested in oral and aural modalities than did the Asian students. In written tests, however, there were no significant differences among groups. This example illustrates how language test performance can vary according to task conditions, and according to cultural background. Many other studies in the SLA literature, in sociolinguistics, and in the language-testing literature also illustrate ways that language use varies according to situational variables. Such variation must be considered in interpreting the meaning of any experiment.

In summary, experimental approaches to research attempt to establish cause-and-effect relationships. Key factors in instructional experimental design involve researcher manipulation of the independent variable, careful control of extraneous variables, and precise measurement of the dependent variable.

CRITERIA FOR ASSESSING
AN L2 EXPERIMENT

In reading reports of experimental research you can use the following questions as a guide to evaluation. The answers will help you assess the quality of the experiment, understand its limitations, and arrive at your own conclusions about the value of the study and the meanings that it will have for you.

1. What is the research question? What are the hypotheses?
2. In what context was the research conducted?
3. What were the theoretical and other orientations of the researcher?
4. Who were the subjects/participants in the study? How many were there and how were they selected? What are their relevant characteristics?
5. What was the independent variable and how was it operationalized?

6. What procedures were used to carry out the study? Was assignment to group random?
7. What means were used to control extraneous variables and to achieve internal validity?
8. What were the dependent variables and how were they defined and measured? How adequate (valid and reliable) were the measures?
9. What analyses were performed and with what results? Can the results be attributed to the treatment? What other factors might have influenced the results?
10. What conclusions were drawn? Are generalizations about the results appropriate?
11. What is the contribution of the study to our knowledge of social and contextual factors in L2 learning or teaching?
12. What are the stated implications for L2 learning in formal contexts?

SAMPLE EXPERIMENTAL STUDY: EFFECTS OF CONTENT-BASED PEER TEACHING

Let us now apply these criteria to a sample classroom experiment. The sample is a study I conducted (Johnson, 1983, 1988) to examine the use and acquisition of English by Spanish-speaking children.[2] I have selected this study because it was conducted in a classroom setting, because it was a true experiment involving random assignment of students to experimental and control conditions, and because it addressed social interactional factors in second language acquisition. The study illustrated that ESL children could successfully teach content activities to monolingual English speakers and that such teaching led to improved English vocabulary comprehension.

1. What is the research question? What are the hypotheses?

This study had two purposes. One was to assess the effects of a content-based, functional instructional intervention on the language use of children in informal social interaction. The second purpose was to examine the effects of this intervention on growth in L2 proficiency.[3] The experimental hypotheses were formally worded in the following format:

1. Limited English-speaking (LES) children who participate in Inter-Ethnolinguistic Peer Tutoring (IEPT) will interact verbally with fluent English speakers to a greater extent than will LES children in a control group.
2. LES children who participate in peer tutoring will make more growth in English language proficiency than will LES children in a control group.

2. In what context was the research conducted?

The study was conducted with children aged five to eight in a university experimental school. The context was described in the report of the research in this way:

> All 34 children were attending a seven-week bilingual program at Stanford's experimental school. . . . The program was bilingual only in the sense that both English and Spanish were used by students and teachers, and a limited number of ESL and SSL [Spanish as a second language] vocabulary lessons were provided. It was a daycamp program with an open-classroom atmosphere and a wide range of activities for the children to choose from, both indoors and outdoors. There were some large group and small group activities directed by teachers, but, for the most part, children were free to choose their own activities and their own playmates. The LES children attended three days a week for a total of 21 days. Of the five teachers, two were monolingual English speakers, two were fluent Spanish speakers, and one had a fair degree of proficiency in Spanish. (Johnson, 1983, pp. 57–58)

The Chicano children were bused to the school for this summer program and made themselves at home quickly. In fact, they dominated a large play area containing a sand mound and a hose. Because all the children enjoyed spraying water, there was continual competition to get access to the hose. Interestingly, the only Spanish that the English-speaking children learned, to our knowledge, was *agua* (water), which they yelled out to claim the hose. This information was not included in formal reports of the experiment, however, because it was not part of the planned study. In a qualitative study, a researcher, observing this phenomenon, might have decided to explore these issues further as part of the study.

3. What were the theoretical and other orientations of the researcher?

The study was based primarily on Wong Fillmore's (1976) work on the role of sustained child-child interaction in L2 acquisition. She illustrated that L2 learners benefitted from interactions with English-speaking children who provided them with useful linguistic input for acquisition. That work also illustrated that the most successful learners of the five she examined in her case studies were those who were able to establish and maintain social contact with peers and adults who gave them the type of input they needed for learning.

Speech act theory and Hymes's notion of communicative competence were used to inform the development of the test of communicative competence. In addition, this experiment was based on the theoretical notion that the informal, social, language-acquisition environment could be affected by how teachers structured experiences for students, and that the cumulative effects of planned, functional L2 use and natural, informal L2 use would promote overall development.

4. Who were the subjects/participants in the study? How many were there and how were they selected? What are their relevant characteristics?

Of the 34 children attending the program, the subjects of the study were 16 Mexican-American children from a local school district who ranged from age five to age eight. All were fluent speakers of Spanish and all spoke at least some English, but were not yet proficient in English.

The other participants in the study were 18 children who neither understood nor spoke Spanish. No data were collected on these students, although they participated in the study by interacting with the LES children.

5. What was the independent variable and how was it operationalized?

The independent variable was content-based ESL instruction. Two types (levels) of content-based learning experiences were provided. In the experimental group, L2 children first learned a content activity (in science, cooking, or art) in a teacher-led small group. Cross-language pairs were then formed and each child carried out the task of teaching the activity to a fluent-English-speaking peer. Roles were alternated so that ESL children were in the high-status role of teacher for half of these sessions. The purpose of the experimental treatment was to

> provide a structured setting for meaningful, natural conversation, through an exchange of information, between a Spanish-dominant student and a monolingual English-speaking student. (Johnson, 1983, p. 60)

Most readers will recognize this as an "information-gap" activity. Language use for tutoring was necessarily English, supplemented by nonverbal communication and contextual information, since the monolingual English speakers could not speak or understand Spanish. Two researchers monitored the implementation of these activities to ensure that they were carried out as planned. We found that the ESL children were very able to teach the content activities to their monolingual English-speaking peers.

In the control group, children learned the same set of activities in a large-group setting from a teacher but did not then engage in any peer teaching.

6. What procedures were used to carry out the study? Was assignment to group random?

A matched-pairs experimental design was used. During the first week, LES children were pretested on three measures of English proficiency and were observed to determine how much they interacted verbally with English-speaking children. They were then matched on the basis of two criteria: (1) overall English proficiency and (2) frequency of interaction in English. Members of the matched pairs were randomly assigned to a treatment group and a control group. These procedures ensured that the two groups were as equivalent as possible.

Step	Procedure
1	Pretest and observe interactions
2	Form matched pairs
3	Randomly assign members of pairs to treatment and control groups
4	Implement treatment and monitor implementation (5 weeks)
5	Conduct observations in unstructured contexts
6	Posttest and observe interactions

Figure 7.2. Temporal Sequence of Experimental Procedures

The treatment was carried out over a period of five weeks. During that time the children were systematically observed in unstructured contexts to assess the frequency and nature of their verbal interactions in English. During the last week of the program, after the treatment ended, the LES children were posttested on the same three proficiency measures used for pretesting, and they were observed again for verbal interaction. The procedural steps are depicted in Figure 7.2.

7. What means were used to control extraneous variables and to improve internal validity?

The purpose of controls in an experiment is to help ensure that any differences in the results between the two groups will be due to differences in the two treatments, rather than to differences in extraneous variables. In this study it was important to control for important extraneous variables that might have a strong influence on outcomes, such as differences in the curriculum tasks or in teachers. The method for imposing these controls is explained:

> A control for curriculum was imposed by providing both groups with the same activities. Teacher effects were controlled by having teachers alternate weekly between the treatment and the control group for the one-hour session. (Johnson, 1983, p. 60)

These controls help improve the internal validity of the study. The more alternative explanations (rival hypotheses) for the results that the researcher can rule out through controls, the more internally valid an experiment is.

8. What were the dependent variables and how were they defined and measured? How adequate (valid and reliable) were the measures?

The effects of the treatment on two dependent variables were studied. The first of these was verbal interaction in English and the second was English language proficiency. Each is explained below.

Observations of Verbal Interaction. We assessed verbal interaction by directly observing the children. They were observed outside the treatment situations at times when they were free to interact with children of their own choice and to use the language of their choice. Each ESL child was observed for a total of 40 minutes before and after the five-week treatment. In addition, during the five-week treatment period, each child was observed for 20 minutes each week. All observations were conducted in five-minute time segments spaced throughout the day. The observation system was formally reported in this way:

> To measure the quantity and type of verbal interactions in which the students engaged, the Language Use and Interaction System (LUIS) was employed. . . . Observers focus on one child at a time and the basic unit they code is the utterance. The instrument allows for recording information concerning:
>
> (1) the type of utterance (whether an initiation or a non-initiation);
> (2) characteristics of the addressee, such as language proficiency, whether a student or a teacher, whether an individual or a group; and
> (3) the language of the utterance (Spanish, English, or code switching).
>
> In addition, information about the setting is recorded, including: location, group size, teacher presence and role, activity, and who selected the activity. Live observations were conducted by two observers, who underwent twelve hours of training. In order to reduce bias, one observer was kept uninformed of the purpose of the treatment and of the hypotheses under investigation. A randomized rotation system was used in order to control for effects due to setting, time of day, and state of alertness of the observers. (1983, pp. 58–59)

This observational method provided quantitative measures of the *amount* of interaction in which children engaged with various interlocutors during situations involving free choice of activities and interactants.

Reliability of the Observers and of the Time Sample. To determine how well the observers agreed with one another we calculated interobserver reliabilities. Reliabilities (correlations) of .76 and .82 were established prior to and at the start of the program. Two additional reliability checks made midway through the program and at the end of the program yielded reliabilities of .74 and .81. These levels are considered adequate, but the data would be considered more accurate if agreement were higher.

In quantitative observational research, it is important to determine not only consistency across observers (interobserver reliability), but also to determine the reliability of the sample of observations. If the amount of time that students are observed is too small, and if their behavior is quite variable, then the results may not provide an accurate view of their overall behavior in the context of interest.

The amount of time sampled, therefore, should be large enough that it can be shown to be reasonably representative of a person's overall behavior in that particular type of context. The procedure used in this study is described:

> In order to determine the extent to which the observed behavior of the children was representative of their behavior throughout the day at unstructured times, a split-half reliability check was performed. For 20 minutes of observation, reliabilities ranged from .36 to 1.00 with a median of .86, indicating that for most students 20 minutes was an adequate sample of behavior.[4] (Johnson, 1983, p. 59)

An explanation of these statistical procedures is beyond the scope of our discussion. The conceptual point, however, should be clear; namely that people (children) are naturally somewhat inconsistent in their behavior, some more so than others. Stated another way, their behavior varies according to situational context and other factors. That is why reliabilities are quite low for some of the children. In experimental research, however, if we wish to characterize subjects' overall behavior in a specified type of context, we need to provide some indication of the extent to which the small amount of behavior we have documented is representative of their behavior at other times in that same type of context.

In summary, we have seen that the reliability of the first dependent variable—verbal interaction in English—was assessed by calculating both interobserver reliabilities and the reliability of the time sample. While interobserver reliabilities are usually provided by researchers, it is less common to find any mention of the reliability of the time sample.

Language Proficiency. The second dependent variable that was expected to be affected by the independent variable was English language proficiency. This was measured by three tests: (1) a test of vocabulary comprehension, the Peabody Picture Vocabulary Test; (2) a test of global proficiency, the Language Assessment Scales; and (3) a test of communicative competence developed by the researcher. Reports of research should describe what the measures assess and how adequate they are. The instruments are described:

> Forty items of the Peabody Picture Vocabulary Test (PPVT), which measures comprehension of vocabulary, were administered. In this test, a vocabulary word is read to the student who then chooses the correct picture from a plate of four pictures.

> The Language Assessment Scales (LAS) is an overall proficiency test with sections on comprehension and production of phonology, vocabulary production, syntax comprehension, and a story retelling task. It was administered and scored according to the publisher's instructions. Interrater agreement for the

pretest stories was .91 and for the posttest stories was .95.

> The Child-Child Communication Test (CCCT) is a functional test designed to measure the kind of language children would . . . learn by interacting with one another in an open-classroom setting. It involves a comprehension-imitation-production task. . . . Each item is based on a picture of two children engaged in dialogue in a school situation. The tester explains each situation briefly in Spanish, then supplies the dialogue in English, and the child is asked to recreate the conversation.

> Each child's speech was recorded and later rated by two independent raters on four criteria: quantity, grammaticality, comprehensibility, and appropriateness, . . .

> The reliability of the CCCT was established through interrater reliability.[5] (Johnson, 1983, pp. 59–60)

One lesson to be learned is that, if possible, it is wise to use proficiency measures with well-established psychometric properties (validity and reliability) and then to establish these again for the current study. Adequate measurement of outcomes is crucial in an experiment, and constructing adequate measures from scratch is not a simple process.

9. What analyses were performed and with what results?

Hypothesis 1. Several analyses were carried out to address the first hypothesis, that is, to determine the effect of peer teaching on the ESL children's amount of verbal interaction in English during unstructured times. Eight statistics from the observation data were calculated for each ESL student for each of the seven weeks of the program. These corresponded with the categories of the observation instrument and included, for example, both the frequency and percent of utterances by ESL students addressed to fluent English-speaking students in English and the frequency and percent of utterances they initiated.

Three analyses were performed: (1) a trend analysis employing linear regression (this involves correlation), (2) a correlational analysis; and (3) *t* tests. Each analysis represented a different method of examining the data, and each produced somewhat different results, although results pointed in the same general direction.

The trend analysis showed no statistically significant differences between the two groups. Visual inspection of the scattergrams and regression lines showed that the treatment group either maintained or increased the frequency and percentage of interaction in English over time, while the control group decreased over time. The correlational results also suggested that the treatment served to prevent the decline in English use with monolingual English speakers that occurred in its absence. The *t* tests at the conclusion of the study yielded significant differences on two of the eight measures of interaction.

In summary, these results meant that the treatment group outperformed the control group in two ways. A greater proportion of their total speech was devoted to (1) initiating verbal interactions with English speakers (including both adults and children), and (2) engaging in verbal interactions with FES children.

Hypothesis 2. The second hypothesis predicted that students in the experimental group would make greater gains in English proficiency than would those in the control group. The application of a statistical test to the results of the CCCT was not warranted because two of the scores were determined to be invalid. There was no apparent difference, however, between the treatment and the control group on this measure. *T* tests for related samples were applied to difference scores on the PPVT and the LAS. There was no significant difference between the performance of the treatment group and the control group on the LAS. On the vocabulary measure, however, the treatment group significantly outperformed the control group, $t(7) = 3.88, p < .005$.

The results of these analyses indicate, then, that there is no evidence that the peer tutoring was more effective than the control treatment in improving most areas of language proficiency. This finding could have been due to the short treatment period. We can conclude, however, that the peer-tutoring treatment was an effective means of improving vocabulary comprehension for these students.

10. What conclusions are drawn? Are generalizations about the results appropriate?

Conclusions regarding effects on interaction were reported in this way:

> The no-treatment expectation in this . . . program was that, without the IEPT treatment, children would gradually decrease both the frequency and percent of their utterances in English to FESs. The study provided some evidence that the effect of the treatment was to arrest this decline and to cause students to either maintain or increase the number and percent of English utterances over time. (Johnson, 1983, p. 65)

Conclusions regarding the effects of the treatment on language proficiency were reported in this way:

> . . . the IEPT technique proved to be an effective method of improving children's vocabulary comprehension. (Johnson, 1983, p. 64)

It is important to note that these conclusions are worded in such a way that they do not imply that the results would hold in other situations. The findings of a small experiment cannot be generalized to different students in different settings learning different languages. In fact, in a related, subsequent study, August (1987) found some similar but stronger positive effects for English growth. She also found that using the same strategy to promote Spanish language development for Chicano children was not effective.

11. & 12. What is the contribution of the study to our knowledge of social or contextual factors in L2 learning or teaching? What are the stated implications for L2 learning in formal contexts?

This study illustrated, first, that the treatment was feasible. That is, when invited to play the role of teacher, all of the ESL children (ages five to eight) in this study were able to draw on their communicative resources to effectively handle the demands of teaching content (e.g., art, science, and cooking activities) to their monolingual English-speaking peers. This basic aspect of the study is consistent with Steinberg and Cazden's (1979) conclusion that children display surprising competence in peer-teaching tasks outside the teacher's direct control.

Second, the findings illustrated that the way teachers structure content-based ESL lessons can have some effect on students' interactions in other informal settings. In other words, variations in participation structure in content sessions can affect how children approach other interactions in the informal social environment. The implication of this notion was summarized as follows:

> One implication . . . is that the informal social environment at school may not be a factor over which educators have no control. Children's social interaction may be influenced by the way educators structure classroom groups and activities. The IEPT technique shows promise as a means of breaking down communication barriers between different ethnolinguistic groups and helping to create an environment more conducive to informal second language acquisition. (Johnson, 1983, p. 66)

This study illustrates some of the ways in which those who conduct experiments attempt to strive for rigor. Authentic instructional experiments of this type are worth doing, but only under certain conditions. They can be valuable provided that both treatment and control activities are educationally sound and provided that all parties involved (including teachers, aides, administrators, researchers, observers, etc.) support the study and work cooperatively in carrying it out. We were most fortunate in this regard. Nevertheless, any instructional experiment or quasi-experiment will be much more valuable if it is supplemented by rich qualitative, descriptive information. For example, discourse analysis of peer-teaching sessions over time would provide valuable information about how students grow in the communicative and academic competence needed to carry out these or other types of cooperative tasks.

CONCLUSION

Second language experiments serve many purposes. In this chapter we have concentrated our attention primarily on the true experiment conducted in an educational setting, pointing out its goals along with its limitations. Its goals are to establish that a very specific set of actions or conditions (the independent variable) is the cause of changes in some outcome (the dependent variable). The methodology involves setting up treatment conditions, assigning subjects to conditions, rigorous control of extraneous variables, and precise measurement of variables.

In designing the study, the researcher makes decisions about procedures before carrying out the experiment. Unlike most case studies, ethnographic studies, and various qualitative approaches, such decisions are not to be altered midstream in an experiment. As Porter (1988) points out, "This is potentially one of its greatest strengths and one of its greatest weaknesses. The strength is that carefully specified experimental procedures allow rigorous control and provide relatively unambiguous results for a limited set of questions. By concentrating on only a few variables, the difficult measurement problems of each can be given careful attention. The weakness is that the original questions may have been misguided" (p. 410). The key point is that if experimenters focus on inputs and outputs without attending to processes and contexts, they may completely miss the important events that most shaped the results. Without rich descriptions of what goes on, there is little basis for adequate interpretation.

Traditionally, experiments have been viewed as powerful because they can establish cause-and-effect relationships, but they are still essentially reductionist. That is, too often the constructs are represented by measures that are insufficiently valid or reliable, and that reduce a complex construct to mere bits and pieces. The direction of this reduction is shaped by the theoretical orientation of the researcher. Thus, the theories and biases the researcher brings to the study affect not only the original question asked but also the way constructs are measured and, finally, the way results are interpreted.

In reading and assessing experiments, readers should carefully consider how constructs were defined and measured, what plausible rival hypotheses might account for the results, and how the study would be different under different situational and contextual conditions. Readers should decide for themselves in what ways results might be generalizable, if at all.

NOTES

1. See Huck and Sandler (1979) for exercises in developing rival hypotheses.
2. I would like to acknowledge and express my appreciation to those who collaborated in carrying out this research: Diane August, Zoe Ann Hayes, Robert Milk, Mary

McGroarty, Ruben Abrica, Frances Morales, Hector Nava, Elly Pardo, Juanita Chavez, Kate Williams, Peter Hood, and Bonnie Chandler; to those who contributed and facilitated: Robert Politzer, Arnulfo Ramirez, Rosedith Sitgreaves, Kast Tallmadge, Oscar Roberts, Dee Irwin, Aphra Katzev, and Susan Hood; to those who sponsored the study: The William and Flora Hewlett Foundation.

3. The complete study involved three hypotheses, but we will discuss two here, omitting the correlational part of the study.

4. Reliability coefficients for 40 minutes of observation were estimated using the Spearman Brown formula. They ranged from .53 to 1.0 with a median of .94.

5. Pearson correlation coefficients, computed for each subscale as well as for the total score of the CCCT, were .79 for grammaticality, .87 for comprehensibility, .91 for appropriateness, .96 for amount of communication, and .93 for the total score. Ideally, the concurrent validity of the CCCT would be established by comparing it to a standard communication test. Since no such test was available, CCCT scores were correlated with LAS scores (pretest: $r = .84$, posttest: $r = .86$) and PPVT scores (pretest: $r = .75$, posttest: $r = .78$).

REFERENCES

August, D. L. (1987). Effects of peer tutoring on the second language acquisition of Mexican American children in elementary school. *TESOL Quarterly, 21*, 717–736.

Barnett, M. A. (1986). Syntactic and lexical/semantic skill in foreign language reading: Importance and interaction. *Modern Language Journal, 70*, 343–349. (This article won an award from ACTFL.)

Barnett, M. A. (1988). Reading through context: How real and perceived strategy use affects L2 comprehension. *Modern Language Journal, 72*, 150–162.

Bejarano, Y. (1987). A cooperative small-group methodology in the language classroom. *TESOL Quarterly, 21*, 483–504.

California State Department of Education. (1982). *Basic principles for the education of language-minority students: An overview.* Sacramento, CA: Author.

Campbell, D. T., & Stanley, J. C. (1966). *Experimental and quasi-experimental designs for research.* Chicago: Rand McNally

Carrell, P. L. (1985). Facilitating ESL reading by teaching text structure. *TESOL Quarterly, 19*, 727–752.

Carrell, P. L. (1987). Content and formal schemata in ESL reading. *TESOL Quarterly, 21*, 461–481.

Cook, T. D., & Campbell, D. T. (1979). *Quasi-experimentation: Design & analysis issues for field settings.* Chicago: Rand McNally.

Cook, V. (1986). *Experimental approaches to second language learning.* Oxford: Pergamon.

Cook, V. J. (1988). *Chomsky's universal grammar: An introduction.* Oxford: Basil Blackwell.

Connor, U. (1987). The eclectic synergy of methods of reading research. In J. Devine, P. L. Carrell, & D. E. Eskey (Eds.), *Research in reading in English as a second language* (pp. 11–20). Washington, DC: Teachers of English to Speakers of Other Languages.

Ellis, R. (1985). *Understanding second language acquisition.* Oxford: Oxford University Press.

Fasold, R. (1984). *The sociolinguistics of society.* Oxford: Basil Blackwell.

Floyd, P., & Carrell, P. (1987). Effect on ESL reading of teaching cultural content schemata. *Language Learning, 37,* 89–108.

Gass, S. M. (1989). Language universals and second-language acquisition. *Language Learning, 39,* 497–534.

Geertz, C. (1984). "From the native's point of view": On the nature of anthropological understanding. In R. Shweder & R. LeVine (Eds.), *Culture theory: Essays on mind, self, and emotion* (pp. 123–136). Cambridge: Cambridge University Press. (Reprinted from the *Bulletin of the American Academy of Arts and Sciences, 28,* 1974.)

Hansen-Strain, L. (1989). Orality/literacy and group differences in second-language acquisition. *Language Learning, 39,* 469–496.

Hatch, E., & Lazaraton, A. (1990). *The research manual: Design and statistics for applied linguistics.* New York: Newbury House/Harper Collins.

Huck, S. W., & Sandler, H. M. (1979). *Rival hypotheses: Alternative interpretations of data based conclusions.* New York: Harper & Row.

Hudelson, S. (1989). *Write on: Children's writing in ESL.* Englewood Cliffs, NJ: Prentice-Hall.

Johnson, D. M. (1983). Natural language learning by design: A classroom experiment in social interaction and second language acquisition. *TESOL Quarterly, 17*(1), 55–68.

Johnson, D. M. (1988). ESL children as teachers: A social view of second language use. *Language Arts, 65,* 154–163.

Johnson, D. M., & Roen, D. H. (1989). *Richness in writing: Empowering ESL students.* White Plains, NY: Longman.

Kagan, S. (1986). Cooperative learning and sociocultural factors in schooling. In California State Department of Education, *Beyond language: Social and cultural factors in schooling language minority students.* Los Angeles: California State University, Evaluation, Dissemination and Assessment Center.

McGroarty, M. (1989). *The "good learner" of English in two settings.* Los Angeles: University of California, Center for Language Education and Research. (Technical Report 12)

McLaughlin, B., & Harrington, M. (1990). Second-language acquisition. In R. B. Kaplan (Ed.), *Annual Review of Applied Linguistics* (Vol. 10) (pp. 122–134). New York: Cambridge University Press.

O'Malley, J. M., & Chamot, A. U. (1989). *Learning strategies in second language acquisition.* New York: Cambridge University Press.

O'Malley, J. M., Chamot, A. U., Stewer-Manzanares, G., Russo, R., & Kupper, L. (1985). Learning strategy applications with students of English as a second language. *TESOL Quarterly, 19,* 557–584.

Oxford, R. (1990). *Language learning strategies.* New York: Newbury House/ HarperCollins.

Pica, T., Young, R., & Doughty, C. (1987). The impact of interaction on comprehension. *TESOL Quarterly, 21*(4), 737–758.

Politzer, R. L., & McGroarty, M. (1985). An exploratory study of learning behaviors and their relationship to gains in linguistic and communicative competence. *TESOL Quarterly, 19,* 103–123.

Porter, A. C. (1988). Comparative experiments in educational research. In R. M. Jaeger (Ed.), *Complementary methods for research in education* (pp. 391–411). Washington, DC: American Educational Research Association.

Robb, T., Ross, S., & Shortreed, I. (1986). Salience of feedback on error and its effect on EFL writing quality. *TESOL Quarterly, 20,* 83–93.

Ross, S., Shortreed, I., & Robb, T. (1988). First language composition pedagogy in the second language classroom: A reassessment. *RECL Journal, 19,* 29–48.

Rutherford, W. E. (1987). *Second language grammar: Learning and teaching.* London: Longman.

Smith, M. L., & Glass, G. V. (1987). *Research and evaluation in education and the social sciences.* Englewood Cliffs, NJ: Prentice-Hall.

Steinberg, D., & Cazden, C. (1979). Children as teachers—of peers and ourselves. *Theory into Practice, 18,* 258–266.

Tallmadge, G. K. (1977). *The idea book of the Joint Dissemination Review Panel.* Washington, DC: U.S. Office of Education and the National Institute of Education, U. S. Department of Health, Education and Welfare.

Tarone, E. (1988). *Variation in interlanguage.* London: Edward Arnold.

Wenden, A. L. (1987). Metacognition: An expanded view of the cognitive abilities of L2 learners. *Language Learning, 37,* 573–598.

White, L. (1986). Implications of parametric variation for adult second language acquisition: An investigation of the pro-drop parameter. In V. Cook (Ed.), *Experimental approaches to second language learning* (pp. 55–72). Oxford: Pergamon.

Wong Fillmore, L. (1976). *The second time around.* Unpublished doctoral dissertation, Stanford University.

Zamel, V. (1987). Recent research on writing pedagogy. *TESOL Quarterly, 21*(4), 697–715.

CHAPTER 8

Multisite, Multimethod, and Large-Scale Research

What kinds of language programs are funded by the U.S. government? How are such programs being implemented and what are their effects on students? What is the impact of immigration and migration on education and what are the experiences of immigrant and migrant students? What are some impacts of technology on L2 learning? These are some of the questions that researchers have addressed or could address in large-scale studies.

The final approach to research that we shall examine is a very loose category that I have termed *multisite, multimethod, large-scale research*. These approaches have been omitted from many discussions of research in L2 acquisition and L2 classroom research because those areas of inquiry have tended to focus on more micro-level issues of interaction. Yet language policy, as a wider societal issue, is an important field of inquiry (Hatch, 1989) as is language planning as it relates to international development education. The effects of language policy on language programs and ultimately on students is powerful. Program evaluation studies are important because they can illuminate the links among policy, classroom practice, and language learning.

In the first section of this chapter we will define this approach and discuss the distinction between research and evaluation. Next we will examine the results of a few multisite, multimethod, and large-scale studies in second language acquisition and bilingual education. We will then briefly review the range of methods used in conducting studies. Finally, we will apply a set of criteria for assessing a study to a specific example of evaluation research, which is a statewide study of the Migrant Education Program.

WHAT IS MULTISITE, MULTIMETHOD, LARGE-SCALE RESEARCH?

Multisite, multimethod, large-scale research refers to large studies in which a team of collaborating researchers collects data from a number of sites and employs a variety of both qualitative and quantitative data-collection and analysis strategies. The team of researchers may be based in a university, in a private research firm, or a school district, or researchers may collaborate across institutions. *Multimethod* studies combine two or more approaches to research in a single study. For example, a study may include qualitative case studies, quasi-experimentation, and quantitative descriptive data collection and analysis. Studies are often *longitudinal,* lasting one to three years or even longer. Budgets for studies that are both lengthy and large in scope might range from $200,000 up to $1 million. Funding for research of this scope is usually provided by *sponsors* such as government agencies or foundations. The purposes of these studies are to answer questions that are important not only to the researchers but also to the sponsor.

For example, the sponsor may want to gather information to describe the operation of a program that it funds. In this case the sponsor would fund a *descriptive study.* Alternatively, a sponsor might fund an *effectiveness study* to learn what programs or what aspects of programs are effective. A sponsor might fund a *policy study* to gather information about language policies and their implementation to inform future policy decisions. Large-scale studies often address major societal and educational issues that are politically controversial, such as the motivations for and effects of language policies, the effectiveness of bilingual education approaches compared to alternative approaches, or the value of varying approaches to multicultural literacy. On the whole, evaluation research has been conducted by dominant groups to study whether programs designed to improve language learning and educational experiences for marginalized groups are effective.

Evaluation versus Research

We can categorize multisite, multimethod studies as either research or evaluation. As both research and evaluation are forms of *disciplined inquiry* and should employ adequate methodology, the distinction between them that is made in the research methodology literature lies not in the methods that researchers use. Rather, the distinction rests in the major purpose of the study. The purpose of an *evaluation* study is to assess the quality, effectiveness, or general value of a program or other entity. The purpose of *research* is to contribute to the body of scholarly knowledge about a topic or to contribute to theory. This distinction in reality, however, is not so neat. Evaluation research that is not designed to contribute to theory could do so, while theory-oriented research could address the value of certain language-learning situations, teaching practices, and programs, serving either an intended or unintended evaluative function.

Research and evaluation differ not only in their central purpose but also in scope and audience. Second language evaluation studies are often much more comprehensive than are research studies. Ideally, an evaluation provides a thorough description of a program in its social context using multiple sources of data. In addition, the audiences for research and evaluation reports differ. While the primary audiences for research are usually academic discourse communities, the audiences for evaluation are the sponsor who requested and funded the study, as well as a number of stakeholders. *Stakeholders* are individuals with an interest in the processes, findings, and uses of an evaluation, and these might include researchers, teachers, professional organizations, political groups, school districts, or agencies. For the interested reader, there is an extensive body of literature on educational program evaluation, bilingual program evaluation, and a growing literature on ESL program evaluation.[1]

USES OF MULTISITE, MULTIMETHOD, LARGE-SCALE RESEARCH

Let us briefly examine the purposes and major findings of several multisite, multimethod, and large-scale studies. These examples include evaluation studies commissioned by a sponsor to assess a program, descriptive studies, and research studies whose major purpose is to add to the body of knowledge.

Studying Pragmatics across Cultures

Our first example is a study of linguistic pragmatics that is both multisite and cross-cultural. An international group of researchers has conducted extensive research into the pragmatic aspects of language use. Their purpose has been to discover how certain speech acts, such as requests and apologies, are realized in different languages. Blum-Kulka, House, and Kasper (1989) provide a full report of this project, which involved speakers of Argentinean Spanish, German, Israeli Hebrew, French, and English. By gathering data in different countries, and using the same theoretical framework and methods, the group identified both cross-cultural variation in speech-act realization and intralingual variation according to aspects of the situation.

The project is illustrative for its use of multiple sites across cultures, rather than for its use of multiple methods, however. The team relied primarily on the discourse completion test as a data-collection technique (see Chapter 5). A key disadvantage of the technique is that it is quite limited in addressing situational context and discourse factors that might affect speech-act realization. The researchers did, however, carry out some work comparing this method of data collection to others such as naturalistic speech and role-play (Rintell & Mitchell, 1989).

This study provides just one example of a cross-national linguistic research project. The important contribution of the work is in illustrating the many issues and problems involved in studying speech acts across languages and cultures. Work in this field is also important for teachers because it helps them understand the complex nature of communicative competence and all that students have to learn to be able to communicate their intentions in a less familiar language and culture.

The L2 Methods-Comparison Studies

What is the best way to learn a language? This simple question, for which there can never be one simple answer, has driven much research on L2 teaching. The best-known example of a large-scale multisite study is the Pennsylvania methods-comparison study in which an audiolingual method (ALM) was compared with a grammar-translation method. Summarizing the results of this and other similar studies, Politzer wrote in 1981:

> Some ten years later, the main message and impact of these studies can perhaps be summarized as follows: (1) They caused or perhaps rather confirmed a healthy skepticism in the pure habit formation type of audiolingualism which had dominated language teaching in the 1950's and early 1960's. (2) They underlined the apparently trivial but nevertheless very important fact that students tend to learn what they are taught. (3) They raised some doubts about the possibility of obtaining conclusive results from large-scale research in comparing methods of foreign language teaching. (p. 24)

Bilingual Program Evaluations

Despite these lessons gleaned from large-scale studies comparing L2 teaching methods, large-scale comparison studies continued to be funded in the United States because policymakers continued to want answers to questions such as: Is method A more effective than method B? The U.S. Department of Education sponsored a number of evaluations of bilingual programs. One lesson from the early evaluations was that there was sometimes more variation within program type than across programs. For example, many programs were struggling with implementation problems such as unprepared teachers, and some so-called bilingual programs involved very little use of the students' L1 for instruction. Bilingual education advocates insisted that complete descriptions of what occurred in classrooms must be an essential feature of an adequate evaluation (Horst et al., 1980a).

Later studies of bilingual education programs focused on the characteristics of successful programs. In one study (Tikunoff, 1985) researchers observed classrooms of 58 effective bilingual teachers at six different sites in the United States. Three common instructional features of these successful classes were highlighted: (1) both English and the students' native language were used in instruction; (2) L2 instruction was integrated with ongoing instruction in the content areas; and (3) teachers drew on students' cultural background. Although these results were less than astounding, the research emphasis on successful programs represented progress in asking better questions. More evaluations of two-way or dual language programs as well as of successful programs are needed, particularly studies that include rich descriptions of classroom processes (see, for example, Swain & Lapkin, 1989).

Aggregate Effects of Federal Programs

While some studies have singled out successful programs, others have attempted to identify the sources of problems. Kimbrough and Hill (1981) studied the effects of multiple federal programs in school districts that had trouble administering them. One important finding was that in some of these problem schools, Hispanic migrant students were pulled out for as many as six or seven special sessions per day. Students who were learning English typically spent half the school day in segregated situations. The potential harmful effects of a lack of continuity and too much disjointedness in the education of students from diverse linguistic and cultural backgrounds have been noted in other studies as well (Ventriglia, 1982, cited in Cazden, 1986).

Crossing the Schoolhouse Border

The educational experiences of culturally diverse students is the topic of an interesting policy report by Olsen (1988) published by California Tomorrow, a nonprofit organization based in San Francisco. The organization was established to address issues facing California's future,

> particularly those public policy concerns related to the state's future as a multi-national society with no ethnic/racial majority group. Economically, educationally and socially, the challenge presented by our changing demographics is to develop new approaches within our public institutions that make diversity workable. (p. 112)

Over a one-year period the California Tomorrow research staff conducted site visits to 29 school districts to interview personnel and gather information about programs and services for immigrant students. They conducted interviews with 360 recently arrived immigrant students aged 11 through 18 and with about

187 professionals involved in their schooling. The report provides a picture of the challenges that students face in cultural adjustment and the kinds of instruction they receive. A follow-up document for practitioners reviews a variety of promising programs for the overall education of immigrant children (Olsen, 1989).

MULTIPLE METHODS

Multisite, multimethod, and large-scale studies such as these may use and combine a wide variety of both qualitative and quantitative methods of data collection and analysis. These methods may include any of those discussed in previous chapters.

Data Collection and Analysis

The following data-collection methods are particularly common in large-scale program evaluations:

- site visits (single or multiple visits to educational institutions, units, classrooms)
- observations (structured, semistructured, open) of classes, lessons, meetings, communicative events, informal interactions, L1 use
- interviews (structured/formal, semistructured, informal/open) with key persons (students, parents, teachers, administrators)
- questionnaires (on attitudes, opinions, perceptions, language use, aspirations)
- test data (language proficiency data, general achievement data)
- written or computer-generated documents and student work (legal documents, program regulations, proposals, planning documents, curricula and books, evaluation reports, student writing)
- quantitative data (grade advancement data; program enrollment; drug use; socioeconomic indicators)

The advantage of using a variety of data-collection methods and gathering data from a variety of sources is that it allows for triangulation and helps the research team build a holistic picture of a program. This kind of broad view is not possible in very small studies or in single-method studies.

In previous chapters we introduced some of the methods of analysis that researchers employ. The key problem for a large study is integrating and making sense of the vast quantities of data that are accumulated. For the qualitative data, perhaps the most important principle is that qualitative data analysis is a continuous and iterative activity. After sessions of observation and interviewing, researchers comb repeatedly through their notes, trying to make sense of them.

They look for patterns, themes, or the clustering of events, processes, and classroom practices. They continually attempt to cross-validate what they have found. That is, they compare data obtained from one source in a particular manner (formal and informal interviews and discussions with teachers, for example) to data obtained from a different source in a different manner (classroom observations, for example) in a continuously interactive way. As qualitative data are analyzed and summarized, these findings are compared to and/or integrated with the quantitative data before final conclusions are drawn.

Meta-analysis and Meta-evaluation

Another type of research that can use the information obtained in multisite, multimethod, large-scale research and other studies as points of departure is the meta-evaluation. Just as metalanguage is language about language, a *meta-analysis* is an analysis of other analyses, and a *meta-evaluation* is an evaluation of evaluations. The purpose of a meta-analysis is to summarize, quantitatively, the findings of a given set of studies using mathematical procedures. Meta-analyses have been carried out for studies of computer-assisted learning (see Dunkel, 1991, for a review) and for bilingual education (Willig, 1985). A crucial principle to keep in mind in reading reports of meta-analyses is that the quality of the meta-analysis can be no better than the quality of the individual studies that it is based on.

Conducting a meta-evaluation involves developing criteria and assessing the quality of evaluations according to these criteria. For example, criteria that we used in a meta-evaluation of local bilingual program evaluations included adequate comparison standards, tests, description of students and programs, testing and scoring procedures, data analysis, and interpretation (Douglas & Johnson, 1981). Other meta-evaluation criteria include adequate scope, cost effectiveness of the study, and the quality and utility of the report. The last criterion is based on the assumption that the product of the evaluation is simply a report. Evaluations can be much more dynamic.

Fourth-Generation Evaluation

Fourth-Generation Evaluation is the title of Guba and Lincoln's 1989 book in which they propose a *constructivist evaluation model.* The model is based on the constructivist ontological, epistemological, and methodological views they have proposed (see Chapter 2). They see evaluation not as scientific and measurement-oriented, but as a fundamentally social, political, and value-laden endeavor involving negotiations among all the participants.

Two key characteristics of their model are: (1) responsive focusing and (2) constructivist methodology. *Responsive focusing,* based on Stake's notion of responsive evaluation, requires that the design of the study emerge as stakeholders discuss and determine the boundaries of the study and what they want from the study. The *constructivist methodology* contributes to responsiveness as it requires that each group of stakeholders deal with the claims, issues, and concerns of all other groups in a hermeneutic dialectic, that is, through negotiations arranged by the evaluators. The conclusions, then, are arrived at jointly.

CRITERIA FOR ASSESSING STUDIES

Because multisite, multimethod, large-scale studies vary so widely, the assessment questions presented below, which are oriented toward evaluation research, can serve only as a general guide. In reading reports of large studies, you should attempt to answer as many of the questions as possible to your own satisfaction, but, because of the broad scope of such studies, only portions can be reported in journal articles or book chapters. As with many ethnographies, the only way to understand the complete study is to read the entire set of reports and/or resulting documents.

1. What were the research or evaluation questions?
2. In what context was the research conducted? Who funded the study and why?
3. What is the program and whom does it serve?
4. What were the orientations of the sponsors, researchers, participants, and stakeholders?
5. Who were the participants in the study? What was the sample of sites, institutions, programs, teachers, students, parents?
6. What data-collection methods were used?
7. What means were used to analyze and integrate data?
8. How were results communicated or reported?
9. What results are presented and what conclusions are drawn?
10. What is the contribution of the study and what are its implications?

We will now use these questions as a guide to examine a sample evaluation study, a study of the Migrant Education Program.

SAMPLE STUDY: AN EVALUATION OF THE MIGRANT EDUCATION PROGRAM

For years the education of language-minority students had been the unique interest and specialty of second language and bilingual educators and researchers. In the last two decades, however, changing demographics have brought these issues to the attention of a much wider community of researchers and teachers. Increasingly higher proportions of students are involved in the learning of additional languages and cultures, and increasingly higher proportions of teachers, not just those in large urban areas, are addressing the challenges of diversity. In fact, in 1989, so-called minorities made up more than half of California's school population, 1 of 6 students in the state was born in another country, and 1 of 4 school children spoke a language other than English at home (Kirst et al., 1989). These state statistics are important for the United States as a whole because 1 out of 9 U.S. children and adolescents between the ages of 5 and 18 resided in California in 1989.

In the climate of educational reform of the 1980s, educators focused attention on students described as "at risk" of not succeeding in school or dropping out altogether (Cook-Gumperz, 1986; Jacob & Jordan, 1987). Scholars such as Cummins (1989) have argued that basic-skills-oriented reform efforts have worked against language-minority students and they have proposed models and approaches aimed at richer, high-quality educational experiences (Cummins, 1984, 1986; Mehan, Moll, & Reil, 1985).

Researchers also began to take a more global look at students, particularly those labeled "at risk" owing to a combination of factors associated with dropping out or with less than optimal success. These factors include parents' educational aspirations for their children, frequent moving, home conditions not conducive to study, health and drug problems, and neighborhood and peer influences. Other scholars have placed their emphasis on the resources that students bring to the classroom and that can benefit all students (Moll, 1989; Ruiz, 1984).

A major group of language learners that has received little attention in the L2 literature is migrant students in the United States. Not only is their schooling interrupted because their parents move from one location to another in search of work, but a large percentage of migrant students need to learn English as an additional language to succeed in school. The Migrant Education Program, funded by the U.S. government, has been a major provider of instructional and other services to migrant students.

I have selected an evaluation of the Migrant Education Program as a sample of a multisite, multimethod, large-scale study. The evaluation presented here was conducted for the State of California. It was a two-year study, focusing on a broad range of issues and employing multiple methods. During the second year it included a sub-study of instruction, involving observations of 86 classrooms throughout the state, to examine the organization of instruction, the organizational contexts for instruction, and interactions among participants in the process. As we go through the series of questions, we will focus on the research at two levels: the overall two-year study and the study of classroom instruction.

1. What were the research or evaluation questions?

The overall purpose of the study was to evaluate the operation of the program. During the first year the research staff focused holistically on all components of the program (these are described below). An important aspect of the first-year study was a formative evaluation of each of the 13 districts studied. The purpose was to provide formative feedback of a confidential nature to participants. Formative studies were also conducted in each region, and at the state level.

In the second year of the study (Noggle et al., 1982, 1983), the research questions focused on the nature of instruction, including the summer school instructional program, with a secondary focus on staff development, needs assessment, and parent involvement. In addition to basic issues such as who teaches migrant students during migrant supplemental instruction and what they teach, we were primarily interested in describing the nature of the interactions among the various participants in the students' education. These included the following interactions between:

1. *Migrant staff and migrant students:* Where is instruction provided? What grouping strategies are used? What methods are used? What language-use policies and practices are employed?
2. *The regular classroom teachers and migrant students:* What languages does the teacher use? How much interaction is there? To what extent is the teacher aware of the progress migrant students are making during supplemental instruction?
3. *The migrant aide and the regular classroom teacher:* How do aides and regular teachers communicate, cooperate, and plan jointly?

On the whole, we were interested not only in describing what was occurring but also in identifying practices that contributed to high-quality instructional environments.

2. In what context was the research conducted? Who funded the study and why?

The context in which this study of classroom practices was carried out was a statewide evaluation conducted over a two-year period by an educational research corporation under contract to the State Department of Education. The study was funded by the federal Chapter I Migrant Program. In addition to a requirement for evaluation in the federal regulations for Migrant Education, California legislation mandated an annual statewide evaluation of the state's program. Evaluations had typically been carried out by individual sites, but the Migrant Education Office of the state decided to pool money and to fund a statewide study. State officials contracted with a private research firm to conduct the evaluation.

3. What is the program, and whom does it serve?

The introductory section of the journal report (Johnson, 1987) provides a description of the migrant students based on data collected during the study.

In general, migrant students in California have at least three characteristics that make them one of the groups of children and youth who are at risk. First, migrant students, by definition, have had their schooling interrupted because of moves. For this reason they often fall behind in school. Migrant students' families generally move because the parents are involved in seasonal agricultural and fishing industries. In 1982–83, for example, about one third to one half of the families of migrant students made at least one move during the school year, while others tended to move during the summer or early fall. Fortunately many returned to the same town or school district, so that in some cases students were able to resume their schooling with the same teachers. (Johnson, 1987, pp. 437–438)

Second, of the third-grade migrant students in California enrolled in 1982–1983, the year in which data were collected, 57% were classified by the state as limited in English proficiency (LEP). Third, as a group, migrant students' academic achievement was low, with those in the third grade (excluding students categorized as non–English-speaking) performing between the 21st and 35th percentile on standardized achievement tests. Their math scores (35) were higher than their English scores (reading, 29; writing, 21), however. The program is described in the following way:

> The Migrant Education Program is a federally funded program designed to assist migrant students in overcoming these obstacles to success in school. In fiscal 1982 the State of California received about $61 million in ESEA (Elementary and Secondary Education Act) Chapter I Migrant funds for the program and served 80,000 students from preschool through high school (Noggle, Garza, Weiner, Abrica-Carrasco, & Johnson, 1982). More than three quarters of these students (78%) were in elementary schools. A total of 32,000 migrant students were served in summer school programs. (p. 438)

At the time of the study, the program comprised 13 components addressing not only instruction but also health, staff development, counseling, needs assessment, parent involvement, and the Migrant Student Record Transfer System (a computerized system designed to keep track of and transfer student records across states and districts).

> The instructional components were designed to be strictly "supplemental" to the regular school program and to focus on the "basic skills." Because about half of the migrant students in California were acquiring English as a second language, much of the instruction was focused on improving English. (pp. 438–439)

The program provided wide-ranging services to students. We saw this as one of its great strengths. However, definitions of the program as "supplemental" and as addressing "basic" skills led to some disjointed and reductionist practices.

4. What were the orientations of the sponsors, researchers, participants, and/or stakeholders?

The principal stakeholders included all of the migrant program personnel, including state, regional, and district-level personnel, and parents. Program personnel were strongly committed to serving migrant students. Many administrators had a long history with the program and were committed to preserving its identity as distinct from other programs. While all were concerned about students learning English and succeeding academically, most did not see L1 use and development as a program goal.

The professional research staff had its own values and orientations. Our collective areas of expertise included second language acquisition, minority education, educational policy, anthropology, and sociology. Three were Chicanos and four were fluent Spanish speakers. In terms of evaluation methods, the entire team was committed to formative approaches and to multidisciplinary perspectives. All were advocates for language-minority students and strong advocates for both bilingual education and anti-racist education. These value orientations affected what we studied. For example, we were interested in examining attitudes toward native-language use as well as how so-called "basic skills" and English were promoted. In at least one instance, the values of the research team created tensions when program practices that team members interpreted as potentially racist were brought out and criticized. On the whole, however, program personnel and the research team shared a general interest in quality education for migrant students.

5. & 6. Who were the participants in the study? What data-collection methods were used?

For the overall evaluation study, we used a methodology based on multiple sources of data. We visited each of 10 regional offices and the State Department of Education, and made three 5-day site visits to each of 11 districts over the course of the year. We conducted on-site interviews with 19 categories of respondents at the state, regional, district, and school levels, including both nonmigrant and migrant staff. In addition we surveyed a sample of 100 districts by mail to gather questionnaire data on program characteristics as well as data on the English language proficiency, grade advancement, graduation, and mobility of migrant students. We also gathered achievement data from the statewide testing program, the California Assessment Program (CAP).

Observation Sample. The procedures used in the study of classroom instruction are described:

From each of the 11 districts to which site visits were made during the second year of the study, three or four schools, those that served the largest numbers of migrant students, were selected, and within each school two classes, on the average, were selected for observation. While a broad range of subject areas and grade levels was observed, 50 of the 86 observations (58%) were of English instruction. (p. 440)

Classroom Observation Instrument. The research staff developed an observation instrument that would allow us to collect both quantitative and qualitative information about classrooms. It is described as follows:

> The classroom observation instrument, constructed by the research staff to obtain a range of information, contained a highly structured section, a semistructured section, and an open-ended section. The structured section allowed for the collection of data on classroom identity, classroom composition, use of staff with students, grouping procedures, type of instruction, language use of migrant aide, language use of regular teacher, and amount of communication with migrant students. The semistructured section contained questions dealing with the interactions between staff and students (rapport, teaching methods, engaged time, contribution of instruction to progress in regular class); between regular teacher and migrant students (knowledge of student progress, communication); and between regular teacher and migrant staff (evidence of joint planning, team teaching, rapport). The unstructured section was open-ended to allow for a qualitative, rich description of classroom atmosphere and events. (pp. 440–441)

Training and Conducting the Observations and Interviews. The training that we instituted to ensure some degree of consistency across observations is described:

> Training sessions were held prior to site visits in order to clarify category definitions and finalize observation and interview procedures. In addition, while site visits were in progress, the Director of the Study of Instruction contacted site visitors by telephone in order to resolve any problems such as lack of clarity regarding the categorization or description of unanticipated circumstances or events. (p. 441)

We were concerned about excessive pullouts and were interested in whether and how migrant staff and nonmigrant staff coordinated instruction across pullout and classroom contexts. This section of the journal report describes how we included this topic in our interviews:

> In addition to the observations, both migrant staff and regular (non-migrant) staff were interviewed regarding instructional practices. Of particular interest was the degree of coordination between migrant staff and the regular classroom

teacher. Thus, when migrant instruction was provided in a pullout setting outside of the students' regular classroom, the observer went back to the regular classroom to attempt to determine the relationship between the migrant supplementary instruction and regular classroom instruction. In interviews with regular teachers, the extent of coordination was assessed. Coordination was also assessed at the school level through interviews with principals, bilingual program personnel, Chapter I personnel, and other related program personnel. (p. 441)

7. What means were used to analyze and integrate data?

Data analysis was time-consuming, multifaceted, and ongoing. Our qualitative analyses of information obtained from interviews and observations had top priority and were recursive. We also carried out quantitative analyses of achievement, proficiency, questionnaire, and mobility data.

Data Integration. Because we gathered a great deal of data from many sources, the methods used to integrate information were important. We summarized our approach briefly as follows:

> Data obtained from one source in a particular manner (on-site interviews with aides, for example) were used to cross-validate data obtained from a different source in a different manner (observations of classroom instruction done during the second year, for example) in a continuously interactive system (Noggle et al., 1982). (Johnson, 1987, pp. 439–440)

Throughout the study we held "crosstalks," discussion sessions in which we compared our findings from field visits, discussed emerging issues, and planned issues to explore and strategies to use in future field visits. These crosstalks were an essential and productive part of ongoing analysis.

Analysis of Classroom Observation Data. In the report, I briefly decribe the procedures we used to analyze the classroom observation data.

> Classroom observation data were analyzed using both qualitative and quantitative means. The data from each of the 86 classroom observations were coded and categorized by two people, the observer and the Director of the Study of Instruction, who also served as observer at some of the sites. The participation of the Director in every coding session served to provide consistency across observers in the coding of the quantitative data and in the categorizing of the qualitative information. (pp. 441–442)
>
> Quantitative data were analyzed using Statistical Analysis System (SAS), a statistical package capable of handling multiple data bases. Analyses consisted primarily of the calculation of frequencies, means, standard deviations, crosstabulations of frequencies, and other descriptive statistics. Qualitative

data were analyzed by summarizing information by category and examining the information, along with related information from other sources, for themes or patterns, and for examples of exemplary practices. (p. 442)

8. How were results communicated or reported?

For the larger two-year study, the research team reported findings in a variety of ways, including interim and final reports to the state. During the first year, the formative aspects of the study involved holding reporting and discussion sessions with each district as well as giving them a report in written form. These reports were confidential and not shared with state personnel.

9. What results are presented and what conclusions are drawn?

One of the most significant findings of the overall study was that migrant staff at all levels were making sincere and dedicated efforts to provide educational continuity for migrant students. The program's broad emphasis on the whole student provided valuable support for students. Even so, we found that an effective partnership between the Migrant Education Program staff and other staff was often missing. This issue had important consequences for instruction. In general, the more that migrant instruction was integrated with mainstream bilingual or all-English instruction, the more effective it appeared to be in helping students succeed in school (Johnson, 1987, p. 449). We will discuss only a few specific results here, drawing primarily from the study of instruction.

Aides as Teachers and Advocates. Uncertified migrant instructional aides provided the majority of supplemental instruction to migrant students. In 99% of the classroom observations, the migrant staff person providing instruction was an aide. While the position of migrant resource teacher was a common one, usually that person's responsibility involved training and supervising aides, rather than teaching migrant students. Qualitative data from interviews and responses to questionnaires, however, indicated that interviewees and respondents would prefer more teaching by certified migrant staff. Indeed, there was a trend toward hiring more certified migrant teachers to work directly with migrant students. The programs judged to be of the highest quality by the research staff were those in which certified migrant teachers worked with students. Because bilingual, migrant, and ESL professionals have long been concerned that students spend too much time being instructed by paraprofessionals, the trend toward more use of qualified teachers was positive.

Most of the aides (96%) were bilingual and/or were at one time members of migrant families themselves. We observed and rated the apparent rapport between aides and their students and found that in 98% of the classrooms, rapport was fair to excellent. Aides seemed to have empathy for migrant students and were committed both to helping them with their school work and serving as advocates for them in their total school experience. The extent to which their advocacy was effective depended to a large degree on contextual factors that are addressed below.

The Content of Instruction. Migrant instruction focused primarily on English, math, and the information needed to pass proficiency tests. Although 90% of the programs provided ESL instruction, only 40% provided native language assistance with reading and writing, and few placed any emphasis on science and social studies. Assistance in science and social studies occurred more often in bilingual education settings or in high school programs. We observed many instances of in-class assistance that was highly relevant to helping students succeed in their high school content classes.

Interactions between Migrant Staff and Migrant Students. Most instruction was provided within the regular classroom. In two-thirds (68%) of the migrant sessions we observed, aides worked with students in the regular classroom, while in 32% of the sessions we observed, they taught in a pullout setting outside of the regular classroom. These pullout groups met in a variety of locations including resource rooms or laboratories (40%), unused classrooms (30%), designated "migrant classrooms" (20%), and sometimes in noisy cafeterias (10%). Aides most often worked with small groups of two to five students (48% of the sessions observed) and with individual students (40% of the sessions observed). They worked with large groups less frequently (12% of the sessions). The aides spent 46% of their instructional time conducting drill, practice, review, or translation activities. A similar percentage of time, 43%, was spent monitoring students' work or explaining the work in progress. As we had expected, only a small proportion of time, 5%, was devoted to introducing new material or new concepts. These data illustrate the clearly supplemental nature of migrant instruction as well as its emphasis on individualized support.

Language-Use Policy and Practice. Migrant staff used English much more than the student's native language in instruction. The unwritten language use policy was: "Use English rather than the native language for content instruction to the extent possible." Our functional analysis of L1 use revealed that when the L1 was used it was used primarily for reviewing and translating functions rather than the introduction of new concepts or material.

When the migrant programs were supplementing bilingual education programs, language use was consistent with bilingual program policy. The unstated bilingual education philosophy was transitional, and our questionnaire results indicated that 80% of school-district staff were satisfied with the role of the Migrant Program in assisting ESL students in the "transition" from the primary language into English. Although the policy of the program was merely to supplement regular instruction, program staff often took the initiative in establishing an ESL program where there was none; they did not, however, take the initiative in establishing a bilingual program where there was none.

Approaches to ESL. Providing ESL was conceptualized as (1) the application of a structured commercial ESL curriculum to the students (2) by a designated ESL provider (3) in a situation, defined by time and location, that was identifiable in the organizational structure of the school. We saw few signs of the purposeful integration of academic content and language learning within the ESL lessons and no evidence of plans for grouping students and structuring interaction throughout the day in ways that would enhance their second language and literacy development. Furthermore, we observed few signs of the use of authentic materials and few opportunities for students to create their own meanings either in writing or speaking.

One change that was taking place, however, was that plans were being formulated to prepare regular elementary classroom teachers to teach ESL in the classroom. On the whole, then, most of the ESL instruction we observed was not communicative in nature and was conducted by teacher aides with much empathy and dedication but with limited training.

Teacher Awareness of Student Progress. It was our belief that the more that regular teachers knew about their migrant students' progress in migrant supplementary instruction, the better they could support the students' overall learning. We investigated this issue directly by first observing students during migrant instruction, and then interviewing their regular teachers regarding the progress their migrant students were making in this supplemental instruction. We rated the extent of their knowledge on a scale of 1 (no awareness) to 4 (considerable awareness).

We found that the location of migrant instruction was associated with level of awareness. As expected, only 17% of those teachers who chose small-group pullout arrangements were rated as having considerable awareness of their students' progress. In contrast, 65% of those teachers who chose to have migrant aides work with small groups in their regular classroom had considerable awareness of the academic progress of the migrant students.

The contrast was even more striking for individuals. The percentage of regular teachers who chose to have individual migrant students pulled out of the classroom and who had considerable awareness of their progress was 0. Those who favored in-class-at-desk and in-class-pull-aside arrangements for individuals were much more knowledgeable about those students. The percentages who evidenced considerable awareness of their progress were 71% and 86%, respectively. These results, from 86 observations, indicate that pullout supplementary instruction was associated with a disjointedness in the students' education.

Interactions between Migrant Staff and Nonmigrant Staff. This disjointedness was found at many levels. Our major finding regarding interactions between migrant and nonmigrant staff, based on information triangulated from many sources, was that in most programs there was little joint planning. We also found a lack of planning at the program level among the various programs serving migrant students, including Chapter I, bilingual education, and Migrant Education. Yet, joint planning was a critical characteristic of the high-quality programs. Those migrant programs that we qualitatively judged as most effective evidenced close communication and coordination among migrant and other staff.

At the school level, those schools that were successful at cross-program planning shared two features: (1) a principal provided active leadership in promoting planning or a resource teacher provided leadership with the principal's support; and (2) some structure was provided for the planning process, such as a committee that held regular meetings. These organizational features created contexts in which collaboration for the benefit of students was encouraged and supported.

10. What is the contribution of the study and what are its implications?

One contribution of the study of instruction was to document that pullout supplementary instructional arrangements were associated with a lack of knowledge, on the part of regular classroom teachers, about migrant students' activities and progress. Pullout arrangements as an organizational structure for migrant education, then, can be counterproductive in many situations if the goal of such instruction is to help students to get along in the mainstream bilingual or all-English curriculum. Often this was a situation over which migrant aides had no control. Because they were to "supplement" regular instruction, they often could only comply with regular teachers' requests about where supplementary instruction should occur. We therefore recommended that qualified, certified migrant resource teachers take a stronger role in instructional leadership.

Another barrier to providing high-quality instructional experiences lay in the migrant program staff's interpretation of "basic skills." Because those migrant programs that operated in the context of a bilingual program were rated by the research staff as higher in quality, we recommended that migrant staff be stronger advocates for the initiation of both effective approaches to promoting L2 development and high-quality bilingual or multilingual programs that build on students' strengths.

CONCLUSION

Perhaps the greatest potential disadvantage of large-scale studies is that if the research questions are somehow misguided, large amounts of public funds might be spent for little benefit. On the other hand, large-scale, multimethod studies can be important in L2 research for several reasons. First, researchers can study programs across many sites, providing a description of the key aspects of an entire program. This breadth is accompanied by some depth when researchers make repeated visits to each site, as we did in this study. Second, a collaborative, team approach to research enriches the study by encouraging multiple and multidisciplinary perspectives.

Third, as we have seen in previous chapters, the use of multiple methods allows researchers to study some of the contextual factors that shape learning opportunities, such as staff characteristics and interaction, program management, and the students' family life. Multiple methods also allow researchers to triangulate, to obtain a more complete and holistic picture of the phenomena under study.

Finally, many of these studies address policy issues. As L2 professionals we are all involved with policy in one way or another. We formulate it, we implement it, we deviate from it, we try to ignore it, we speak out against it, or we change it. Because national, state, and local language policies and language-program policies have a profound effect on institutions, teachers, and students, these policies and how they are carried out in day-to-day interactions constitute an important topic of L2 research.

NOTE

1. For discussions of program evaluation in education and the social sciences see Cronbach, 1982; Eisner, 1985; Fetterman, 1984; Guba and Lincoln, 1989; and the journal *Educational Evaluation and Policy Analysis*. Discussions of ESL and bilingual education program evaluation can be found in Beretta, 1986; Genesee, 1987; Hakuta, 1986; Horst et al., 1980a, 1980b; Nunan, 1988; Swain and Lapkin, 1982; and Tallmadge, Lam, and Gamel, 1987.

REFERENCES

Beretta, A. (1986). Program-fair language teaching evaluation. *TESOL Quarterly, 20,* 431–444.

Blum-Kulka, S., House, H., & Kasper, G. (1989). *Cross-cultural pragmatics: Requests and apologies.* Norwood, NJ: Ablex.

Cazden, C. (1986). ESL teachers as language advocates for children. In P. Rigg & D. S. Enright (Eds.), *Children and ESL:* Integrating perspectives (pp. 9–21). Washington, DC: Teachers of English to Speakers of Other Languages.

Cook-Gumperz, J. (1986). *The social construction of literacy.* Cambridge: Cambridge University Press.

Cronbach, L. J. (1982). *Designing evaluations of educational and social programs.* San Francisco: Jossey-Bass.

Cummins, J. (1984). *Bilingualism and special education: Issues in assessment and pedagogy.* Clevedon, England: Multilingual Matters. Co-published in the United States by College-Hill Press, San Diego.

Cummins, J. (1986). Empowering minority students: A framework for intervention. *Harvard Educational Review, 56,* 18–36.

Cummins, J. (1989). The sanitized curriculum: Educational disempowerment in a nation at risk. In D. M. Johnson & D. H. Roen (Eds.), *Richness in writing: Empowering ESL students* (pp. 120–133). White Plains, NY: Longman.

Douglas, D., & Johnson, D. M. (1981). *An evaluation of Title VII evaluations: Results from a national study.* Paper presented at the Annual Meeting of the National Association for Bilingual Education, Boston.

Dunkel, P. A. (1991). The effectiveness of computer-assisted instruction and computer-assisted language learning. In P. A. Dunkel (Ed.), *Computer-assisted language learning and testing: Research issues and practice.* New York: Harper Collins/Newbury House.

Eisner, E. (1985). *The educational imagination: On the design and evaluation of school programs.* New York: Macmillan.

Fetterman, D. M. (1984). Guilty knowledge, dirty hands, and other ethnical dilemmas: The hazards of contract research. In D. M. Fetterman (Ed.), *Ethnography in educational evaluation* (pp. 211–236). Newbury Park, CA: Sage.

Genesee, F. (1987). *Learning through two languages: Studies of immersion and bilingual education.* New York: Harper & Row.

Guba, E. G., & Lincoln, Y. (1989). *Fourth-generation evaluation.* Newbury Park, CA: Sage.

Hakuta, K. (1986). *Mirror of language.* New York: Basic Books.

Hatch, E. (1989, February). *Multidisciplinary perspectives in SLA.* Plenary address presented at the Second Language Research Forum, Los Angeles.

Horst, D. P., Douglas, D. E., Friendly, L. D., Johnson, D. M., Luber, L. M., McKay, M., Nava, H. G., Peistrup, A. M., Roberts, A. O. H., & Valdez, A. (1980a). *An evaluation of Project Information Packages as used for the diffusion of bilingual projects* (Vol.2) (Report No. VR-460). Mountain View, CA: RMC Research Corporation. (ERIC Document Reproduction Service No. ED 193 954)

Horst, D. P., Johnson, D. M., Nava, H. G., Douglas, D. E., Friendly, L. D., & Roberts, A. O. H. (1980b). *A prototype guide to measuring achievement level and program impact on achievement in bilingual projects* (Report No. VR-46). Mountain View, CA: RMC Research Corporation. (ERIC Document Reproduction Service No. ED 193 955)

Jacob, E., & Jordan, C. (1987). Explaining the school performance of minority students. [Special Issue]. *Anthropology & Education Quarterly, 18*(4).

Johnson, D. M. (1987). The organization of instruction in migrant education: Assistance for children and youth at risk. *TESOL Quarterly, 21,* 437–459.

Kimbrough, J., & Hill, P. (1981). *The aggregate effects of federal education programs: Summary.* Santa Monica, CA: Rand.

Kirst, M., et al. (1989). *Conditions of education in California.* Berkeley, CA: Policy Analysis for California Education.

Mehan, H., Moll, L., & Reil, M. (1985, June). *Computers in classrooms: A quasi-experiment in guided change.* Final report to the National Institute of Education. La Jolla: University of California, San Diego.

Moll, L. (1989). Teaching second language students: A Vygotskian perspective. In D. M. Johnson & D. H. Roen (Eds.), *Richness in writing* (pp. 55–69). White Plains, NY: Longman.

Noggle, N. L., Garza, H. A., Weiner, F. S., Abrica-Carrasco, R., & Johnson, D. M. (1982). *The education of California's migrant students: An evaluation of the Migrant Education Program—technical addendum.* Mountain View, CA: RMC Research Corporation.

Noggle, N. L., Garza, H. A., Weiner, F. S., Abrica-Carrasco, R., & Johnson, D. M. (1983). *The education of California's migrant students: An evaluation of the Migrant Education Program—final report.* Mountain View, CA: RMC Research Corporation.

Nunan, D. (1988). *The learner-centred curriculum: A study in second language teaching.* Cambridge: Cambridge University Press.

Olsen, L. (1988). *Crossing the schoolhouse border: Immigrant students and the California public schools.* San Francisco: California Tomorrow.

Olsen, L. (1989). *Bridges: Promising practices for the education of immigrant children.* San Francisco: California Tomorrow.

Politzer, R. L. (1981). Effective language teaching: Insights from research. In J. E. Alatis, H. B. Altman, & P. M. Alatis, *The second language classroom: Directions for the 1980's* (pp. 23– 35). New York: Oxford University Press.

Rintell, E. M., & Mitchell, C. J. (1989). Studying requests and apologies: An inquiry into method. In S. Blum-Kulka, J. House, & G. Kasper, *Cross-cultural pragmatics: Requests and apologies.* Norwood, NJ: Ablex.

Ruiz, R. (1984). Orientations in language planning. *NABE Journal, 8,* 15–34.

Swain, M., & Lapkin, S. (1982). *Evaluating bilingual education: A Canadian case study.* Clevedon, England: Multilingual Matters.

Swain, M., & Lapkin, S. (1989). Canadian immersion and adult second language teaching: What's the connection? *Modern Language Journal, 73,* 150–159.

Tallmadge, G. K., Lam, T. C. M., & Gamel, N. N. (1987). *The evaluation of bilingual education programs for language-minority, limited-English-proficient students: A status report with recommendations for future development.* Mountain View, CA: RMC Research Corporation.

Tikunoff, W. (1985). *Applying significant bilingual instructional features in the classroom.* Rosslyn, VA: National Clearinghouse for Bilingual Education.

Willig, A. (1985). A meta-analysis of selected studies on the effectiveness of bilingual education. *Review of Educational Research, 55,* 269–317.

CHAPTER 9

Researchers, Teachers, and Inquiry

Donna M. Johnson and Lihe Chen

This book has focused on alternative approaches that researchers use to conduct inquiry. We have most often used the term "researcher" to refer to one who does research in universities and other research institutions, usually as a major part of a professional role. A growing number of researchers and scholars are advocating teacher involvement in research, and an evolving teacher-research movement (sometimes called "action research" in the field of second language acquisition and teaching), is underway. These scholars have suggested that teacher involvement in research is an effective way to bridge the gaps between theory and practice and contribute to knowledge. Cochran-Smith and Lytle, for example, propose that

> What is missing from the knowledge base for teaching . . . are the voices of the teachers themselves, the questions teachers ask, the ways teachers use writing and intentional talk in their work lives, and the interpretive frames teachers use to understand and improve their own classroom practices. (Cochran-Smith & Lytle, 1990, p. 2)

Because teachers are so close to students on a daily basis, their own inquiry from their unique perspectives can make an important contribution to knowledge about teaching and learning (Cochran-Smith & Lytle, 1990; Miller, 1990). In addition, teachers who conduct their own research build a richer understanding of their work lives and gain the confidence, knowledge, and support needed to make important changes (Miller, 1990; van Lier, 1990).

What are the roles of language teachers in relation to research? Are teachers merely an audience for researchers? Are they simply to consume, apply, and

212

learn from the research of others? Or should teachers do research themselves? What contributions can teacher-researchers make to knowledge and what are some pitfalls that they should be aware of? As the teacher-researcher movement has gained momentum, issues such as these have received increasing attention in a wide variety of publications (Nunan, 1989). The purpose of this chapter is not to propose definitive answers to such questions but rather to explore some of the issues under discussion.

ROLES OF TEACHERS
IN RELATION TO RESEARCH

Teachers Reading and Applying Research

In Chapter 1 we argued against a mechanical consumer model of applying research. In the traditional model, researchers conduct research, and the role of the teacher is that of a passive recipient of findings who is expected to "apply" those findings in the classroom. One problem with this notion is that it is based on the assumption that studies provide unequivocal answers to questions. Most often they do not. High-quality studies provide important new insights, but they always raise many questions as well. They set us wondering about issues that were formerly outside of our awareness. Second, results are often not widely generalizable. Intelligent judgments must be made about the ways in which a study may or may not apply to a different set of learners in a different task or learning situation or in a different cultural setting. A third problem with the consumer model of applying research is that, as reader-response theory suggests, readers of studies gain different insights from the same study. For example, after reading Gibson's (1987) study of Punjabi high school students, one reader might "apply" what he learned by trying to find out more about his own students' family values and views of success. Another reader might restructure her stereotypes about Asian high school students.

Readers of a research report, then, construct highly personal meanings from the text depending on their experiences, background knowledge, current interests, and purposes for reading the study. Because readers construct their own meanings, we have proposed a model of applying research as re-seeing learners, the learning process, and the teaching process. This anti-consumer model of benefitting from research implies a deep respect for the everyday practical knowledge of teachers and its role in building new understandings. Seeing learning and teaching through new lenses and from different perspectives can then lead to new attitudes and to new kinds of action aimed at improving practice. Often there are inconsistencies between what we know, what we believe, what we would like to do, and what we actually do. One way that we work out these tensions is to act on the new ideas we formulate from reading pertinent research. Such action may occur only after some time, however, as new ideas often percolate for a long time before we integrate them into what we do.

Teachers Doing Research

In addition to teachers' roles as active constructors of knowledge from the research they read and hear reported, many researchers, teachers, and teacher-researchers alike advocate new and expanding roles for teachers in the research process. These roles include teachers initiating and conducting research themselves, participating in teacher inquiry groups, or collaborating with university professors in joint projects.

Some teachers may feel that L2 teachers and L2 researchers have very little in common, however. To many teachers, the results of research seem either irrelevant for teaching or inaccessible. Irrelevant—because too often statistical models, linguistic categories, trends, an advisor's wishes, and governmental politics, rather than the issues that perplex teachers and cause them to wonder, detemine research questions. Inaccessible—because some research is cloaked in what teachers see as elitist veils, such that knowledge of advanced statistics and the details of the latest controversy in linguistic theory are required simply to comprehend the report (Johnson, 1987). It is not surprising that teachers see research as irrelevant and inaccessible when the real audience for most research reports, particularly those published in journals, is not teachers but other researchers.

Yet, teachers and researchers do have many common aims. Both aim to continually improve classroom learning experiences for L2 users. That is, one of the goals of most L2 researchers is to contribute to knowledge that will ultimately inform classroom practice, while dedicated teachers are continually on the lookout for theory, research, and ideas that can help them rethink and improve their L2 programs and classes. In fact, many of us are both re-searchers and teachers. Yet if researchers write for other researchers, how are the gaps between research and teaching, and between theory and practice, to be bridged?

Many propose that the teacher-as-researcher movement holds the greatest promise for linking theory and practice in ways that are meaningful to teachers. Van Lier (1990), in fact, following Stenhouse (1975), claims that "if significant and lasting improvements in classroom second language learning are to be achieved, this can best be done by teachers and learners doing their own research in their own classrooms" (p. 174). We will now take a look at several of the issues under discussion in the teacher-research movement. These issues include defining teacher-research, collaborative arrangements, methods and standards, topics of research, and the goals of the movement.

WHAT IS TEACHER-RESEARCH?

The teacher-researcher movement has its philosophical foundations in and builds on a wide range of thinking. Its rationales are grounded in views of the social construction of knowledge, feminist theory, post-structuralism, curriculum theory, research as praxis, and critical theory (Brodkey, 1987; Miller, 1990; Schubert, 1990). The movement is also based on conceptions of teachers as reflective practitioners, intellectuals, and theory-makers (Schon, 1983; Giroux, 1988). Its goals, which are political as well as intellectual, are linked to notions of emancipation, empowerment, liberation, and democracy (Giroux, 1988).

While the philosophical basis for the movement seems cohesive, conceptions of teacher-research as action vary widely. For example, Bissex (1986) defines a teacher-researcher as one who observes, questions, and learns in the context of his or her own classroom and who, as a result, becomes a better teacher. For Bissex, teacher-research involves taking notice of and attempting to understand what occurs in the classroom. As she suggests, "Everything that happens in a classroom can be seen as data to be understood rather than causes for blaming or congratulating ourselves or our students" (Bissex, 1986, p. 483). The teacher-researcher notices problems as well as successes, but problems can become questions to investigate and occasions for learning. As a result, "new approaches to teaching are no longer just risks, but opportunities for learning" (Bissex, 1986, p. 483). The classroom, then, is a learning laboratory for the teacher. This view of teacher-research is quite broad, with a strong emphasis on conscious reflection. It differs little, however, from how many would define a good teacher as a reflective practitioner. Most thoughtful teachers try out new approaches to creating optimal learning situations; they carefully observe what happens; and they modify their practice based on what they have learned.

Cochran-Smith and Lytle (1990) take a somewhat different perspective. They concur that teachers' desire to make sense of their classroom experiences motivates their inquiry and that teacher-researchers adopt a "learning stance or openness toward classroom life" (p. 3). Their conception of teacher-research is more precisely defined, however, as "systematic and intentional inquiry carried out by teachers" (p. 3). This view goes further toward distinguishing teacher-research from good teaching. By "intentional" these writers mean that research is planned rather than spontaneous. They offer less guidance, however, in defining "systematic," stating that teacher-research involves "gathering and recording information, documenting experiences inside and outside of classrooms, and making some kind of written record" (p. 3).

Cazden, Diamondstone, and Nasso (1989) further define the nature of teacher-research, suggesting that

> To engage in it, the teacher takes time out from the demands for action in an immediate, ongoing situation, and—alone or with colleagues—reflects on her

practice outside the flow of events, in frozen time. She finds ways to collect for such reflection documentation of her teaching and of student learning. . . . (p. 2)

This conception of teacher-research implies that not only does it involve intentional inquiry, but that it also requires time away from teaching to engage in research.

In summary, the view of teacher-research offered by these authors is that it is conducted by teachers, either alone or with others. It involves gathering and recording information from their own classrooms and school life, and then reflecting on what was learned. Views on whether it requires significant time away from normal teaching functions differ, however, as do views on what counts as systematic. These are related issues, and not trivial ones, if research, as distinct from teaching, is defined as disciplined inquiry.

Yet arriving at a precise distinction between high-quality, reflective teaching and teacher-research is not the most important concern of most who write about the movement. The distinction is a matter of degree, and the movement is defining itself as it evolves. Its nature, parameters, goals, and forms are being constructed by the community of interested professionals. Perhaps more important in characterizing the movement is the Freirian notion of research as tapping sources of knowledge not previously recognized as legitimate (Miller, 1990, pp. 73–74). That is, if what is missing from the research on classroom language learning is the voices of teachers themselves, then the movement provides ways for teachers' voices to be heard and valued. It is primarily a political movement aimed at self-empowerment. This is accomplished by creating forums for teachers' voices. Given the richness and cultural diversity of L2 teachers' experiences and perspectives, the insights they offer can make many important contributions to the movement.

ISSUES IN TEACHER-RESEARCH

Figure 9.1 depicts some of the many issues under discussion in the teacher-as-researcher movement. These issues include: Who participates in doing teacher-research? What are various options for participation and collaboration? What topics do teacher-researchers study? Do they tend to neglect certain topics? In what settings is inquiry carried out? What research methodologies are most appropriate? What are the purposes of teacher-research and who are the audiences? How might research be publicly shared? What is the real value of the teacher-researcher movement?

Figure 9.1 is similar to Figure 1.1, which illustrates factors involved in the L2 research endeavor. The accompanying discussion in Chapter 1 focused on how research varies according to the institutional, disciplinary, and other

Sociopolitical and Sociocultural Contexts

National and cultural groups
Status and roles of teachers and researchers

Purposes and Goals

Contribute to knowledge
Professional growth
Emancipation
Change practice/working conditions
Democratize inquiry

Initiators/Impetus	**Support and Funding**
Grassroots: teachers	Professional organizations
Professional organizations	Federal, public
University-based researchers	Networks, groups
Schools: Inservice training	Released time

Institutional Settings

Own class, school, institute
Collaboration across settings

Characteristics of Research Process

Topic (teacher-generated, other-generated)
Participants (teachers, researchers, students)
Particular perspectives of participants
Resources available (time, videos, etc.)
Methodology (ethnographic, quasi-experimental)
Data sources
Standards for quality
Scope

Audiences	**Diffusion**	**Uses of Results**
Self	Books	Student growth
Institution	Newsletters	Reflection
Teachers	Conferences	Professional growth
Wider communities	Professional organizations	Change practice
Support groups		Change structures
Administrators		Planning

Figure 9.1. Issues in Teacher Inquiry

contexts in which it is conducted. For example, research carried out in a university setting may differ in purpose, topic, and intended audience from research conducted in a private research firm. These same notions provide a useful framework for analyzing teacher-research. We will address some of these issues in an effort to point out the uniqueness and value of teacher-research while exposing some potential dilemmas that teacher-researchers might face.

The L2 Teacher's Perspective

Teachers, especially L2 teachers, have some unique contributions to make to research. Clearly, teachers know their own students well. Through daily interactions with them, they have firsthand information about their struggles and progress in learning and using a language. Teachers also have a particular perspective on the contexts in which they work, both the multiple synchronic contexts, such as curriculum, families and community, institutional pressures, and the diachronic contexts. They know what their students did yesterday and last month and how their attitudes and approaches to learning change. These insider perspectives can be essential for examining learning.

It might be said of all teachers that they have at least these perspectives to contribute. Second language teachers have more and different perspectives to offer, however. Because they are bilingual and bicultural, or multilingual and multicultural, L2 teacher-researchers in ESOL, bilingual, and immersion classrooms have much to contribute in examining issues that require gaining an emic view. If the teacher-researcher, or any researcher for that matter, does not understand and speak the language of the students he or she is studying, it may be difficult or impossible to truly see phenomena from the students' perspective. Gaining a real understanding requires construing the meanings of events or actions from the students' point of view. As Geertz (1984) has pointed out, empathy is not enough, although it helps. Second language teachers' linguistic abilities, as well as their cultural sensitivity and knowledge, give them a particular advantage in understanding the learners' perspectives. This understanding is important for studying sociolinguistic and cultural issues as well as issues in cognition.

Collaborative Arrangements. How might L2 teacher-researchers carry out inquiry in ways that draw on their own perspectives and abilities? A variety of individual or collaborative arrangements are possible. Teachers may inquire alone, in collaboration with other teachers, and/or in collaboration with university-based or other professional researchers.

Within each of these arrangements, the roles that teachers play can vary widely. For example, teachers may play a fairly passive role, simply providing access to students and helping to facilitate data collection. On the other hand, they may be equal partners, or even leaders, in determining the focus and parameters of a study and the methods to be used. As Cochran-Smith and Lytle (1990) point out, there are many fine examples of published cooperative studies in the qualitative/interpretive paradigm, such as work by Heath and Branscombe (1985) and Edelsky and Smith (1984). Such cooperative research provides "valuable insights into the interrelationships of theory and practice" (Cochran-Smith & Lytle, 1990, p. 3).

The warning that Cochran-Smith and Lytle offer regarding cooperative arrangements is that the researcher may predetermine the role of the teacher in the research process. They see this as a problem if the teacher's perspective is framed and mediated through the researcher's perspective. When this occurs, much of the teacher's unique contribution (i.e., his or her own perspective) can be lost. As a result, the teacher may play a minimal role in the generation of knowledge about learning and teaching.

Various other researchers suggest that more egalitarian relations will help avoid this problem. Lunsford and Ede (1990), for example, have studied modes of collaboration and focused on the problems of collaborative arrangements that are hierarchical: "This form of collaboration is linearly structured, driven by highly specific goals, and carried out by people who play clearly assigned roles" (p. 235). They found, in one study of writing, that the hierarchical mode of collaboration was inefficient. Moreover, it also was not satisfactory, either to those at the top or to those at the bottom of the hierarchy. Instead, Lunsford and Ede advocate a dialogic mode of collaboration, viewing it as both essential to the production of knowledge and to the satisfaction of participants. Lunsford and Ede concur with Miller (1990) who argues for a more dominant and egalitarian role for the teacher in cooperative research arrangements. Miller advocates a democratic, collaborative inquiry that is equitable and consensual.

Related to the issue of hierarchical forms of collaboration is another caution that needs mention—the potential exploitation of teachers by university-based researchers. This is not an issue in the fine projects with which we are familiar. Nevertheless, the danger is present if researchers tell teachers that they should or must do research. Outside of graduate courses, only teachers can decide if they want to engage in research and with whom. The question to be asked is: Who will benefit and how? We will return to that issue below.

Collaborating across Settings. Many discussions of the teacher-researcher, as we indicated above, depict a reflective inquirer working in the confines of one classroom. Yet one of the values of collaboration is that it builds on the contributions of each participant in describing and explaining phenomena. Various possibilities are available for collaborating across settings.

First, teachers of ESOL can study their own students in varied situations. Much can be learned from inquiry in the classroom of cooperating colleagues. It is particularly enlightening, for example, to learn how language learners cope with academic content in various classes. The work of the high school teacher-researchers in Adamson's study (in press) revealed detailed information about their students' strategies and needs in content courses. One history teacher learned, for example, why her essay tests, rather than her multiple-choice tests, allowed students to show more of what they knew. Hawkins's work (1988) provides one model for examining L2 learning across settings and illustrates how learning can result from scaffolded interaction. (Both of these studies are discussed in Chapter 4.)

In addition to studying their own students in different classes, two teachers might collaborate to study students in one another's classes. Hymes's (1981) technique of ethnographic monitoring is a particularly useful one for this purpose. For example, the ethnographic monitoring that Carrasco (1981) describes offers an excellent way for teachers to work reciprocally and to offer one another an "expanded awareness" of their students. What is unique about such monitoring is that the teacher-researcher is able to see students in situations in which their own teacher is not present. For example, the researcher might observe a student in free time or in a student-led activity. The knowledge gained provides a more complete picture of a student's full range of abilities. Language teachers have a particular advantage in this kind of research. When two teachers, one who is trilingual in Chinese, Amoy, and English, and one who is bilingual in Spanish and English, collaborate, they have much to offer one another. Each can provide an "expanded awareness" of the students who speak those languages to the teacher who does not speak them.

Settings for teacher-research need not be confined to one's own class, or even to other classes within the same institution. Teachers who step out of teaching temporarily to study for an advanced degree in another country can expand the awareness of the teachers they work with by providing much needed cross-cultural perspectives. For instance, an experienced teacher from Japan, conducting a research project in collaboration with a monolingual English-speaking teacher, can offer important cultural information to help interpret students' attitudes and actions. Second language teacher-researchers should also consider conducting inquiry in settings that offer the potential to expand their own cross-cultural understanding and sensitivity, goals that are crucial for professional development.

Student Participation. Another nontraditional aspect of teacher-research is its emphasis on student participation in research. Because the world of the good teacher is very student-centered, it is not only important but motivating for teacher-researchers to embrace the students' perspective. Some teacher-researcher teams have actively and successfully involved students in the research process, not simply in the interests of research, but in the interests of student learning (Heath & Branscombe, 1985). Inquiry into our students' points of view can only be enlightening. What do our students know and want to know about L2 learning and teaching? How could that kind of knowledge add to our ability to help them learn? There is still much to be done along these lines, and L2 teacher-researchers have a great deal to contribute in this area.

Methods and Standards

What research approaches and techniques can teachers most profitably employ? Most teacher-research is qualitative or interpretive in orientation (Cochran-Smith & Lytle, 1990). The movement generally advocates these methods, but not because they are less rigorous, as some would claim. Qualitative methods are advocated in part because, as Erickson (1986) suggests, the primary significance of interpretive methods for classroom research is the content these methods allow us to address, such as the meaning-perspectives of learners and the classroom as a social and cultural environment (p. 120). These topical goals, combined with L2 teachers' particular abilities and perspectives, make qualitative approaches particularly appealing and appropriate.

Teacher-researchers can use nearly all of the approaches and techniques discussed in this book, although descriptive studies, case studies, and ethnographic techniques, such as ethnographic monitoring, are particularly accessible and useful. A wide variety of data-collection techniques, especially those discussed in the case-study chapter, are useful. Examining L2 students' dialogue journal writing has been one of the most productive areas of teacher-researcher collaboration. Peyton and Mackinson (1989), for example, collaborated to study how students with varying degrees of English proficiency communicated with one another on a local-area network. By recording and analyzing the students' written discourse, they discovered how writers were able to vary language use for differing partners and how their English developed. Teacher-researchers we have known have used introspective, retrospective, and think-aloud procedures to examine their students' reading and writing processes. These teachers have found that the results changed their attitudes toward their students and led them to implement more sensitive and effective teaching strategies.

A number of methodological approaches not typically used in L2 research could offer insights as well. Eisner's (1985) *educational connoisseurship* is one of these. Rich, artistic renderings of classroom events, particularly from very different cultural perspectives, can be illuminating. A modified application of Denzin's (1989) *interpretive interactionist method,* which attempts to "make the world of problematic lived experience of ordinary people directly available to the reader" (p. 7), might help us further see how acculturation, language use, and personal histories are related. The choice of an approach and of techniques should depend on the expertise the teacher brings to the research endeavor and the purpose of the project.

Most advocates of the teacher-researcher movement reject quantitative methods and associated positivist thinking (see Chapter 2). Bereiter (1989), on the other hand, laments the reluctance of what he calls the "coalition" to use research methods such as experiments to validate empirical claims. He urges teacher-researchers to test out theoretical claims through comparative experiments that examine educational outcomes. We agree with the qualitatively oriented advocates that correlational and experimental methods are less accessible, generally reductionist, less feasible, and therefore less useful for teacher-research projects. On the other hand, sensitively used small-scale experiments, quasi-experiments supplemented with adequate description, and short task-based experiments can be appropriate for teacher-research. It is crucial that the expertise and interests of the inquirer be considered as well. We know a teacher-researcher who came to the field of L2 acquisition and teaching with a master's degree in computer science. His research interests lay in developing a computer program for practicing for the TOEFL and examining its effects on students by using both computer-generated quantitative data and personal interviews. The expertise that he brought to his inquiry was appropriate for the questions he raised, although quite different from the expertise of his teacher colleagues.

Regardless of the methodologies chosen, a related question is: Should teacher-research be held to the standards of the established (and evolving) traditions of research? Clearly, if teacher-research is held to these standards and fails to meet them, it will receive little audience from the academic research community.

To avoid this problem, some have suggested that teacher-research should be considered a new genre. Cochran-Smith and Lytle (1990), for example, propose that teacher-research be considered its own genre with its own defining features. They do not, however, suggest what those features might be. Myers (1985) as well proposes that a different set of standards is called for. He suggests that "teacher research will be judged on the basis of its clarity of language, its organizational consistency, and its goodness-of-fit with the intuitions of the teacher community, both in its definition of problems and in its findings" (p. 5).

There are serious problems with the standards that Myers suggests, particularly from a cross-cultural perspective. Research is generally communicated through writing, but notions such as clarity, organizational consistency, and means used to achieve coherence are culturally variable (Smith, 1987; Grabe & Kaplan, 1989). Indeed, they are variable across reviewers for the same journal. A criterion of goodness-of-fit with the intuitions of the teacher community can be very dangerous when prevailing commonsense intuitions are simply wrong.

For example, the commonsense notion (supported by some correlational research) that parents' educational level predicts students' academic success fits well with the intuitions of many, but is not necessarily true for a cultural group (Gibson, 1987) or any individual. The intuitions of many teachers who are not knowledgeable about SLA are often misguided. Commonly shared teacher intuitions may also include damaging cultural stereotypes that should not be held up as standards, but combatted. To claim that research is good if one teacher's experience fits another's may work against the generation of new knowledge. In some cases, it is precisely those insights that are counter-intuitive that most contribute to knowledge, particularly in cross-cultural situations. Our view is that the developing standards for teacher inquiry are more likely to center on issues of validity, the freshness and vividness of insights, and the impact of these insights on teachers and students. Ultimately, guidelines for what is valued are being socially constructed through dialogue in the teacher-researcher community.

Topics

One of the most exciting and refreshing aspects of teacher-research for us has been the questions that teachers ask. These questions, which often critically challenge theoretical claims in the literature, come directly out of teachers' own experiences. Cazden and her colleagues (1989) conducted a survey of topics of teacher-research on writing. They found that studies focused on topics such as teacher–student conferences, revision, writing to explore meaning (in learning logs, for example), writing in the content areas, and relationships between personal and informational writing. These topics, not surprisingly, tend to focus on the actions and interactions of students and teachers.

Some suggest that certain topics have been excluded from teacher-research. Bereiter (1989) suggests that there is a reluctance to examine how the mind works (p. 8). He sees the systematic exclusion of topics in the cognitive psychology of writing as a serious limitation of teacher-research and suggests that knowledge about topics such as writing systems and anaphora, for example, can prove quite valuable for teachers in unpredictable ways. Bereiter attributes the aversion to cognitive topics to a "clash of cultures" between the humanities and the social sciences. He states:

> The alliance that has developed between teacher-researchers and researcher-researchers is an alliance based on a strong feeling for the humane values of written expression. At least on the part of some of the researcher-researchers, however, this feeling seems to be accompanied by the aforesaid aversion to poking into how the mind works. They read into cognitive research all sorts of prescriptive and value implications that aren't there. (Bereiter, 1989, p. 8)

Bereiter also predicts that teacher-researchers who are interested in studying topics in cognition using experimental methods will be estranged from their colleagues. Unfortunately, this last concern may be well founded. Yet, the choice of topics to pursue should be up to the teacher, not something that is imposed from outside and from above. Researchers do not facilitate teacher empowerment by dictating topics and methods.

We have found in our experience that, while most teachers conducting pilot research projects within graduate courses do choose to examine overt teacher–student interactions, some are intensely interested in examining how the mind works. The second author of this chapter, for example, decided to explore how his own six-year-old son, a native Chinese who had just arrived in the United States, comprehended English messages. By showing him video cartoon stories in English and discussing his understanding of the stories in Chinese, Lihe discovered how his son's young mind handled the seemingly incomprehensible input. He discovered how his son drew inferences based on his cultural experiences both in China and in the United States.

Even if certain topics are generally excluded from teacher inquiry, we do not view this as a problem. Just as university researchers define their own areas of interest (some SLA researchers may not address sociocultural context; some ethnographers may not write about UG), teacher-researchers carve out their own domains of inquiry. Teachers might not raise questions about highly theoretical linguistic issues, for example; yet teachers do raise questions that point to flaws and limits in SLA theories and they raise a host of other insightful questions that go unaddressed in the literature. Teachers' questions and their insights grounded in experience cannot be ignored, and the contributions that come from their own perspectives should inform all of us, enriching both teaching and research.

Goals of Teacher-Researchers

The goals of teacher-researchers are multiple and controversial. One goal is professional development. Inquiry can be extremely valuable to individual teachers who wish to reflect and improve on their own teaching and thus grow in personal professionalism. What they learn through research may affect their practice in specific ways, it may affect their attitudes or expectations about students' abilities and growth, or it may affect teachers and students in completely surprising ways that manifest themselves immediately or only over time.[1] As one teacher said to us after completing a pilot research project on dialogue journal writing with adults, "What I learned about my students from their journals was absolutely mind-boggling. I'll never be the same again." For this teacher, professional growth was the goal, although later she was invited to share her findings with a wider audience of adult ESL teachers.

Personal professional growth is one legitimate and worthy goal. In fact, NCTE (the National Council of Teachers of English) in 1990 funded teacher-research projects aimed at personal growth. TESOL (Teachers of English to Speakers of Other Languages) did not provide such grants to teachers. Rather, TESOL announced an award for a classroom-based teacher-research project. The purpose of the award is to recognize excellence in teaching through inquiry, specifically inquiry that focuses on practices and principles of language learning and use in the classroom. TESOL has also promoted teacher inquiry and collaborative inquiry though publications at the local and national levels.[2]

Beyond personal growth, however, the purpose and value of teacher-research are still multiple. Locally, not only can one's own classroom be improved, but projects can also result in school improvement. For example, they can produce evidence that may convince school administrators of the value of certain approaches to learning.

By the same token, on a broader level, school districts, language institutes, and the L2 teaching profession in general can expect to benefit from the most insightful of these inquiries when teachers share them with broader communities through conferences, support groups, newsletters, electronic mail, books, and articles. The audience for reports of projects may be primarily other teachers, but many proponents of teacher-research have argued that the academic world also needs to listen to the voices of teachers (Cochran-Smith & Lytle, 1990). Our view is that teacher-research projects are yielding insights that are of benefit to all of us.

Another goal of teacher-research is to democratize inquiry. Some feel that the teacher-research movement has grown in reaction to academic environments they view as exclusive and elitist and in which theory is not developed democratically. By conducting their own research, teachers can contribute to knowledge in their own way. A related but stronger rationale for teacher inquiry has been that of emancipating teachers. By asking their own questions and exploring them in their own ways, we have seen many teachers gain a new sense of their own creative power. As Miller (1990) puts it, they come to see themselves as "challengers and creators rather than just transmitters and receivers of others' construction of knowledge" (p. 3). Bolstered with a new confidence through knowledge gained firsthand, teachers then play stronger roles in initiating critical dialogues and changing structures they find oppressive to themselves, to their colleagues, and to their students. These structures might involve mandated but poor-quality curricula, unsatisfactory pullout arrangements, a lack of materials, or inferior working conditions.

However, we sense in some of the current writing about the movement a tendency to impose a concept of empowerment on teachers. That is, we hear researchers telling teachers how they should strive to be empowered. We feel each situation is unique. In the United States, what would be emancipating for an L2 teacher in a high school might be quite different from what would be emancipating for a teacher in a language institute or center. Even more significantly, the notion of emancipation through teacher inquiry may be seen very differently across cultures. Indeed, it would not be surprising to see that what is valued in teacher-research in the United States is not valued in another society. The meanings, values, and outcomes of teacher inquiry, including its role in emancipating teachers, must be determined by teachers themselves in their own sociocultural settings, just as the decision of whether or not to do research is up to the teacher.

NOTES

1. Consider, for example, the changing attitudes of teachers who are knowledgeable about issues such as the variability of children in undergoing a "silent period" and how long it takes to learn an additional language well.
2. TESOL and its affiliates have promoted teacher-research by providing forums in Newsletters (e.g., "Explorations in Teacher Research" in the *AZ-TESOL Newsletter* and "Asking Questions" in the *TESOL Newsletter*). The new *TESOL Journal*, devoted to teaching and classroom research, provides an additional forum as do books (e.g., Peyton, 1990).

REFERENCES

Adamson, H. D. (in press). *Academic competence: Theory and classroom practice.* White Plains, NY: Longman.

Bereiter, C. (1989). Beyond lived experience in writing research. *The Quarterly, 11*(4), 7–8. Berkeley: University of California, National Writing Project and Center for the Study of Writing.

Bissex, G. (1986). On becoming teacher experts: What's a teacher-researcher? *Language Arts, 63,* 482–484.

Brodkey, L. (1987). Writing critical ethnographic narratives. *Anthropology & Education Quarterly, 18,* 67–76.

Carrasco, R. (1981). Expanded awareness of student performance: A case study in applied ethnographic monitoring in a bilingual classroom. In H. T. Tueba, G. P. Gutherie, & K. H. Au (Eds.), *Culture and the bilingual classroom: Studies in classroom ethnography* (pp. 153–177). Rowley, MA: Newbury House.

Cazden, C., Diamondstone, J., & Nasso, P. (1989). Teachers and researchers: Roles and relationships. *The Quarterly, 11*(4), 1–3,25–27. Berkeley: University of California, National Writing Project and Center for the Study of Writing.

Cochran-Smith, M., & Lytle, S. L. (1990). Research on teaching and teacher research: The issues that divide. *Educational Researcher, 19*(2), 2–11.

Denzin, N. K. (1989). *Interpretive interactionism.* Newbury Park, CA: Sage.

Edelsky, C., & Smith, K. (1984). Is that writing or are those marks just a figment of your curriculum? *Language Arts, 61*(1), 24–32.

Eisner, E. (1979). *The educational imagination.* New York: Macmillan.

Eisner, E. (1985). *The educational imagination: On the design and evaluation of school programs.* New York: Macmillan.

Erickson, F. (1986). Qualitative methods in research on teaching. In M. C. Wittrock (Ed.), *Handbook of research on teaching* (3rd ed.) (pp. 119–161). New York: Macmillan.

Geertz, C. (1984). "From the native's point of view": On the nature of anthropological understanding. In R. Shweder & R. LeVine (Eds.), *Culture theory: Essays on mind, self, and emotion* (pp. 123–136). Cambridge: Cambridge University Press.

Gibson, M. (1987). The school performance of immigrant minorities: A comparative view. *Anthropology & Education Quarterly, 18,* 262–275.

Giroux, H. A. (1988). *Teachers as intellectuals: Toward a critical pedagogy of learning*. Granby, MA: Bergin & Garvey.

Grabe, W., & Kaplan, R. B. (1989). Writing in a second language: Contrastive rhetoric. In D. M. Johnson & D. H. Roen (Eds.), *Richness in writing* (pp. 263–283). White Plains, NY: Longman.

Hawkins, B. A. (1988). *Scaffolded classroom interaction and its relation to second language acquisition for language minority children*. Unpublished doctoral dissertation, University of California, Los Angeles.

Heath, S. B., & Branscombe, A. (1985). "Intelligent writing" in an audience community: Teacher, students, and researcher. In S. W. Freedman (Ed.), *The acquisition of written language: Response and revision* (pp. 3–32). Norwood, NJ: Ablex.

Hymes, D. (1981). Ethnographic monitoring. In H. T. Tueba, G. P. Gutherie, & K. H. Au (Eds.), *Culture and the bilingual classroom: Studies in classroom ethnography* (pp. 56–68). Rowley, MA: Newbury House.

Johnson, D. M. (1987). Explorations in teacher research. *AZ-TESOL Newsletter*.

Lunsford, A., & Ede, L. (1990). Rhetoric in a new key: Women and collaboration. *Rhetoric Review, 8*, 235–241.

Miller, J. L. (1990). *Creating spaces and finding voices: Teachers collaborating for empowerment*. Albany: State University of New York Press.

Myers, M. (1985). *The teacher-researcher: How to study writing in the classroom*. Urbana, IL: National Council of Teachers of English and ERIC Clearinghouse on Reading and Communication Skills, National Institute of Education.

Nunan, D. (1989). *Understanding language classrooms: A guide for teacher-initiated action*. Englewood Cliffs, NJ: Prentice-Hall.

Peyton, J. K. (1990). *Students and teachers writing together: Perspectives on journal writing*. Alexandria, VA: Teachers of English to Speakers of Other Languages.

Peyton, J. K., & Mackinson, J. (1989). Writing and talking about writing: Computer networking with elementary students. In D. M. Johnson & D. H. Roen (Eds.), *Richness in writing: Empowering ESL students* (pp. 100–119). White Plains, NY: Longman.

Schon, D. A. (1983). *The reflective practitioner: How professionals think in action*. New York: Basic Books.

Schubert, W. H. (1990). Teacher lore: A basis for understanding praxis. In C. Witherell & N. Noddings (Eds.), *The stories lives tell: Narrative and dialogue in educational research and practice*. New York: Teachers College Press.

Smith, L. E. (1987). *Discourse across cultures: Strategies in world Englishes*. Englewood Cliffs, NJ: Prentice Hall.

Stenhouse, L. (1975). *An introduction to curriculum research and development*. London: Heinemann.

van Lier, L. (1990). Classroom research in second language acquisition. In R. Kaplan (Ed.), *Annual Review of Applied Linguistics* (Vol. 10) (pp. 173–186). New York: Cambridge University Press.

CHAPTER 10
Concluding Remarks

The purpose of this book has been to examine six approaches to L2 research to illustrate alternative ways to address research questions. In addition, we have addressed roles of teachers, not only as readers and interpreters of research but also as inquirers. To conclude, we will briefly discuss three issues: research types, linking method to purpose, and some goals for L2 research.

RESEARCH TYPES AS EVOLVING FRAMEWORKS

The six approaches to empirical research outlined in Chapters 3 through 8 are simply central types. They are not intended to be all inclusive, for clearly other types of research have been neglected. Nor are they intended as "pure" types. We have focused on the most central features of each of the six types, while giving some indication of the range of variation. The approaches are not homogeneous, self-contained, or unchanging, nor should they be. Rather, they are loose frameworks held together by evolving philosophies, purposes, and methods. Their fluid boundaries are continually changing as communities of researchers redefine the types of inquiry they value for the issues that interest them.

As we have seen in the studies used for illustrative purposes, most real studies do not fit one type in any rigid way. Rather, many researchers combine approaches. For example, a survey may be primarily descriptive and quantitative, but may also involve in-depth qualitative interviews with a small sample to search for explanations. An experiment may be supplemented by qualitative analyses of interactions. A case study may employ both qualitative and quantitative analyses of discourse. In fact, some of the most creative and interesting studies do not simply fit a rigid model, but draw on and create methods to suit the issues under study.

LINKING METHOD TO PURPOSE

The value of any particular method that is constructed, then, lies in how well it answers a particular research question in a particular situation and whether it offers important insight. Answers to these issues are not only a matter of personal judgment; they are also a matter of consensus among the members of a research community.

My view is that it is not productive to completely discount any particular research approach. A strong commitment to one, accompanied by a complete rejection of another, can lead to exaggerated dichotomies, polarized thinking, and intolerant and exclusionary attitudes. To claim that a particular approach is not useful is to claim that the types of questions that particular approach can best address are not important to ask. We should reject this sort of thinking.

I believe it is more productive to take the attitude that methods should fit the purposes of inquiry. We cannot afford, *a priori,* to rule out certain questions as not important. Second language professionals who favor ethnographic research should not ignore, for example, the insights that come from small-scale experiments on issues such as the role of universal grammar in L2 learning and whether the teaching of less universal aspects of language generalize to more universal ones. Insights about these topics have not been coming from ethnographic studies of classrooms and communities, but through carefully designed small-scale experiments.

Nor should those who favor qualitative research ignore what quantitative surveys can offer. Educational, sociolinguistic, and demographic surveys can provide important information about the broad social contexts for language learning. For instance, if one wants to know what languages are taught in U.S. elementary and secondary schools, a quantitative survey approach is appropriate. Although surveys are devalued by some qualitative researchers and experimentalists, neither of those methods suits this research question. Surveys, correlational approaches, and experiments can be useful for gaining insights into certain issues.

On the other hand, those who favor quantitative methods in the hypothetico-deductive paradigm cannot afford to devalue and ignore the insights that flow from methods emphasizing rich contextual description and cultural interpretation. Ethnographic work that helps us understand how social and cultural processes relate to L2 learning in particular situations is extremely useful to teachers in helping them understand what to expect from students. Such research also provides a rich basis for improving SLA theories that seek to explain connections between cultural factors and language learning. Moveover, research on how teachers can create learning environments that demonstrate cultural sensitivity and, at the same time, expand students' cultural awareness is crucial in today's world. These insights come primarily from qualitative and anthropologically oriented work rather than from correlational or experimental work. In conclusion, we must assess research methods for how well they suit research purposes, while continually remaining open-minded about how different ways of knowing from different points of view can be useful in searching for answers to the questions we consider important.

L2 RESEARCH FOR WHAT?

My final comment has to do with the questions we deem important. The purposes of L2 research in formal institutional settings are broad. They encompass not only micro-level topics in classroom interaction and psycholinguistic issues aimed at SLA theory development but also broader issues related to language learning in society. As mentioned in Chapter 5, the continually changing demographics in U.S. society have made issues such as cultural diversity in the classroom, second language acquisition and literacy development, and successful academic experiences for all students the concern not only of ESL, foreign language, and bilingual education professionals, but of the wider community of educators. As these issues have become the concern of all educators and the focus of numerous reports from diverse fields outside of education as well, the roles of applied linguists and language educators in addressing them have become even more important. Tucker (1990) suggests that applied linguists need to take stonger roles in applying their expertise to language issues in educational, occupational, and social settings.

> From my perspective . . . applied linguists have been presented with a challenge from outside the profession to demonstrate the applicability and the relevance of this field and to help address and resolve pressing social concerns. If applied linguists do not respond to the challenge, they run the serious risk that others with good intentions, but little training, will plunge ahead and leave them watching from the sidelines. (p. 243)

We must consider what the body of research in our field has to say to these pressing problems, what it should have to say, and how adequate our inquiry methods are for addressing the issues we consider most important. Some have suggested that L2 inquiry methods are shifting from a humanities to a social science orientation, with a concomitant rise in quantitative research (Henning, 1986; Lazaraton, Riggenbach, & Ediger, 1987; Santos, 1989; Swales, 1988). Yet the social sciences have not only used more sophisticated quantitative methods but have also embraced an increasingly wide variety of qualitative/interpretive methods. Moreover, for L2 studies conducted in formal educational contexts, the influences of qualitative educational, sociolinguistic, and anthropological approaches to research have been powerful and much needed (van Lier, 1988; Watson-Gegeo, 1988). The trend, then, has been toward greater use of qualitative methods in L2 research conducted in educational settings. I feel we must make even greater use of these approaches if we are to adequately address language learning in its sociocultural contexts, and by doing so make more meaningful contributions to addressing the educational and social challenges that face us in multilingual, multicultural societies.

REFERENCES

Henning, G. (1986). Quantitative methods in second language acquisition research. *TESOL Quarterly, 20*, 701–708.

Lazaraton, A., Riggenbach, H., & Ediger, A. (1987). Forming a discipline: Applied linguists' literacy in research methodology and statistics. *TESOL Quarterly, 21*, 263–277.

Santos, T. (1989). Replication in applied linguistics research. *TESOL Quarterly, 23*, 699–702.

Swales, H. (1988). 20 years of TESOL Quarterly. *TESOL Quarterly, 22*, 151–163.

Tucker, G. R. (1990). Summary. In R. B. Kaplan (Ed.), *Annual Review of Applied Linguistics* (Vol. 10) (pp. 243–250). New York: Cambridge University Press.

van Lier, L. (1988). *The classroom and the language learner*. London: Longman.

Watson-Gegeo, K. (1988). Ethnography in ESL: Defining the essentials. *TESOL Quarterly, 22*, 575–592.

Appendix: Resources for L2 Research

This Appendix is organized in three parts, according to the steps you might take in conducting a review of the research literature in an area of interest. The sources in the first section, titled "Indexes and Abstracts," will help you find articles by topic or author. The "Surveys of Research" listed in the following section contain articles and book chapters that provide comprehensive reviews of the research literature on a particular topic. The third section, "Journals," describes the content of the major journals in second and foreign language learning and bilingual education.

INDEXES AND ABSTRACTS

Language Teaching: The International Abstracting Journal for Language Teachers and Applied Linguists. London: Cambridge University Press.

This abstracting journal is published quarterly in England by the Centre for Information on Language Teaching and Research (CILT). It provides abstracts of significant recent articles related to the teaching and learning of second or foreign languages. The abstracts are organized into four broad categories: (1) language learning and teaching—theory and practice; (2) teaching particular languages; (3) research in the supporting

---

This Appendix is based on a bibliography originally prepared by Ruth Dickstein, University of Arizona Library, and subsequently revised and expanded by Margaret Olsen, Joy Egbert, Parvaneh Farzad, Norman Johnson, and Donna M. Johnson.

sciences; and (4) language description and use. Each issue contains one state-of-the-art article. The articles that are abstracted are selected from a list of some 400 journals from all parts of the world.

Linguistics and Language Behavior Abstracts. Ann Arbor: University of Michigan.

This is a scholarly reference work that provides abstracts on articles from more than 1,000 publications in 30 languages. Some of the subjects covered include language acquisition, reading, speech and language, and verbal learning.

U.S. Education Resources Information Center. *Resources in Education* (RIE). Washington, DC: Government Printing Office.

This is an index and abstracting service to the ERIC document collection. ERIC documents include non-copyright materials such as conference papers, curriculum guides, research reports, and other hard-to-find documents. The RIE indexes these documents by author, insititution, document type, and subject, as listed in the *Thesaurus of ERIC Descriptors*. Subjects relevant to L2/FL/BE include second language learning and instruction, English for special purposes, migrant education, applied linguistics, multilingualism, and language dominance.

MLA Bibliography. New York: Modern Language Association of America.

This reference work is generally considered a source of literary criticism. However, each index includes a section (in Volume III) on linguistics, which contains abstracts of articles in scholarly journals. The range of subjects covered includes the origin of language, bilingualism, language processing, and psychoacoustics.

Current Index to Journals in Education (CIJE). Phoenix, AZ: Oryx Press.

CIJE indexes and abstracts over 750 education and education-related journals. The articles are indexed by the terminology used in the *Thesaurus of ERIC Descriptors*. There is also an author index as well as an index of journal contents.

Education Index. New York: H.W. Wilson.

This is a basic index to over 240 education-related periodicals, proceedings, and documents, organized by author and subject categories. One useful feature is a book review section containing reviews of individual authors and titles, as well as special articles and sections of books about education.

Psychological Abstracts. Washington, DC: American Psychological Association.

This index is primarily concerned with the psychological aspects of learning and education. It provides summaries and citations of books, documents, and articles in over 900 journals on psychology, psychometrics, statistics, motivation, and counseling.

Sociological Abstracts. San Diego, CA: Sociological Abstracts, Inc.

This index provides abstracts of articles from journals that address second language acquisition, including the *NABE Journal* and the *Journal of Language and Social Psychology*, as well as other journals addressing topics in sociology. It provides comprehensive coverage of the field of sociology and its subfields.

Social Science Citation Index. Philadelphia: Institute for Scientific Information.

This index is a comprehensive source of information published in journals concerned with all aspects of the social sciences. It is divided into three parts (in separate volumes). The "Source Index" provides full bibliographic details on articles indexed as well as citations included in each article. The "Citation Index" lists, by author, who is being cited, by whom, and where. The "Permuterms Subject Index" is a keyword analysis of the titles of articles listed in the "Source Index."

SURVEYS OF RESEARCH

Annual Review of Applied Linguistics. Cambridge: Cambridge University Press.

Published annually, this review is a collection of state-of-the-art articles on a different theme each year. Recent themes have been international bilingualism, communicative language teaching, second language acquisition, and discourse analysis. Each article in a volume provides an overview of important research in an area as well as a useful annotated bibliography.

Handbook of Research on Teaching, 3rd ed., 1986, New York: American Educational Research Association/Macmillan.

The *Handbook* provides comprehensive reviews of research on teaching, particularly advances made since the previous edition in 1973. Broad areas include theory and method of research on teaching, research on teaching and teachers, social and institutional contexts of teaching, and differences among learners. Particularly relevant chapters include teaching bilingual learners, classroom discourse, reading, composition, teacher education, qualitative methods, and observation.

Review of Research in Education. Itasca, IL: F.E. Peacock.

This review is a yearly publication of the American Educational Research Association that offers critical analyses of several major areas of educational research per issue. Within each general area, a number of specific issues (chapters) are presented and reviewed. Topics covered in Volume 14 (1987) included early childhood education, improving the teaching force, writing instruction, and gender and minority issues. Each chapter includes a substantial bibliography.

Handbook of Reading Research. White Plains, NY: Longman, 1984.

The *Handbook* is a compilation of reports of research on reading, and over 350 journals are reviewed. It contains sections on methodological issues, reading processes, and instructional practices. Topics such as the history of reading research, the design of experiments, and individual differences are addressed. Author and subject indices and extensive reference lists are included.

JOURNALS

Anthropology & Education Quarterly. Washington, DC: The Council on Anthropology and Education.

Concerned with the application of anthropology to research and development in education, this quarterly relates anthropological data, theories, methods, and insights to educational problems, practice, and institutions. The contents address multicultural education programs, cultural systems, school and community interaction, migration issues, and minority status in education. It includes articles, commentaries, and book reviews.

Applied Linguistics. Oxford: Oxford University Press.

Sponsored by the American, British, and International Associations of Applied Linguistics, this journal promotes a principled approach to language education and other language-related concerns by encouraging inquiry into the relationship between theory and practice. Applied research topics include L1 and L2 learning and teaching; bilingualism and bilingual education; discourse analysis; translation; language testing; and language teaching methodology. Published quarterly.

CALICO Journal. Provo, UT: CALICO, Brigham Young University.

This journal is published by the Computer Assisted Language Learning and Instruction Consortium (CALICO), an international clearinghouse of applications of high technology to the teaching and learning of languages. The journal features articles, reviews, and information pertinent to the field of computer-assisted language learning. Published quarterly.

Canadian Modern Language Review. Ontario: Canadian Modern Language Association.

The dual focus of this journal is linguistic theory and teaching pedagogy. It publishes articles, book reviews, and other material of interest to teachers of French, German, Italian, Russian, Spanish, Ukrainian, and English at all levels of intruction. Published quarterly.

College ESL. New York: City University of New York.

This new journal will publish articles on the education of urban immigrant and refugee adults in college settings. Topics include instructional practice; curricular innovation; research; teacher education; cultural issues; and ethical, legal, and political issues.

Computer Assisted Language Learning (CALL). Norwood, NJ: Ablex and Oxford: Intellect Books.

This is a new international journal published three times a year. It addresses topics such as pedagogical principles in CALL; computer-assisted composition; software analysis; applications of artificial intelligence (AI) to language teaching. Emphasis is on a variety of technologies.

Discourse Processes. Norwood, NJ: Ablex.

This multidisciplinary journal includes articles on discourse in different settings, language development, cognitive development, and language. Its emphasis is on both psycholinguistic and sociolinguistic analyses of discourse. Published quarterly.

ELT Journal. Oxford: Oxford University Press in association with The British Council and with the International Association of Teachers of English as a Foreign Language (IATEFL).

This journal is a quarterly publication for those in the field of teaching ESL or EFL. It is concerned with practical factors in English-language teaching around the world as well as theoretical issues that are relevant to practice. It includes articles, book reviews, and information relevant to everyday classroom practice. Each issue contains several articles devoted to a single topic. In 1988, for example, these topics included teacher training and learning strategies.

English for Specific Purposes. New York: Pergamon Press.

An international journal, it publishes articles and research notes on specialized varieties of English and on methodology. Topics include discourse analysis, SLA in specialized contexts, ESP (English for specific purposes) curriculum development, and teacher training. It also includes book reviews. Published semiannually.

Foreign Language Annals. Hastings-on-Hudson, NY: American Council on the Teaching of Foreign Languages (ACTFL).

This journal contains articles relevant to the teaching of foreign languages (including English) at all educational and age levels. It includes program descriptions, descriptions of successful teaching methods, reports of research, and information pertinent to the ACTFL organization. Published bimonthly.

IRAL. Oxford: Oxford University Press.

The International Review of Applied Linguistics in Language Teaching is devoted to problems of general and applied linguistics. It publishes articles in English, French, and German.

Issues in Applied Linguistics. Los Angeles: University of California at Los Angeles.

This new semiannual journal is published by graduate students of the UCLA Department of TESL & Applied Linguistics. One of its aims is to encourage publication of work by graduate students. Topics include language acquisition, language analysis, language education, language testing, language use, and research methodology.

JALT Journal. Japan Association of Language Teachers.

This is the scholarly journal of the Japan Association of Language Teachers. It features articles on language learning and teaching with particular emphasis on teaching and programs in Japan.

Journal of Intensive English Studies, Tucson: University of Arizona, Center for English as a Second Language.

Aimed at an audience of faculty and administrators of intensive programs for ESL/EFL, this journal publishes theoretical, empirical, methodological, and practice-oriented articles as well as review articles. Topics include program design and evaluation, curriculum development, classroom organization, program administration, teacher training, and second language and culture learning and instruction. Published semiannually.

Journal of Language and Social Psychology. Clevedon, Avon: Multilingual Matters.

This journal is a forum for discussions of social-psychological approaches to the study of language. Topics have included language attitudes, cognitive factors mediating production and L2 learning, and relationships among language, individual differences, and social situations. Published quarterly.

Journal of Multilingual and Multicultural Development. Clevedon, Avon: Multilingual Matters.

This journal focuses on issues of multilingualism and multiculturalism throughout the world. It publishes articles on theory, research, and practice in multilingual and multicultural education. Articles draw on the related fields of sociology, psychology, anthropology, linguistics, and the disciplines of psycholinguistics and sociolinguistics. The journal includes articles, book reviews, and briefs of work in progress. Published bimonthly.

Language Arts. Urbana, IL: National Council of Teachers of English.

Published monthly, September through April, this journal emphasizes practical applications of theory for English teaching, especially in elementary classrooms. Each issue includes articles on a particular theme. Themes in 1988 included, for example, drama as a learning medium, purposes of schooling, critical literacy/critical thinking, and the reflective practitioner. The journal often publishes one or more articles relevant to child second language and literacy development.

Language and Education: An International Journal. Clevedon, Avon: Multilingual Matters.
International in focus, this journal publishes articles on mother-tongue education and second language and literacy development in classroom settings. The journal also has a book review section.

Language in Society. Cambridge: Cambridge University Press.
Published quarterly, this scholarly journal of sociolinguistics is concerned with all branches of speech and language as aspects of social life. Articles cover a range of topics from linguistic to social, and reflect the interrelationship of theory and methodology in language development. Some issues are devoted to developments and research in a particular country or region. Also included are book reviews, briefs of work in progress, and reader responses to recent publications.

Language Learning. Ann Arbor: University of Michigan.
This journal publishes empirical research in the field of second language learning and applied linguistics. It includes research in psycholinguistics, sociolinguistics, anthropological linguistics, language pedagogy, and second language acquisition. Published quarterly.

Linguistics and Education: An International Research Journal. Norwood, NJ: Ablex.
The purpose of this journal is to provide a forum for researchers who examine educational processes from a linguistic perspective. Topics include classroom interaction, language diversity in educational settings, language policy and curriculum, written language learning, language disorders, and the application of linguistics, sociolinguistics, psycholinguistics, discourse analysis, social semiotics, conversational analysis and ethnomethodology, among other language and linguistically based perspectives, to educational issues.

The Modern Language Journal. Madison: University of Wisconsin Press, National Federation of Modern Language Teachers Associations.
This publication is devoted primarily to research in methods, pedagogy, and applied linguistics pertaining to modern languages, including TESL. Its intended audience is teachers of foreign and second languages. It publishes articles, reports, book reviews, and essays. Published quarterly.

NABE Journal. Washington, DC: National Association for Bilingual Education.
This journal serves as a forum for research, policy analyses, evaluation studies, and essays related to bilingualism and schooling in the United States. It focuses on research and pedagogical theory in bilingual education, ESL, foreign language instruction, and first, second, and dual language learning.

Pragmatics and Language Learning. Urbana: University of Illinois at Urbana-Champaign.
This refereed journal publishes research in pragmatics, communicative competence, literacy, discourse analysis, and conversational analysis. Its focus is on the interaction of pragmatics with the learning and/or teaching of a second or foreign language in varied contexts. Published annually.

RELC Journal. Singapore: Southeast Asian Ministers of Education Organization (SAMEO), Regional Language Center.

A journal of language teaching and research in Southeast Asia, it publishes articles on theory, research, methods, and materials related to language learning and teaching in Southeast Asia. The journal also contains book reviews.

Research in the Teaching of English. Urbana, IL: National Council of Teachers of English.

This is an interdisciplinary journal that publishes original research articles representing the variety of methodologies and modes of inquiry current in the field of English-language teaching. It includes studies of the interrelationships among reading, writing, and oral language.

Review of Educational Research. Washington, DC: American Educational Research Association.

This journal provides critical reviews of educational research literature on both theoretical and methodological issues. Some recent topics (1987) have included historical research on Chicano education, revision in writing, and stratification in secondary schools. The journal supplements and updates the information in the *Encyclopedia of Educational Research* and the *Handbook of Research on Teaching.* Published five times a year.

Second Language Research. London: Edward Arnold.

This journal focuses on the relationship between second language acquisition data and generative grammatical theory. It also publishes studies in neurolinguistics, semantic theory, and sociolinguistic theory as they relate to "theory formation in psycholinguistic acquisitional issues." The journal grew out of the *Interlanguage Studies Bulletin,* started in 1976. Articles in 1985–1986 addressed topics such as universal grammar (UG), the limits of hypothesis testing, transfer, markedness, parameter setting in L1 and L2, and parsing. Published semiannually.

Studies in Second Language Acquisition. Cambridge: Cambridge University Press.

This journal is devoted to issues and problems in second language acquisition and foreign language learning. The majority of its articles are reports of empirical research or theoretical papers. Those pedagogical papers that are included are based on current theoretical research. Topics of recent articles have included markedness theory, interlanguage fossilization, language transfer, and pragmatics. Published triannually, this journal also includes book reviews. Yearly thematic issues have been published on topics such as lexical acquisition and language testing.

System. Oxford: Pergamon Press.

Subtitled "International Journal of Educational Technology and Applied Linguistics," *System* is devoted to applications of technology and systems thinking to issues in foreign language teaching and learning. Articles come from a wide variety of countries. Published three times a year.

TESOL Journal. Alexandria, VA: Teachers of English to Speakers of Other Languages (TESOL).

This new quarterly journal focuses on teaching and classroom research. Its articles emphasize methodology, materials and curriculum design, teacher education, program administration, classroom observation and research, and teacher-conducted inquiry. The journal also publishes reviews of textbooks, programs, and other teaching resources.

TESOL Quarterly. Alexandria, VA: Teachers of English to Speakers of Other Languages (TESOL).

This quarterly journal includes articles, brief reports, book reviews, book notes, and information on topics pertinent to teachers of ESL, EFL, and Standard English as a second dialect. The journal represents a variety of cross-disciplinary interests, both theoretical and practical. Topics include psychology and sociology of language learning and teaching; issues in research methodology; curriculum design and development; instructional methods, materials and techniques; testing and evaluation; professional preparation; and language planning.

World Englishes. Oxford: Pergamon Press.

Subtitled "A Journal of English as an International and Intranational Language," this journal is devoted to the study of the forms and functions of English, both native and non-native, in diverse cultural and sociolinguistic contexts. Articles focus on language, literature, and the teaching of English as a primary or additional language, as well as topics such as bilingualism, sociolinguistics, and Creoles. Published three times per year.

Index